WRITING DIASPORA

Studies in Migration and Diaspora

Series Editor: Anne J. Kershen

Studies in Migration and Diaspora is a series designed to showcase the interdisciplinary and multidisciplinary nature of research in this important field. Volumes in the series cover local, national and global issues and engage with both historical and contemporary events. The books will appeal to scholars, students and all those engaged in the study of migration and diaspora. Amongst the topics covered are minority ethnic relations, transnational movements and the cultural, social and political implications of moving from 'over there', to 'over here'.

Writing Diaspora
South Asian Women, Culture and Ethnicity

YASMIN HUSSAIN
University of Leeds

ASHGATE

© Yasmin Hussain 2005

All rights reserved. No part of this publication may be reproduced, stored in a retrieval system, or transmitted in any form or by any means, electronic, mechanical, photocopying, recording or otherwise without the prior permission of the publisher.

Yasmin Hussain has asserted her right under the Copyright, Designs and Patents Act, 1988, to be identified as the author of this work.

Published by
Ashgate Publishing Limited
Wey Court East
Union Road
Farnham
Surrey, GU9 7PT
England

Ashgate Publishing Company
Suite 420
101 Cherry Street
Burlington
VT 05401-4405
USA

Ashgate website: http://www.ashgate.com

British Library Cataloguing in Publication Data
Yasmin Hussain
  Writing diaspora : South Asian women, culture and
  ethnicity. - (Studies in migration)
  1. English literature - 20th century - History and criticism
  2. English literature - Women authors - History and
  criticism 3. English literature - South Asian authors -
  History and criticism 4. Women in literature 5. South Asians
  in literature 6. South Asians - Great Britain - Intellectual
  life 7. East Indian diaspora in literature 8. Group identity
  in literature 9. Minorities in literature 10. Sex role in
  literature
  I. Title
  820.9'8914041

Library of Congress Cataloging-in-Publication Data
Yasmin Hussain.
  Writing diaspora : South Asian women, culture, and ethnicity / by Yasmin Hussain.
      p. cm. -- (Studies in migration)
  Includes bibliographical references and index.
  ISBN 0-7546-4113-9
  1. English literature--South Asian authors--History and criticism. 2. English literature--Women authors--History and criticism. 3. South Asians--Great Britain--Intellectual life. 4. Motion pictures--Great Britain--History. 5. Women--Great Britain--Intellectual life. 6. Emigration and immigration in literature. 7. Women and literature--Great Britain. 8. Asia, Southeastern--In literature. 9. South Asians in literature. 10. South Asians in mass media. 11 Immigrants in literature. 12. Ethnicity in literature. I. Title. II. Series.

PR129.A785Y37 2005
820.9'9287'0954--dc22

2005008912

Transfered to Digital Printing in 2012

ISBN 978-0-7546-4113-1

Printed and bound in Great Britain by the
MPG Books Group Ltd, UK

Contents

Preface vii
Acknowledgements ix

1 Introduction 1

2 Identity and Gender Across Generations of British South Asians 19

3 Black British Feminism and the Birth of South Asian Women's Writing 33

4 The New Woman in South Asian and Diasporic Literature 53

5 *Bhaji on the Beach* and *Bend it like Beckham*: Gurinder Chadha and the 'Desification' of British Cinema 71

6 *Brick Lane*: Gender and Migration 91

7 Childhood in *Anita and Me* 111

8 Conclusion 131

Bibliography 135
Index 143

Preface

The migrant experience does not end with the first point of settlement. It is handed down through the generations, consciously or unconsciously making its contribution to the way in which those in the diaspora negotiate their existence through societies in which they, and their cultures, are in the minority. *Being* in the diaspora means *living* in a cross-cultural context, one in which change, fusion and expansion are inevitable. Those aware of the complexities of this recognise the need to redefine their identity and the necessity to discover a medium through which to articulate their progress.

In their process of defining and redefining their identity and the struggle this involves, South Asian women in Britain have had to confront the combined issues of gender and ethnicity. The procedure has produced a range of female voices which, in recent years, have echoed through the mediums of literature and film. In this pioneering volume, Yasmin Hussain deconstructs the work of a selection of South Asian women whose output, 'has been shaped by the specifics of the British South Asian experience and context'. Hussain readily points out that the term 'South Asian' is inclined to suggest an 'imagined community', one which itself needs deconstructing into its constituent parts of, India, Pakistan, Bangladesh and Sri Lanka. Thus, through Hussain's guidance, we are able to listen to the South Asian female voice and, in addition, identify the cultural contrasts that exist within the South Asian continent.

Combining the theoretical with specific case studies, the author provides an intellectual foundation together with an astute literary and cinematic critique. Many of us have watched *Bhaji on the Beach* and *Bend it like Beckham*, and yet how many deconstructed director Gurinder Chanda's explorations of racial, ethnic, religious and gendered identities, or the dynamics of the ethnic minority family in contrast to that of the indigenous white? Did we pick up on all the nuances that are written into Meera Syal's novel, *Anita and Me* (subsequently filmed) and the comparative strengths and weaknesses in Monica Ali's hotly debated *Brick Lane?*

In this volume, Yasmin Hussain successfully argues for the existence of, 'A body of creative works in recent literature and cinema that express the distinctive identities of British South Asian women.' By so doing she has highlighted the difference that being a South Asian woman in the Diaspora makes to creativity and to the inclusion of minority cultural expression within the mainstream. A reading of this book not only extends our awareness of the growth in literary and cinematic diversity, it also enhances our understanding of the migrant experience and its influence on the generations to come.

Anne J. Kershen
Queen Mary, University of London.

Acknowledgements

There are a number of friends, colleagues and relatives who have offered support, love, words of encouragement and have shown interest in the development of my ideas. Many of these need to be thanked individually.

Firstly, this book is dedicated to my parents with love and gratitude. Their continual support and encouragement through often difficult times has been the driving force in the completion of this piece of work. Their belief in my ability has been inspiring and no words can fully express my debt. To my brothers and sister, Ali, Aftab, Nusrat, Abid, Alam, I am grateful not only for practical support but more importantly for their solidarity and confidence that has sustained me through the inevitable difficulties of persevering with a doctoral thesis and subsequently this book.

The work on which this book is based was originally developed for a PhD that I completed at the University of Bradford. I gratefully acknowledge the support of my supervisor John Harrison. His critical dialogue, although incisive and demanding, was always delivered in the spirit of encouragement and challenge. I am extremely grateful to Paul Bagguley for his commitment and assistance in transforming the PhD into a book – he has been generous with his time and I thank him for his patience and enthusiasm. Thanks also to my colleagues in the old Social and Economic Studies department at the University of Bradford, in particular Charles Husband, Yunas Samad, Michael Mullan, and Jane Hammond. My colleagues in the School of Sociology and Social Policy at the University of Leeds need to be acknowledged for their support. Nasim Shah, Bano Murtuja, John Roberts and Ruth Pearson also need to be credited for their words of encouragement.

To my parents

Chapter 1

Introduction

Britain's South Asian ethnic minorities are largely the product of an influx of immigrants, which began in the 1950s as a movement of intending sojourners who instead became settlers, creating a new life for themselves in a different social context (Anwar, 1979). Since their arrival, they have raised new generations whose personal lives and self-images have been conditioned by circumstances very different from those familiar to their parents. The first immigrant generation transplanted into Britain's ways of being, seeing and living that were determined partly by the experience of imperialist domination and partly by resistance to it. Those who settled in Britain, and more especially their British-born descendants, have participated in the evolution of a new self-image and identity – the British South Asian way of being. This self-concept is influenced by the British social and political environment and includes responses to the rejection and oppression experienced by non-White minorities (Grewal, 1988).

These pressures and resistances have brought about considerable changes in the identity of South Asian women in Britain. The majority culture harboured notions about South Asian communities and the place of women within them which were frequently distorted by stereotypical images and ethnocentric perceptions of women in the context of western values of independence and individuality, which South Asian cultures were seen as denying. However, from within the minority groups themselves, inherited ideas of South Asian identity and women's roles were also being questioned, not only by the men who were supposedly the privileged guardians of imposed identities but also by the women themselves who rejected the identities prescribed for them. Consequently South Asian women have redefined the very idea of South Asianness and South Asian womanhood within both the minority and majority cultures as they give voice to their resistance to oppression. The creative output from these women documents this struggle.

Changes in South Asian communities' understandings of themselves affects their culture in a number of ways, including cultural formation, reproduction and dissemination (Gilroy, 1993). The negotiation of identities is fundamental to South Asian women's writing in cross-cultural contexts. It is the convergence of multiple places and cultures that re-negotiates the terms of South Asian women's experiences, a process which in turn negotiates and re-negotiates their identities (Davies, 1994). It is against this background of change and expansion that this book aims to decipher questions of identity, by examining certain types of emotional reaction among women as they appear in creative works by the South Asian women who form the British diasporic community. The works deconstructed within this book have been produced by women living in Britain whose subjects and methods are shaped by the specifics of the British South Asian experience and context (Macauley, 1996).

The notion of a 'South Asian identity' promotes a unity and solidarity among the 'imagined community' of the South Asian diaspora. People from the various South Asian cultures have been treated typically as one monolithic people by the West. For instance, all South Asians were defined in Britain as 'Indian' before 1945, and subsequently re-defined as Pakistani and Indian. Bangladeshis were only categorised as such from the 1970s onwards when West and East Pakistan were divided so that Bangladesh emerged as an independent nation. The term 'South Asian' also functions as an umbrella term, often abbreviated to 'Asian', to unify diverse peoples against common obstacles, in the name of empowerment and coalition-building (Iyer, 1997). Yet the differences ethnically, culturally, religiously within the term 'South Asian' are vast. The majority of Britain's current South Asian population can be placed within four broad categories, Gujaratis and Punjabis from India, Punjabis from Pakistan and Bangladeshi (Ballard, 2002). Those who form the Gujarati population are drawn from the coastal districts in Saurashtra and the Gulf of Cambay, with 80 per cent Hindu and the remainder Muslim. The Punjabis from India, are from the Jullundur Doab, with the majority being Sikh and the remainder either Hindu or Christian. The other substantial body of Punjabis are from areas in Pakistan such as Mirpur, Jhelum, Rawalpindi and Gujrat Districts as well as smaller numbers from Faisalabad and Lahore. The overwhelming majority of Bangladeshis are from the district of Sylhet (Ballard, 2002).

There are a number of differences within these ethnic groups, for instance lifestyles, dress, diet and language. Furthermore, their responses to new social and economic environments are also different, with diverse employment patterns and marriage practises for example (Ballard, 2002). However, irrespective of this diversity there are similarities; for all those categorised as South Asian, the multiplicity of languages has always been a part of their history, and this often entails an acceptance of difference, and an open-ness to different cultural influences. This does not take place at the expense of established cultural ties, nor does it challenge self-identity (Iyer, 1997). This book illuminates the basic patterns and principles that are characteristic of women's lives in the diasporic communities of Pakistanis, Indians and Bangladeshis in Britain. These run across the whole pan-ethnic category of South Asian, thus allowing them to be treated as an amalgamated identity. The differences between the ethnic categories are highlighted when they emerge as important.

The South Asian identities expressed in the work examined in the following chapters are not religious or national identities, but the collective concerns of women who have roots in South Asia and are living in the diaspora. These issues, including migration and settlement, self-identity, the role of the family and marriage, feature in all of the works to varying degrees regardless of whether the author is Bangladeshi, Indian or Pakistani; Hindu, Muslim or Sikh. The details may be specific to religion or nation, but as will become apparent in what follows the broad themes are shared by South Asian women in the diaspora.

Works of fiction, cinematic screenplays and poetry are essentially products of unique individual imaginations and as such might be challenged as admissible evidence in a sociological study, especially if the works were considered in isolation from each other and outside a theoretical framework. They are, however, entirely relevant to the sociology of culture. The creative works featured in this study are in a real sense eyewitness accounts: not literal autobiographies, but representations of aspects of the lived experience and preoccupations of each author which she recognised as relevant to lives other than her own. They deal with authentic concerns about individual and group identity, framed largely by social relations which position people in terms of ethnicity and gender. By identifying these common themes and the different ways they are addressed in these creative works, we can uncover some of the major issues in the real lives of British South Asian women. The works considered within this book are all by women whose parents originated from India, Pakistan and Bangladesh, and almost all have been either born or brought up in Britain.

This book examines the identities of South Asian women in Britain and the extent to which these permeate through the products of their creativity in the form of literature and film. These works are informed by a historical perspective and are concerned with putting forward an interpretation of the world as experienced by British South Asian women themselves. Similarities in the treatment of issues of identity are highlighted with respect to the thematic concerns and the stylistic techniques used. These women are concerned with the relationships between image, identity, culture, power, politics and representation and the differences between images and reality, policy and practice are made apparent.

The propriety or the motives in associating the personal lives of authors with their writings is problematic. Are imaginative writings attempts to find satisfaction by releasing pre-occupied thoughts? This study accepts the fact that individuals reveal themselves in whatever they read and write. Its purpose is to relate the quantity and temper of imaginative writing to the assumption that what has been written and read for pleasure is a fair index of the interests and attitudes widely shared among contemporary British South Asian women. Diasporic writing as a creative genre encapsulates the shared social and psychological preoccupations of whole dispersed generations and their offspring. The creative product, whether in the form of visual or text media, have opened up new ways of thinking in both peoples' lives and scholarly work. It is within this literature that diaspora is used as a social and political tool for expressing immediate grievances, those of which are intimately concerned with identity and the quest for individuality.

It is significant that the emergence of this creative endeavour has reworked the language of representation. Women authors 'pen' themselves into their own history: they articulate differences in a narrative which is also expressed in their own terms of reference and which highlights ignorance from within the majority and minority communities (Parmar, 1990). Among the themes they address are the different ways that aspects of the 'host' or 'majority' culture are perceived by women brought up and educated within that culture, compared to the perceptions and valued judgements of their elders. Culture is not genetically inherited but is instilled by upbringing within a given cultural context or a given set of parallel contexts, within which the individual has to learn about such ideas as race and gender. White society's ignorance related to both their gender and race becomes a core issue within the writing of British South Asian women and an underlying feature of their everyday lives. However, it is the way in which they deal with these issues of contention that is the essence of the writing, as it shows a battling of self-worth alongside preconceived notions of identity which are interwoven within stereotypical notions of South Asian womanhood found in wider British society. Thus the identity which is explored is not only specific and individual but embraces a collective identity of South Asian women in Britain.

What is interesting to note is that the dynamics within the South Asian women's diaspora develop according to the historical circumstances and alternating environments in which it is situated. The creative works become sites within which active identification appears through their creative works; these women engage in constant practical ideological work – of marking boundaries, creating transnational networks, articulating dissenting voices – at the same time that they re-inscribe collective memories and utopian visions in their public ceremonials or cultural works (Werbner, 1990). Women's identities are shaped by rejection or acceptance on the basis of identity. The positioning of women when they first arrived in the UK where they were subjected to ethnocentric pathologisation forced them to assert their identity within their creativity. The quest for identity is therefore played out as a means of expressing self-identity, and this identity is not a product of economic determinants, but one arrived at through the multi-axial configurations of power which permeate their lives.

British South Asian women writers are creating new ways of representing their individual and collective identities. In the exploration of identity, gender is of course at the very centre of their preoccupations. They write from a particular time and place, from a particular combination of experiences and influences, and from the rich variety of their creative works it is possible to identify their concerns and their feelings as to what constitutes their identity as young British South Asian women.

The creative works considered in the subsequent chapters serve as evidence of the shared preoccupations of whole generations of South Asian women, within South Asian and the diasporic communities. Whilst social and political grievances are expressed in the writings, the women also succeed in expressing intimately personal concerns, many of which are centred on questions of identity. For all the differences between the works to be surveyed here, the theme of searching for identity is pervasive and brings the many different protagonists into a questioning confrontation with her own heritage as well as the cultural mores of the society in which she finds herself. The quest for individuality, the theme of the journey through space and time, the acceptance or rejection of categorisation, confrontation with patriarchal constraints and the tendency to seek self-definition in terms of comparison with the behaviour or identities of others, are recurring themes in the creativity of British South Asian women. Here is a body of literature which is striking not only in terms of its growth as a creative genre, but in its value as a compelling body of sociological evidence about the South Asian diaspora.

Diaspora

The concept of diaspora is central to this book, so it is appropriate at this point to reflect on its meaning and on what this work has established about its usefulness to the understanding of South Asian women's identity. The impact of globalisation on the world's economies means that there have been profound changes in the composition of local, regional and national cultural practices. The break-up of metanarratives and the arrival of new genealogies for spatial fixity, new diasporic communities and the corresponding emergence of new subjectivities; indicates that diaspora has taken on a new dimension (Brah, 1996). Diaspora has becomes a breeding ground for new sociological concepts within scholarly work. The rise of migration, nomadism, religious movements, urbanisation and pilgrimages have all helped precipitate the arrival of new sociological constructs of culture. In recent times diaspora has penetrated the discipline of sociology and provides new ways of thinking about race and ethnicity. The advent of hyphenated identities and multinational attachments reveal not so much loopholes in the traditional ways of analysing culture, but previously uncharted territory within the discipline itself (Werbner, 1997). Consequently, earlier anthropological conceptualisations of culture are rendered inadequate and inappropriate models for analysing the heterogeneous composition of group collectivities in contemporary society.

A growing scholarly literature has responded to the evident expansion of the concept and discourse of diaspora and attempts to probe its salient features and limits (Safran, 1991; Tololyan, 1991 and 1996; Hall, 1990; Gilroy, 1993; Clifford, 1994; Brah, 1996; Werbner, 1990). Vertovec (1996) suggests four ways of approaching the idea of diaspora within this literature. The first, and most literal, is that of a social category: for example, referring exclusively to the experience of the Jews, who dispersed throughout the world over the centuries. This concept of diaspora often focused on a forced displacement and therefore was centred on negative experiences in terms of alienation, loss and victimisation. Whilst their ancestral dispossession is an overwhelmingly negative concept, the idea of the Jewish diaspora describes a community whose socio-economic, cultural, familial and political networks cross boundaries of states, and preserve a common shared identity. Although transformed by the influences of surrounding cultures; for many the dream of return to the 'homeland' provided a fundamental principle of identity.

The same model has been applied to other groups often seen as forcibly dispersed, such as the African-American or Armenian diasporas. As a social category, diaspora has created a theoretical framework within which categories including immigrants, ethnic minorities, refugees or migrant labourers cannot be wholly included because the circumstances of their displacement do not necessarily reach back through generations to define collective identities.

It is possible to emigrate, whether temporarily or permanently, without acquiring a diasporic identity. For example, North African day-labourers who regularly cross the Mediterranean to harvest crops in Southern Spain, move to a seasonal workplace and then return to a home, which they have not really left in cultural terms. Another example is an Irish person who migrates to England or the USA and successfully melts into the surrounding culture, not seeking out the company of her compatriots and deliberately losing her accent. By contrast, in Vertovec's second way of thinking about diaspora, membership of a diasporic community implies a self-conscious attachment to the place of origin as well as a sense of being somewhere else; a sense that one can share with others whose roots are left behind in the same country. To that extent, a first generation immigrant may have a choice as to whether or not to become part of a diaspora. There is less of a choice for daughters or sons when the parents have clung to their cultural and linguistic roots; these people, and their offspring, if they retain that sense of identity, constitute a diaspora, but the term diaspora is sometimes applied rather loosely to cover all individuals who share a 'foreign' heritage within the host culture (Vertovec, 1996).

The third sense in which the word is used is that of diaspora as a mode of cultural production. Cultural identity is fluid, produced and reproduced so that it often results in 'hybrid' forms of expression. In the British South Asian example, this might include bhangra music or curry houses, neither of which could have come into existence without the interaction of different cultures; each marks the presence of the diasporic community within the majority culture and the way that each has influenced the shape of the other (Hall, 1990; Vertovec, 1996).

For instance, bhangra music has signalled the development of a self-conscious and distinctively British South Asian youth culture. This originates in the Punjab and celebrates the rhythms of the dhol and dholki drums, and is associated with major social occasions, including the harvest festivals. However, in the context of Britain, bhangra music has been reinvented, with bands bringing in sound sampling, drum machines and synthesisers to produce new forms of the bhangra beat, different from the raw dholi sounds found in the bhangra music in its pure form in the Punjab. Again this has developed so that other influences from hip-hop and house music have been incorporated, producing northern rock bhangra and house bhangra (Bennett, 2000).

This cultural approach sees the diaspora(s) as part(s) of the 'host' culture(s) and vice-versa. These musical forms are important for the South Asian youth culture, as they cut across nationalities, religion, caste or class and the way they subvert such intra-community divisions is essential when discussing the relevance to British South Asians of the notion of diaspora as a mode of cultural production. This is comparable to the articulation of black diasporic culture in Britain as being about finding alternative ways of defining British identity (Clifford, 1997).

Finally, Vertovec (1996) suggests a fourth approach, diaspora as a 'problem'. Transnational communities may be, and often are seen, as problems or threats to state security and to the social order when seen from right-wing perspectives within the 'host' countries (Vertovec, 1996, p. 54). Here, the individual's connection with the country of origin calls into question their loyalty to the host country. The existence of hybrid cultural forms and multiple identities are viewed as diluting or undermining the traditional norms of the indigenous population. This has taken its most recent expression in official concerns about South Asian communities in Britain since the 2001 'riots' (Hussain and Bagguley, 2005).

Each of these four approaches to the understanding of diaspora is valid in its own way, and indicative of diaspora as a transnational network of dispersed individuals. These individuals are connected by ties of co-responsibility across the boundaries of empires, political communities or nations (Werbner, 1990). Yet despite their dispersal, they share a collective past and common destiny, and hence also a simultaneity in time. The novels, stories and films examined elsewhere in this book include characters and situations defined in terms of a resentful yearning for the ancestral homeland, or a sense of belonging to more than one home, or the cross-fertilisation of two cultures, or the experience of coming into conflict with the majority culture.

Diaspora as a sociological concept takes account of a 'homing' desire – that is, a need for belonging to an identity rooted in a geographical origin – as opposed to simply a desire for a 'homeland' in the sense of returning to, possessing or reconquering a physical territory (Brah, 1996). The dream of returning to the homeland provides a fundamental principle of the diasporic identity. This way of thinking about diaspora puts the ideas of 'home' and 'dispersion' in a creative tension with each other, 'inscribing a homing desire while simultaneously critiquing discourses of fixed origins' (Brah, 1996, p. 193). Diasporas emerge out of migrations of collectivities and are places of long-term, if not permanent, community formation. The traumas of dislocation and separation, coupled with instances of hope and new beginnings are collided with individual and collective memories. These memories which over time become reconfigured and reassembled according to the historical circumstances in which they have been situated. Therefore, should origins be treated in essentialist terms or as a matter of historical displacements?

Those who feel they are being impoverished often tend to embrace the consciousness of the diaspora. While this pertains to an idealised and romanticised image of the homeland, they are merely embracing a 'primary diaspora' (Safran, 1991, p. 88). Black communities often relate exclusively to primary diasporas since they no longer have a clearly defined cultural heritage to preserve, they have been uprooted and dispersed by imperialism and slavery over the centuries. Black diasporas find alternative ways of defining their identities within the 'situatedness' in which they find themselves. This can be conceived of as a new creative output within the concept of diaspora, since they have effectively created new 'exclusive' cultural standpoints, i.e. Black English, Black Islam, Rap music, ghetto-orientated lifestyles, which are very different from the post-war Jazz and blues era, which depicted a peculiar inclusiveness of black culture (Gilroy, 1993). Whereas South Asians have a stronger sense of identity, in a majority of circumstances, they have only been uprooted once from the country of origin, their sense of origin is even stronger. Consequently their works have more similarity with works from South Asia although they remain distinctively diasporic.

Irrespective of this, these new diasporic imagined communities are essentially products of White hegemony, since they have been legitimised through the dominant economic and political means. These new diasporic formations are a means for re-defining origins, or integrating origins in the context of the new historical situation they find themselves within.

It is important to note that diasporas around the world are not identical. Each diaspora is a formation of many journeys and therefore has its own history and its own particularities. It becomes an interweaving of disparate narratives: South Asians in Britain have a different history from South Asians in Canada. The social, economic, political and cultural conditions that mark the trajectories of the journey made from one national culture to another are important when analysing the different formations of diaspora globally. For instance, has the diaspora evolved through conquest, colonisation, or from the capture or removal of a group through slavery or labour, or resulted from desertion of their home as a result of expulsion and persecution within the home country? Whilst the conditions of leaving are important when deconstructing the concept of diaspora, so too are the conditions of arrival and settlement (Vertovec, 1996).

The concept of diaspora is entwined with the concept of power, because power determines the relations between minorities and majorities and often determines their insertion within the social relations of class, gender, racism and sexuality (Brah, 1996). The situating of a group within a country in terms of its economic, political and social structure is also critical to its future interpretation. This relational positioning allows a deconstruction of the power which operates to determine the differences between one group and another with respect to the position that it holds within the cultural framework. Configurations of power shape the location of migrants within their own diasporic space and also the conditions of existence within it. These are critical to determining the future condition or 'situatedness' (Brah, 1996, p. 182) of migrant communities. Therefore each diaspora has to be analysed in its own historical specificity, and its relational positioning to that of other diasporas and more importantly the dominant group in society (Brah, 1996). Different diasporas suggest different narratives. The means of acquiring self-identity within diasporic communities is thus a 'creative' output, since it positions itself relationally to that of others and accordingly attempts to reach a milieu in which the chosen identity can sustain a high degree of autonomy.

Central to the concept of diaspora is the image of a journey; however, not all journeys can be understood as diaspora. Diasporic journeys are not the same as casual travel; they are about 'settling down and putting roots elsewhere' (Brah, 1996 p. 182) – crossing geographical and mental borders. These discussions of diaspora are inevitably bound up with the notion of 'borders and territories' – the arbitrary lines of social, cultural and psychic demarcation. Borders are politically and ideologically constructed as well as forming an analytical category. They have always been used as a means for reflecting upon the indigenous condition of social relations within a restricted area. However, both borders and diaspora are concepts constructed around references to the theme of locations, displacement and dislocation. They act as metaphors for psychological, spiritual, class and racialised boundaries which signify the locality of subjectivities. They are metaphors and narratives which remain firmly entrenched in the power relations indigenous to particular areas.

Borders mark out social, cultural and psychic territories, which are patrolled to defend against those whom they construct as outsiders, or even aliens. Each border has a unique narrative, irrespective of the commonalties it has with other borders. The border is regulated so that those who are alien and those who do not share similarities are excluded. The advent of new migrations, and the creation of new divisions of labour means that these localised narratives are becoming fragmented, rudimentary and enveloped. The changing nature of capital mobility in our globalised world, coupled with the centrifugal tendencies of the new information technologies, suggest that borderlines are becoming increasingly untenable (Brah, 1996). The cultural and generational conflicts depicted in some of the fictional narratives studied here have much to do with borders – defining borders, like Meena's mother criticising English squalor in *Anita and Me* (1996), or transgressing them like Meena herself who wants nothing more than to be like her English friend Anita.

The advent of new subjectivities and hyphenated identities are issues dealt with within South Asian literature since they describe the possibilities of new identity formations within ethnic and minority cultural spaces. This relates to how we might understand diasporic activities. According to Brah, different historical and contemporary contexts of diasporic activity must be understood not separately or comparatively, but 'in their dia-synchronic relationality' (1996, p. 190).

Diasporas are distinctive in that they exist outside states with fixed boundaries and clearly defined categories of inclusion and exclusion (Werbner, 2002). They reproduce and extend themselves without any centralised command structures (Werbner, 1990). Although diasporas are relatively autonomous of any centre, paradoxically they continue to recognise the centre and to acknowledge at least some obligations and responsibilities to it. This responsibility exists through gestures of 'giving' or khidmat, public service, thus the diaspora is in one sense not a multiplicity at all but a single place which is the world. Consequently, South Asians form a diaspora of the 'imagination' (Ghosh, 1989, p. 76), embodying an 'epic' relationship between centre and peripheries. For example South Asians in Britain have built a British South Asian diasporic community oriented towards their homelands. They send money home, consume popular cultural products from there and reproduce rituals and ceremonies. In many respects they form a conventional diaspora focused on the idea of a national homeland. However, they have also redefined themselves, so that there are formations of religious diasporas, within which the Muslim diaspora is better organised than others (Werbner, 2002).

The creative output of South Asian women in the diaspora, despite the features that it shares with that of South Asia, differs in one crucial respect. The South Asian women authors place their protagonists within familiar and essentially unchanging cultures and surroundings, which the characters by and large share with the generation that has gone before them. In the diaspora, by contrast, even the displaced generation of parents finds itself navigating within a social context that differs entirely from that which they share with their own parents, except in so far as they can preserve or re-create islands of South Asia within the host country; or to put it another way, a means of isolating their children from the life that surrounds them from day to day. Their children, the British-born generation, are further removed from the conventions of the South Asian cultures, whilst not wholly assimilated into the surrounding indigenous culture. Conflicts arise between the British born generation and their immigrant parents, which are compounded by the layers of difference between the surrounding British majority culture and that of the British South Asian communities. Thus the creative works of diasporic writers address multiple levels of contradiction and conflict around issues of collective and individual identity.

The protagonists within both South Asian and diasporic genres have sought self-realisation either in conformity or rebellion. They find self-determination through enacting an identity within which they can comfortably live even if this means radically changing the sense of self. The changeability of individual identities is another recurring motif in the novels and films considered in the chapters that follow. Personal identity emerges as the product of a process embedded in a past but open to the possibilities of the future. For women in the South Asian diaspora today, the shaping of the future itself becomes a constituent element of individual and collective identity. As individuals, they want self-realisation to take place in the here and now rather than in some hypothetical, imagined future or by the recreation of a mythological past which informs the hopes and expectations of their parents.

Since the collective 'we' of any social grouping is heterogeneous and differentiated internally, how does the collective 'we' within minority and ethnic communities become reified into singular entities? The exclusive and repressive nature of the majority tends to necessitate the existence of a collective 'we' insofar as that particular diasporic space wants to sustain a high degree of autonomy (Brah, 1996). As a result, bipolar positions or binary oppositions, emerge, i.e. White/Black, male/female. These discourses do not exercise themselves in isolation to one another, they interlink through signifiers, i.e. class, gender and ethnicity, which are prominent issues in South Asian's women's literature. This prompts new creative and discursive formations within the concept of diaspora.

The subsequent chapters, by detailing commonalties in the works by South Asian women, make it possible to distinguish distinctively British literary and cinematic genres. By the same token, exploration of the different approaches of individual authors has highlighted the plurality of identities amongst British South Asian women. As the diasporic genre has grown over the years, authors have become notably more exploratory and assertive and less dependent on cultural rootedness in South Asia. Contemporary writers include some who portray lesbians, not only within the majority but also within the minority cultures. The portrayal highlights their exclusion from both cultures, due to race and religious and cultural prejudice. The existence of this very literature is a landmark in the evolution of South Asian women's writing in Britain as it not only focuses on sexuality, which was previously a taboo area, but takes it one stage further by looking at lesbianism: these writers are rejecting the boundaries of what may permissibly be discussed as well as extending the possible boundaries of self-definition.

The creative works of British South Asian women can help to highlight the differences and conflicts that occur not only between but also within cultural groups. The plurality of identities expressed in these creative works can help to demolish the monolithic stereotypes of South Asian womanhood and of South Asian communities in general. These creative works highlight aspirations and expectations which deserve to be encouraged by those who find themselves in the position of educating or advising South Asian women. The literature provides many insights into the issues that arise within South Asian women's lives. For instance, marriage is commonly perceived as the consequence of abandoning individual ambition and surrendering to inherited cultural norms. Furthermore, the literature analysed here highlights the widespread prevalence of multi-cultural skills, such as the routine familiarity with two or three languages – English, Punjabi, Sylheti/Bengali and Arabic amongst Pakistani Muslims for example – which ought to be considered as a valuable measure of the intellectual gifts South Asian schoolgirls bring to British society.

The growth of creative work produced by the minority ethnic constituencies in Britain is constrained by political, cultural and economic considerations, yet this canon of work has substantially increased from the mid-1980s and the 1990s. Perhaps it is only to be expected that a generation of British South Asian women living through such a complex and multi-layered transition, should give rise to a rich body of creative work centred on the exploration of identity. Social scientists and indeed policy makers ought not to overlook works of the imagination as authentic and valuable evidence of the issues at large in the lives of British South Asian women. Their creative output already forms a large and growing body of evidence that provides insights into the complexity of British South Asian women's lives and their hybrid identities. As oppositional world views, values and material forces come into alignment with each other, the process under which they interact becomes internally reworked, forcing the displacement of old processes and the creation of a new. As mentioned previously, the development of bhangra music in Britain suggests that new forms of hyphenated or hybrid collective identities are evolving as a direct result of this.

Cultural Hybridity

In terms of the 19th-century and early 20th-century discourses of 'scientific' racism, hybridity was seen as a threat to the concepts of purity and exclusivity, positioned negatively as contaminating culture. Fears were expressed about the 'degeneration' which might result if different races mingled freely (Cashmore, 1996). However, the term has since then moved out of the discourse of race and become situated within a more neutral zone of identity; it has been recognised as having positive features (Papastergiadis, 1997).

The overlapping of identities that characterises the diasporic experience creates a cultural hybridity. The term can usefully be applied to British South Asians, because individuals formed within that context do not have identities that are reducible either to one element – Britishness – or another – Asianness. As Meena found, in *Amritvela* (1988), going to India brought her to an awareness that her identity did not fit into the surrounding culture, whereas her experience of racism in Britain underlined her difference from the indigenous population. In each setting, the hybridity of her identity was brought out by contrasting it with different aspects of itself.

Papastergiadis (1997, p. 258) argues that the 'positive feature of hybridity is that it invariably acknowledges that identity is constructed through a negotiation of difference'. Hybridity brings to light narratives of origin and encounter. The conventional value of the hybrid has always been dependent on its relation to the value of purity, which is determined by the success of inclusion and exclusion. The negative associations given to hybridity often notably emanate from a confusion of subject positions.

However, do the discourses of hybridity contained within the supposedly more neutral zone of identity still carry connotations of 'race'? Is hybridity a product of the transforming nature of diasporic communities, the confluence of narratives and new re-awakening of subjective positions or is it the cause of such transgressions? The problem with diaspora as a concept lies in its inherent tendency to appropriate its conditions of life to that of the host country. Hybridity however offers new discourses and methodologies for locating diasporic communities in their concrete conditions. In order for hybridity to merge two cultures, or more, a narcissistic sense of inclusion (contentment with identity) and a transgressive sense of extension (adapting to surroundings) are prerequisite conditions. Although adapting to new surroundings may be seen as an unnecessary susceptibility under the guise of the cultural hybrid, to incorporating western elements into their identity, it may also offer new possibilities for cultural spaces of understanding.

As oppositional world views, values and material forces come into alignment with each other, the process under which they interact becomes internally reworked, forcing the displacement of old processes and the creation of new ones. For instance, as mentioned earlier, bhangra music or the advent of the curry houses in Britain suggest that new forms of hyphenated or hybrid collective identities are evolving as a direct result of this. However, what are the limits of hybridisations, creolisation or hyphenation models in their direct challenge to previous holistic constructs and essentialist notions of culture?

Hybridisation, according to Bhabha (1994), is intrinsic to all forms of racial transformation and traditional renewal. Bhabha argues that hybridity is not limited to the cataloguing of difference and the sum of its parts, but emerges through the process of opening 'a third space', where elements of diverse origins encounter each other and a mutual transformation results. For example, in *The Red Box* (1991), Raisa and Tahira both struggle to negotiate their own spaces between the majority culture and parental convention, in neither of which they can feel entirely at home. This third space is an open, expansive space encouraging the assimilation of contrary signs and metanarratives which obviously remain a necessary precondition for the articulation of cultural differences and the inscription of cultural hybridity. In fact, in all of the novels surveyed, cultural hybridity is developed as a problematic concept: the process of identity formation is premised on boundaries between 'us' and 'them'. The hybrid figures born of crossing or transgressing such boundaries become indecisive about their identity, at times appearing lost. In theory, the hybrid may be manifested with strength and vitality if the individual succeeds in creating a positive 'third space'; however, it is noteworthy that none of the central protagonists in the fiction surveyed quite succeeds in this enterprise. Nevertheless, the intervention of the 'third space' as a sociological concept within the treatment of diasporic communities, ensures that we begin to understand the current trends whereby, 'the meanings and symbols of culture have no primordial unity fixity; that even the same signs can be appropriated, translated, rehistoricised and read anew' (Bhabha, 1994, p. 37). The overlapping elements of identity within the characters portrayed in this body of diasporic literature form sites of potential conflict and tension, which is presumably what makes them attractive as fictional constructs: they embody in their hybridity the subtle complexities of human life (Papastergiadis, 1997).

Gilroy's critique of Black culture implements the 'third space' as an appropriate model for understanding its historical transgression. Apparently as a way of assimilating themselves into British culture, for Black people it has become not so much a process of acculturation but one of cultural syncretism. This has produced a diasporic dimension to Black life where emerging contradictions and continuities within the culture have made it difficult to ascertain its roots: 'the effects of these ties and the penetration of Black forms into the dominant culture means that it is impossible to theorise black culture in Britain without developing a new perspective on British culture as a whole' (Gilroy, 1987, p. 156).

The opening up of the 'third space' within the concept of diaspora denotes the dia-synchronic relationality of cultural ties. This means that cultural practices can be detached from their roots and used to found and extend new patterns of 'metacommunication' (Gilroy, 1987, p. 217) which attribute substance and collective identity to imagined communities. The intervention of Black culture into the traditional scope of the dominant articulations of power means that new genealogies are being created in the synthesis and transcendence of previous styles. Therefore, terms such as ethnicity and minority are no longer strictly amendable to fixed categories. Hall contests the boundaries of ethnicity and defines identity as paradoxically both inclusive and subjective-specific; 'we are all ethnically located and our ethnic identities are crucial to our subjective sense of who we are' (Hall, 1988, p. 5). The political, historical and social conditions in which we are born into shape the outlook for ensuing identity formations and also diasporic community formation.

Post-colonial theory is key to understanding the new diasporic community formations in our contemporary age. It allows for the detachment of forms from existing practices and their reformation, or indeed 'transmigration' into new forms into new practices, new diverse logics and the creation of new forms of boundary. Nevertheless, these concepts are also in danger of celebrating the very reification they seek to suppress and challenge since hyphenation is anchored in ethnicity, which could easily shift to an essential category, having continuity in time and space and thus undermining its relational character. Hybridity ascribes cultures and identities with dynamism and fluidity, yet they remain firmly entrenched in territorial ideas, which are limiting. Therefore, rather than being practice bound, the sources of identity ultimately remain pre-given and restricted by national or transnational territorial constructs (Brah, 1996).

By producing a sense of locality in a multi-faceted, contradictory environment of national political formation and global electronic mediation, these new types of oppositional discourse, bolstered by creative diasporic writers are being articulated by a self-defeating logic. Nonetheless, the resilience of localised cultural categories in contemporary society has come about largely through the intervention of the 'third space' and new diasporic communities. The dynamics of cultural transmission suggests that the criss-crossing links between different cultural categories and the slow juxtaposition of bipolar world views breeds new localised identities and communities of a more egalitarian, pluralistic, and participatory kind.

Analytical Themes

What can the creative work considered in the following chapters tell us about British South Asian women that was not already widely known? The answers are themselves challenges for further research into an area that is in a constant state of evolutionary change and for which change is itself a fundamental constituent. The creative output reflects and contributes to the plurality of individual and group identities amongst British South Asian women. It constitutes a body of evidence that serves to challenge stereotypical notions of a unified and unchanging female 'South Asianness' in Britain.

The contrast between South Asian and diasporic women's writings highlights some of the ways in which South Asian women brought up in western cultural surroundings undertake a quest for individual identity. This quest for identity is characterised by multi-dimensional contradictions which exist within the specific geographical framework within which they live. Choices have to be made between the languages of the home and of the outside world, between South Asian and British social mores, between parental expectations and individual desires, between religious heritage and secular surroundings, between different senses of homeland, between different perceptions of class belonging and, at least in some cases, between inherited notions of sexuality as a preordained biological imperative, governed by religious law and custom, and an alternative view of sexuality as just another changeable dimension of personal identity. These conflicts encourage women not only to feel freer to explore within boundaries but even to extend the number of boundaries within which they explore, in search of self.

Education emerges as an important aspect of the women's lives: it gives them status, value and respect. Access to educational opportunities affords a young woman of the diaspora possibilities of social advancement that may not have been available to previous generations of women in her family. The latter has implications for her desirability as a marriage partner and her self-esteem.

The question of marriage raises the issue of conflicting expectations between partners from different cultural backgrounds, particularly in the case of cross-cultural marriages, whether between two South Asians – one from the diaspora and another from South Asia – or between one South Asian and someone from a different South Asian background, or another background altogether. As some of the novelists illustrate, culture shock can subvert and even destroy such marriages.

A further point that figures in much of the diasporic creative writing is the emergence of new forms of hyphenated or hybrid collective identities – for instance, British South Asian – that find expression not only in the writings themselves and the visual arts, but also in phenomena such as bhangra music, cross-cultural foods and fashions. South Asian young women in Britain are of course exposed to the mass media, which acts as a powerful influence on self-perception, whether in offering role models or in giving rise to resentment and alienation. The television and cinematic work of Meena Syal, possibly the most influential South Asian woman in the British media, not only provides a platform for the concerns of women of the diaspora but also offers a positive role model for young women who may wish to pursue a career in the creative arts.

The identities of South Asian women in Britain are shaped in part by rejection or acceptance on the basis of ethnicity. The experience of racism is not necessarily confined to hatred or contempt emanating from within the ethnic majority towards the minority, but it may also have origins among South Asians themselves in the form of disdain towards the 'uncultured' majority.

One factor that is notable precisely for its absence from the literature surveyed is that of caste. Whether or not caste prejudice is eroding within the diasporic communities is a subject that deserves further research. Some British South Asians consciously choose to abandon considerations of caste as part of their lives, but as the advertisements in the minority press show, it still figures in many instances in the choice of marriage partner – perhaps influenced by parental concerns. Nevertheless, it would appear on the evidence of the fictional narratives considered here that caste does not figure prominently within the self-identifying concerns of diasporic womanhood.

By integrating the different dimensions of their hybrid cultural heritage, the women whose work is considered in the following chapters have produced changes within the meaning of the diasporic identity. The diasporic literature highlights that purity as an uncontaminated notion does not exist but has its origins in diversity and difference (Gilroy, 1993). The creative works articulate a challenge to the notion of 'Asianness' as a homogeneous and simple category, and to the notion that these genres of writing and film owe their origins merely to a response to racist and sexist inequalities; instead, as it expands and develops, they are becoming more preoccupied with 'universal' human themes located specifically within the diasporic experience.

Networks of artists and writers have been developed, in particular during the 1980s and 1990s which have served to shape not only their political agenda, but also their critical discourse. The confidence with which the women write is apparent and it may be anticipated that this will increase. Thus, as the twenty-first century unfolds, old categorisations will no longer be tenable. The literature will undoubtedly continue to change in combinations of form, content and the identity it expresses. As the assertion of British South Asian identity increases in quality and quantity the boundaries between this hybrid identity and that of the indigenous population may well erode to the point where the British identity itself includes and embraces that of its South Asian heritage component. In this way the creative output of British South Asian women can contribute to the construction of a new and inclusive discourse of post-racist Britishness.

Inter-generational conflict is a central theme of many of the works considered below. Chapter 2 outlines the sociological aspects of identity, relating them to the first generation of British South Asians and then the second and subsequent generations, with an emphasis on the women within the two groups. The chapter emphasises the emergence of distinct first- and second-generation identities among British South Asians, and establishes these as the basis for the thematic concerns of the novels and films created by second generation British South Asian women.

'Black' as a category has been frequently used to describe individuals of South Asian descent. The term is discussed in Chapter 3 with reference to feminism and its role in stimulating the creative writings of both African Caribbean and South Asian women. The failure of mainstream feminist discourse to include those from ethnic minority backgrounds is analysed and Black British feminism is discussed in relation to the experiences of ethnic minority women. The analysis highlights the redefinition of Black identities as culturally plural, rather than fixed with regard to political campaigning. It is suggested that the impact of Black feminism can be seen in the writings of these women in terms of thematic concerns and style.

The emergence of the New Woman is considered, with a comparative analysis of her role in South Asian and South Asian diasporic literature in Chapter 4. This New Woman represents a change occurring within the female protagonists' lives, where questions of identity are raised and an understanding of the self is gained through self-analysis. This change brings both emotional and physical consequences for the women. Whilst the two South Asian and diasporic canons of literature are different primarily due to geographical locations, the depiction of the New Woman is a phenomenon common to both. By identifying the similarities and differences in the way the New Woman within these literatures is created, we may reach a more adequate understanding of the specificity of the identity-related concerns of diasporic women compared to those of women living in the subcontinent. In particular, the representation the New Woman in the diasporic context also reflects the impacts of migration and racism in Britain.

Some of these key issues of identity are explored through Gurinder Chadha's films *Bhaji on the Beach* (1994) and *Bend it like Beckham* (2002). The former film was the first mainstream work to be directed, written and produced by a British South Asian woman and symbolises the development and increasing commercial attractiveness of South Asian women's creativity in Britain. Their distinction from other films focusing on the South Asian community lies in their representation of the female characters. *Bhaji on the Beach* concentrates not only on the cultural characteristics that define the South Asian community in Britain but also on the extent of their Englishness (Grice, 1994). *Bend it like Beckham* similarly features the question of national symbols and identities through football. The following analysis examines the influence that the indigenous culture has had on the individuals' lives and concludes with a re-definition of British identities as susceptible to movement and change, more specifically a hybridisation of identity. In this way it is argued that these films involve the 'desification' of British cinema. 'Desi' means authentically South Asian, with reference to its geographical and social origins, but it also has a deeper meaning of being rooted in the South Asian community, carrying with it connotations of pride and self-worth. For instance, when it is argued that Gurinder Chadha's films 'desify' British cinema, it means that the themes, music and language of British film is transformed through the introduction of South Asian elements, so that this is a specifically British South Asian form of hybridisation.

Chapter 6 examines Monica Ali's novel *Brick Lane* (2003), another example of the recent commercial success of British South Asian women's creativity. The analysis of this novel focuses particularly on the trauma of migration, the strains of transnational sisterhood and the difficulties of settling in a hostile society. However, the novel was severely criticised by the Bangladeshi community when it was published. Ali's positioning as an author outside of the community that she attempted to represent limits the novel's authenticity. Although trying to represent the concerns of Bangladeshi women, the novel ultimately fails to achieve this due to Ali's lack of familiarity with the issues she is discussing.

The influential work of Meena Syal features in Chapter 7, in a study of her novel *Anita and Me* (1996). The issues of childhood, race and culture are focused upon here, since they represent areas that are of central importance within the novel. The midlands mining village where it is set, Tollington, is a focus for the family and its responses to White society. In this way Tollington symbolises White Britain in the 1970s. The novel highlights the process of hybridisation through the experiences of the child protagonist Meena, who learns who to come to terms with her parents' culture whilst growing up with White friends.

Chapter 2

Identity and Gender Across Generations of British South Asians

Introduction

South Asians in Britain are an heterogeneous group made up of individuals from various parts of the world, some originate directly from South Asia, some from different parts of Africa but mainly East Africa, and a few from Fiji, Mauritius, the West Indies and other parts of the British Empire (Ramdin, 1999). According to the 2001 census (ONS, 2003), South Asians in Britain number over 2.2 million, with Indians just over 1,035,807 as the largest group, followed by Pakistanis 714, 826 and Bangladeshis 280,830. Each of these groups differ in several respects, they belong to different ethnic, religious and linguistic groups, consequently evolving different forms of cultural and social life. Whilst South Asians shared and continue to share many common features, the differences between them are beginning to emerge in several areas of life. Differences in housing patterns, unemployment rates, attitudes to marriage and socio-economic disadvantages vary across ethnicity. Furthermore, a shift in identification from culture to religion has created a further barrier.

This chapter describes the network of social aspects which shape the identities of the South Asian population in Britain. The identity structures of the children of South Asians are considered in relation to those of their parents, who came over to Britain in the 1950s and 1960s. This is achieved by describing the complex network of social processes that shape the identity of specific generations of South Asians in Britain. Changes between the generations both affect their expressive cultures in very important ways, and are major themes in the texts themselves.

First-Generation Settler-Citizens

For the first generation settler-citizens, identity has been overwhelmingly influenced by the immigration process. The demand for labour within the post-war British economy instigated the large scale of Indian and Pakistani immigration to Britain. The traumas of migration, dispersal and exile from their native country as well as the discrimination they experienced have become potent forces in the formation of their political and social relations; this differs from their children (Gilroy, 1993). Not only does it provide different social and cultural changes, but their definition as a minority group is an important factor that contributes highly to immigrant's experiences. These factors, coupled with the reasons behind immigration and the adaptation and assimilation process that follows, profoundly affect the individual's concept of self.

For first-generation immigrants, their participation in British society was limited due to both the external constraints of prejudice and discrimination and the internal constraints embedded within cultural values and norms. Furthermore, the notion of return had contributed to their exclusion – the mythology that they were in Britain to save, invest and return to the subcontinent (Anwar, 1979). This contributed to how they acted and created a specific relationship between the individual and society (Verma et al., 1986). Making money was the prime objective, so that South Asian employees became known as hard workers. With a very basic education, they were forced to lower their sights in the employment market, holding unskilled jobs as labourers in mills and factories, working long hours in poor conditions for relatively little pay. South Asians were more cautious about adapting to British society, only doing so when it was functionally necessary. Furthermore, discrimination was experienced in all spheres of social life, including employment and housing in which physical and cultural traits were held in low esteem by the dominant segments of society (Ramdin, 1999).

From the perspective of the host country, immigration into Britain was nothing new, but so-called 'coloured' immigration on a 'mass' scale from 1948 was presented as a novel dimension compared to that of the Jews, Irish, or of European-heritage citizens of the 'White' Old Commonwealth. Cultural differentiation was determined by reference to skin colour and significantly contributed to their reception by the host country. The differences evoked curiosity and ignorance that often manifested itself in discrimination. Furthermore, Britain's colonial subjects arrived in the country just at the very time Britain's power was in obvious decline (Hutnik, 1991). Prejudice and discrimination became a common experience for the racially visible minorities. As the concept of the empire became an issue for many individuals so did the morality of imperialism, and the notion of the White man's burden fuelled simple racial prejudice. Racial violence and racism became a dominant part of British national politics. It became a national sport to beat up 'Pakis', as all South Asians were known with the years between 1971-1976 – known as the 'Paki-Bashing' era. Violent and other anti-immigrant movements were also achieving prominence, such as the British Campaign to Stop Immigration and the National Front (Anwar, 1979).

Between 1958 and 1968, racism was institutionalised, legitimised and 'nationalised' with immigrants officially relegated to the status of second-class citizens (Fryer, 1984). It soon became apparent that decisions at political and administrative levels which involved considerations of race were weighted towards subordinating and maintaining control over racial minorities (Carmichael and Hamilton, 1967).

The racism experienced brought with it a potential threat to the continuity of the group identity, forcing minority groups to define and emphasise their own ethnicity, by seeking support from their own kinship and friendship networks in Britain (Verma et al., 1986). This succeeded in enhancing the individual's self-consciousness of their minority group membership and strengthening their in-group cohesiveness and solidarity (Hutnik, 1991). These networks continue to determine a dominant pattern of activity in almost all fields of social interaction among the South Asian population in Britain, helping to facilitate the immigration and settlement within British society. However this networking also resulted in their encapsulation within, and isolation from, the dominant society (Anwar, 1979).

However, the racism and inferiority complex cannot be treated simply from a sociological perspective, it has to be located historically. The historical roots of racist practices within Britain have been conditioned if not determined by the historical development of British imperialism. South Asians are former colonial subjects, belonging to a group whose country was once ruled by Britain. From the beginning of the post-colonial South Asian presence in Britain therefore, the type and quality of social relations and interaction between the South Asians and the British indigenous population was circumscribed by the history of colonialism and imperialism and its aftermath. This contributed to their reactions in Britain and that of the receiving country.

The relationship between the immigrants and the host society was largely premised on the immigrants' presumed intention to return to the homeland. Their migration was seen as temporary, their motives were supposedly economic. Pakistani and Indian migrants started off as 'sojourners' intending to spend time working in Britain, make money, then return and invest their savings in buying some more land for farming or setting up a small business. But the idea of returning home for permanent settlement failed to materialise with immigrants staying longer than anticipated. The reason that brought about this change was that the identity of the migrants changed. They were no longer sojourners, who planned to return to their home society but 'settlers', who intended to remain permanently abroad (Dhaya, 1973).

With an overwhelming majority of the migrants from rural origins, a gradual change occurred, with Pakistani migrants no longer remaining Pakistani village peasants (Akram, 1974). Immigration involved a change in social position from that of a peasant to that of an industrial worker. They found themselves not only favouring the better standards of living in Britain and but also becoming attuned to industrialisation. However, the most significant change was that with the arrival of their wives and children, it became increasingly difficult to contemplate going back home. Even today, the idea of returning home for permanent settlement lingers amongst migrants; however, it has become what Mohammed Anwar refers to a 'myth', more of a fantasy than a reality (Anwar, 1979).

First Generation Women

The extensive literature concerning South Asian migration to Britain has largely ignored the concerns of, the roles assigned to and played by, women. Although immigration legislation has had an important impact on South Asian women, literature addressing the immigration of African-Caribbean and South Asian workers has often ignored gender (Parmar, 1982). The literature assumes that immigrants are male who produce male children, yet the number of women entering Britain rapidly increased during the 1960s (Lomas, 1973). This was the case for Pakistani and Indian women; however, reunification of spouses and children is still taking place for some among the Bangladeshi population.

Whilst the very act of bringing South Asian women into the sociological literature seems to symbolise a move towards multiculturalism, this can also serve to help racism become institutionalised (Trivedi, 1984). There were differences in how the women perceived themselves and how others perceived them. To South Asian women, the individualism and independence so valued in the West appears selfish and irresponsible. Yet their positioning within the ancestry culture was focused upon, therefore on the rare occasions when reference was made to women, the literature used ethnocentric and pathological categories (Dahya, 1965; Uberoi, 1965; Khan, 1976, Kabeer, 2000). The description of South Asian women in Britain was particularly vulnerable to ethnocentric distortion; they were perceived from the perspective of essentially Western values so that the emphasis on independence and individuality and the comparability of the sexes evoked stereotypical images. These texts conceptualised South Asian women as subjugated by the arranged marriage system, economically and emotionally dependent on their husbands. Furthermore, they were conservative upholders of traditional social norms, who not only felt threatened by British norms and values themselves but shared worries about Britain's influence on their children (Trivedi, 1984).

South Asian women's stereotyped representation within the Western framework has been paralleled by their cultural invisibility, which attributed a dominant role to men and an inferior status to women (Wilson, 1978). Yet, in reality, within the South Asian family the 'position' of women is crucial: the woman is the centre of the household. The positioning of immigrant South Asian women was largely determined by the fact that they did not initiate migration but rejoined their husbands later as legal dependants arriving as wives or daughters, rather than for independent reasons. But once in England, these women experienced changes in their identity (Bell, 1971).

Having been accustomed to family support, these women initially found themselves isolated after marrying and moving into the marital home in Britain. They experienced separation from their husbands for many years only to find themselves without the security of the family and the emotional support of other women, when joining their husbands. Although this isolation proved a problem initially, it was countered by positive qualities. They experienced independence, and found themselves in control of their own lives. Having been in an environment where the mother-in-law and other elders took control in the running of the household, these women experienced greater control over the socialisation of their children and the running of their homes. Moreover, the lack of emotional and physical support by others in the family strengthened the relationship between a husband and his wife, leading to the development of confidence and self-assurance (Trivedi, 1984).

Economic circumstances brought several further changes. The rise in the cost of living, high mortgage repayments, high rents, the desire for a better environment for the children plus the desire for independence meant that greater numbers of South Asian women, in particular those of Indian origin, entered the labour market (Uberoi, 1965; Dahya, 1965; Khan, 1976). According to the 1971 Census, 40.8 per cent of women from India were working, in comparison to just 20.7 per cent of women from Pakistan (Parmar, 1982). The reasons for these variations are not clear. Although factors such as employment opportunities must play some part in determining the entry of specific women within the labour market, socio-cultural and religious factors must also be taken into account. More specifically, it seems that the figures for Indian women were especially influenced by data for those of Sikh and Hindu origin. However, when they started to go out to work, language barriers restricted their contact with White British working women. Although Sikh and Hindu women may have been more outgoing than Pakistani and Bangladeshi women, their very exposure to a wider sphere of influence may have entailed other difficulties, confusion and stresses, which have in turn affected family life, as Kalra (1980) found among Sikh women in Southall.

The majority of these women came from societies where women were involved in labour both inside and outside the home, but what was new in Britain was that they had not worked in an industrial situation. For Sikh and Hindu women, wage labour brought new experiences, baffling and exciting, because for the first time, they had an independent economic identity. They found themselves in an environment where independence meant that they were now able to determine their own future and develop their own individuality (Parmar, 1982). But in working, these women found themselves facing greater obstacles and difficulties regarding childminding than English women (Ethnic Minority Community Relations Council, 1975). Ethnic minority mothers failed to access the services they desired, because they had less access to subsidised or free services, while many White minders refused to take Black and South Asian children. Additionally, they had problems in finding access to childminders near their homes. When the government introduced language classes and health and child care education, these were criticised by the community it sought to help because they helped South Asian women adopt English habits and were primarily seen as attempts to help them to become more integrated (Parmar, 1982). The minority communities themselves also set up language classes to teach their children Urdu or Bengali, as well as running religious classes where children learnt the language of their religion; Punjabi for the Sikhs, Hindi for the Hindus and Arabic for the Muslims (Kershen, 2000).

Sociological literature about South Asian women (e.g. Khan, 1976) generally focuses on the socio-cultural features of South Asian communities as a source of restriction, as opposed to the institutional power relations that have served to oppress and exploit them. The South Asian community with its cultural, religious and communal factors becomes easy to blame for the subordinate position held by South Asian women within the British social structure. Whilst restrictions within the community no doubt do, to some extent, constrain South Asian women within patriarchal and ideological and traditional assumptions, these texts fail to consider the economic, political and ideological structures that also reproduce South Asian women as a particular category (Parmar, 1982).

Trivedi (1984) argued that in reproducing stereotypical ideas about the South Asian woman as being passive, non-working, controlled by her family's wishes and unable to assert her own ambitions and desires, these authors fail to look at the ways in which institutional racism permeates British society and affects the position of South Asian women. The late 1970s were marked by the attempts to develop critical analysis of the experiences of South Asian and African Caribbean women, in the form of Amrit Wilson's *Finding A Voice: Asian Women In Britain* (1978) and M. Prescod-Roberts and N. Seele's, *Black Women Bring It All Back Home* (1980). Generally, the image of women as militant or within a political movement is absent; passivity and submissiveness dominate this conceptualisation. Their participation in protests and revolts and their roles in transforming social relations in both Britain and India reveal a different image from that of passivity (Jayawardena, 1982).

In employment, South Asian women were not seen as part of the working class. Imperialism, under-development, sexual inequality and racism have meant that the majority of women from the sub-continent were pushed into unskilled or semi-skilled jobs in the form of 'sweatshops' or sewing clothes at home simply because they had no particular work skills. Whilst it became important for them to work, since their economic contribution was important, being part of the workforce created self-confidence and a growth in self-reliance, giving them the courage to claim their rights through political organisation. They defied orthodox thinking inside and outside the community by being at the forefront of struggles, and they organised to gain better wages and conditions. Demonstrations were staged, for example at Grunwick and Chix, in which South Asian women, in particular Indian women, actively campaigned alongside others (Ramdin, 1999).

South Asian women also began to challenge both the state and the family. They fought against the racism of the state and resisted its attempts to institutionalise their position as dependants of men without an existence of their own (Trivedi, 1984). This notion came about legally as immigration legislation allowed women entry into Britain only as dependants of male workers. These rules and practices were racially and sexually discriminatory, subjecting women to humiliating and coercive interrogations to establish their credentials as dependants of men. The harassment faced by women and children because of this placed them in a vulnerable situation, having to prove their legal status as a wife or fiancée, or that the children accompanying them were actually theirs. This dependency on men became entrenched and perpetuated beyond immigration for the women as it often trapped them in violent relationships with men. Such women have campaigned for an independent political right of existence against this dependency, ensuring that a woman who finds herself unable to live with the man she had come to join in Britain is not deported.

As far as the family was concerned, recurring individual cases of deportation or an individual woman's attempt to have her children join her have resulted in numerous campaigns. South Asian women resisted the state in its attempts to control and define family relations within the South Asian community. This intrusion, seen as political as well as personal, has provided an arena of debate and discussion as well as an impetus to organise collectively up to the present day (Parmar, 1982).

Domestic violence was another issue around which the women organised themselves (Griffin, 1995). It was presented as a different dimension where the

South Asian family provides a major source of oppression. Ultimately the setting up of refuges by battered South Asian women has been a contentious issue, and has been opposed from various sections within the South Asian community. Cultural traditions lay at the roots of women's subordination, but a change occurred in attitudes to correspond to Western industrialisation. It signalled something different, that although very few South Asian women contemplated life on their own, it meant they had an alternative means of escape (Trivedi, 1984).

Whilst women radically transformed and politicised relations within the South Asian community, there were problems in being politically active. Through political campaigning and participating in struggles affecting Black women in Britain, South Asian women broke away from the set roles prescribed to them by the majority and minority society. It was not how women were supposed to behave. South Asian women who organised groups and highlighted the struggles faced the prospect of being portrayed as different from their community (Trivedi, 1984).

There have ultimately been significant changes in the identity structures of first-generation South Asian women, which were largely dependent on age. The older women had a fixed idea of their identity and were less likely to change; it was the middle-aged women going out to work who brought about changes. They have shown that despite the relations that constructed their roles as subordinate, they did not suffer in the passive way indicated by the images that dominate their roles. They have developed their own form of resistance, taken control of their own lives and developed their own ideas about British life and Britain. Yet at the same time they do not cut themselves off from their historical and cultural traditions. These are maintained and, in fact, relied upon as a means of support (Parmar, 1982). But the experience of these women in terms of their contact with the host society in turn influences their aims and aspirations for the children they raise (Afsar, 1989).

Discrepancies in their treatment are being addressed by the women themselves. Having become involved in the Black women's movement, and worked with other ethnic minority women for rights within employment and reproduction, these women have broken away from the set roles prescribed to them by society (Trivedi, 1984). They continue to provide essential organisational support and back-up to women who are fighting for political rights in Britain. A more contemporary example is the Southhall Black Sisters, a resource centre and Back women's group involved in struggles over racism, domestic violence and forced marriages (Gupta, 2003).

Subsequent Generations

The overwhelming difference between the subsequent generations and the preceeding generation is the environment in which they have grown up. Whilst South Asians may be connected by a common 'race', a national origin and arguably a common history, growing up in a country that is culturally, socially and religiously different from the ethnic culture maintained within the home environment has a significant impact on the individual's concept of self. The second generation's understanding of life is very different to that of the previous generation (Jones, 1992; Hutnik, 1991; Watson, 1977).

Their hyphenated identity becomes expressive of commonality and national loyalty that serves as a symbol of belonging. There is genuine value in having dual nationality. For this generation the hyphenated term British-South Asian identity not only symbolically describes the encapsulation of the group from the wider society, or a disassociation from the indigenous culture, but an amalgamation of both that describes their cultural identity. The British-South Asian identity represents two distinctively different cultures; that of those born or brought up in Britain, and that practised at home. They are linked to their parents by religion and language, but by growing up and undergoing schooling in this country, they also come under the influence of other, strong, distinct but very different cultural patterns of White British society (Taylor and Hegarty, 1985).

Differences between the generations arise from exposure to the integrating services of the majority society from birth. Experience of the education system and the employment sphere influences their attitudes and relationships. The child is confronted with both cultures at the same time and begins to absorb totally different values of family life and society. Whilst pupils of South Asian origin live in two different cultural groups, this can have its disadvantages and can affect their performance: it has, however, frequently given them an impetus to work even harder. The education system is a means through which children can join the established social order and gain access to better occupations and lifestyles, since it promises economic and social rewards via the acquisition of credentials and qualifications (Richmond, 1988). Education also implants the seeds of individualism and liberalism in the South Asian child's mind (Hiro, 1991).

Having been educated alongside their White and Black colleagues they demand equal rights within the majority culture. Their attempts to compete are stronger than were those of their parents. In acknowledging Britain as their home, they are cultivating their own distinct values, interests, meanings and ambitions within English society. For young South Asian people in the UK, identity is informed by how they identify with their parents' ethnic, cultural and religious values within the broader British culture (Modood et al., 1994). Outright rejection of their parents' ethnic and religious identities is rare among the second generation, although partial acceptance as well as reinterpretation of some values does occur (Drury, 1991). It is not a question of forsaking one identity for another and choosing between a 'Western' or 'South Asian' way of life (Modood et al., 1994). The idea of hybrid identities thus emerges (Papastergiadis, 1998). In the diaspora, the second and subsequent generation finds itself navigating within a social context which differs entirely from that which they share with their own parents. Young British Asians are therefore best understood as mobile in linguistic, religious and cultural terms (Ballard, 1994).

Academic, policy and lay discussion tend to overemphasise 'cultural conflict' between young people and their parents (Brah, 1992). They pathologise the South Asian communities identifying 'inter-generational conflict' as one aspect of a 'crisis' in British-South Asian communities (Hussain and Bagguley, 2004)

Literature on inter-generational relations, although describing social change, presents a picture of cultural retention and successful negotiation of identities (Anwar, 1998; Ballard, 1994). However, the 'riots' that occurred in 2001 showed that the new generation of young men in particular, are shunning the acquiescent attitude of their parents and elders and demanding radical change. The younger generation, already alienated by the discrimination that exists in Britain, are aware of their own position and their own rights in Britain. Education has heightened their awareness of these rights and their assertion of them. This second generation has political values of equality, higher expectations of education and the labour market, but is disillusioned in the face of continuing racism (Hussain and Bagguley, 2004).

The public political assertiveness of second and subsequent generations of British Pakistanis, as seen in incidences such as the 'riots', is grounded in their identification with British citizenship and its associated rights (Bagguley and Hussain, 2003). In contrast, the apparent public political 'passivity' of the older generation is rooted in their status as economic migrants, their perception of British citizenship as 'temporary', a status that they feel could be revoked at any minute. One aspect of their perceived public passivity, then, lies in their dependency as economic migrants and their view of their own citizenship (Bagguley and Hussain, 2003). However, these generational differences do not constitute a 'crisis' or deep rooted 'inter-generational conflict'. Rather, the changing political economy of ethnic groups, rising levels of education, geographical and social mobility within Britain, cultural hybridization and new forms of citizenship and ethnic identification are producing new forms of generational difference. Furthermore, religious affiliation seems to be far stronger within the second and subsequent generations of Pakistani and Bangladeshi communities than the Hindu and Sikh groups. Allegiance to Islam is apparently stronger and rooted in their readings about Islam, rather than learning about their religion through a largely oral culture (Samad and Eade, 2002).

Language has played, and continues to play, an important role in the integration process. Identity and language are entwined to such an extent that a closer examination of South Asian communities reveals linguistic social divisions, which are also generational. For the first generation, their communication with White British people was reliant upon their economic roles, and was influenced by racism and negative stereotyping (Kershen, 2000). For the second generation their education has ensured that they have a different relationship with White Britain. Their retention of their mother tongue, except in specific circumstances, and their acquisition and fluency in English also creates a different relationship with their parents. Marriage within the South Asian groups is also a principal means by which boundaries are maintained. Issues of identity and belonging to a particular community are central to this process of boundary maintenance, and linked to debates about cultural traditions embedded in distinct languages, religions and regions (Samad and Eade, 2002).

Great emphasis is placed on education by South Asian parents, irrespective of the gender of the child. Education is viewed as a means of improving life chances and is regarded as self-defining and personally empowering (Anwar, 1998).

Parents are keen to see their children do well and not to miss out on the opportunities they, the parents, did not have (Bhatti, 1999). But there was a gender differentiation, initially only the boys were encouraged in their education by their parents. Spending money on educating sons was deemed more important than daughters; however, in contemporary society, the mothers were more keen to see their daughters succeed academicaly and professonally. Many older women without formal qualifications themselves are keen for their daughters to succeed academically and professionally. The positive role played by fathers is also important, which challenges stereotypes of 'restrictive' South Asian fathers. Overall, parents are now becoming more supportive of their daughters' pusuit of their educational goals as well as their integration within the employment market (Ahmad and Modood, 2003).

The process of schooling in the United Kingdom has resulted in a different view of religions. The vehicle for this transformation is the linguistic change that has taken place. This seems to be especially the case for young Muslims educated in British schools and universities. This means that their access to information is primarily through English, which excludes them from the oral traditions of their parental generation (Samad and Eade, 2002). They question the understanding of Islam as perpetuated by a culture that refers back to the Quran and the *Sunnah* (custom and tradition associated with the Prophet), at the same time as applying methods of *ijtihad* (independent inquiry) to fashion arguments in pursuit of their agendas (Hansari, 2002). This move away from oral traditions as the prime source of religious information also parallels the shift away from ethnic identification (Samad and Eade, 2002). Individuals often now assert their religious identifications more readily than their ethnic identifications, so they are Muslims first and then Pakistanis or Bangladeshis second. This strategy has been relatively successful, not only in challenging Muslim communities' demands for adherence to customs and traditions generally but also on gender issues (Hansari, 2002).

The dominant Western picture of Muslim women's submissiveness and oppression is far removed from the lived experience of most Muslim women in Britain. The popularity of the *hijab* (head covering) among young women has symbolised this assertion of female Muslim identity. As Alibhai-Brown has commented, to see the *hijab* 'merely as a symbol of subordination would be to miss the subtle dialect of cultural negotiation' (Alibhai-Brown, p. 216).

British-South Asian Identity – Women

Young South Asian women born or brought up in Britain express both their ethnic identities and their Britishness, and have attempted to create an equilibrium in which they are complementary. The result contains facets of the indigenous majority culture as well as the ethnic minority culture. More recently, the upsurge in religious identification has also become a defining aspect of identity, especially for Muslim women, who express a more active identification with the religion through external codes such as dress. This generation of women is far more confident with external expressions of ethnicity and religion than that of the preceding generation of women. The literature and art they have produced and their contributions to all fields of life are witness to this. Yet achieving their targets becomes a difficult task when cultural constraints are so strong. Choices for South Asian young women are much more complex than for their male or White counterparts. South Asian women's choices are influenced not just by structural factors but also cultural expectations. There is a commitment by women to the duties ascribed by culture, for instance, their willingness to submit to the demands of the family, which makes them vulnerable to control.

South Asian cultural practices, particularly in the rural areas of the subcontinent (where a substantial proportion of the first generation originated from) have strong patriarchal ideologies (Samad and Eade, 2002). The ideology of segregating women is so powerful that young girls from an early age are secluded from men and boys and their movements are restricted to the private sphere. This regulation of young women's movement is implemented by mothers, elder sisters and mother-in-laws, and this clearly shows how women internalise patriarchal ideology and then become its enforcers (Report of the Pakistan Commission on the Status of Women, 1989 quoted in Samad and Eade, 2002). It is the mothers who educate their daughters to conform so that women become the symbols of the culture; they become representatives of South Asianness. The break with traditional concepts of familial unity and the close mother-daughter ties are difficult and fraught with guilt and tensions. The rejection of such values and the adoption of the Western values are threatening and are tied to the idea of izzat or honour. Izzat in Britain faces a new range of threats; for example, should women be allowed to go onto further education, enter employment or choose their own marriage partner?

These issues also have negative effects on individual South Asian women. Alarmingly, the suicide rate amongst young South Asian women aged between 16 and 24 is three times the national average, and that of South Asian women between 25 and 34 is twice the national average, reflecting the intense social pressures (Siddiqui, 1995). Whilst the pressures of arranged marriage and 'surviving' these marriages may be large contributory factors, the lack of services and resources would appear to be key factors. Consequently, some women are not only frightened of leaving their communities, which will more than likely reject them, but are also frightened of entering into a majority culture that frequently isolates and discriminates against them (Parmar, 1982).

Marriage is a contentious issue within South Asian communities, and one that has attracted a lot of media attention. Whilst there are variations in the way marriages are arranged and the degree of consultation that takes place with daughters, this is largely influenced by geographical ties (Afsar, 1989). Whilst women who are born and brought up in England are sceptical about romantic love and Western style marriage, they feel that they should be consulted when considering their own marriages. Marriage without allowing the daughter to interact with her partner is often recognised as a means of punishment. It dictates a specific parental behaviour that is carried out in extreme cases to rid them of a daughter whom they suspect could lead to the loss of their 'face' within the South Asian community (Afsar, 1989).

Whilst effective navigation between the culture of the school and the culture at home (Ballard, 1994) is applicable irrespective of gender, it is more so for women. Ethnicity becomes overtly presented through dress, language and behaviour. After going out to school in uniform, once at home, girls are expected to change into traditional clothes. Wearing traditional South Asian dress signifies that a girl subscribes to the values and codes of behaviour of her community. The act of changing clothes is a metaphor for the hybridised identity. Young women grow up internalising the two cultures, as South Asian young women have a strong relationship with youth culture – wearing fashionable clothes is important – but within the context of religious and cultural identifications.

There are some women who have emerged as powerful, articulate and assertive advocates for women and for their community. These women have gone on to higher education and emerged as teachers, social workers, youth workers and housing campaigners. They appear comfortable in shalwaar kameez or jeans, speak South Asian languages as well as English, and have carved out independent lives with their own flats and cars, yet remain closely attached to their families (Bunting, 1993). However, others have rejected early marriages and have no clear sense of what is expected of them anymore. There is fear mixed with the sense of freedom, and an attempt to accommodate the conflicting demands of both Eastern and Western culture. This leaves many of the women in very exposed positions. Despite the issues surrounding South Asian women and their identity, undoubtedly there is a new generation emerging who are politically active, who are working alongside or have taken over the work started by their previous generation.

Even when employed, the problems facing such women increase. South Asian women are often seen as one of the most excluded and disadvantaged groups in the labour market. These women have the lowest levels of labour market participation (albeit growing), and the lowest levels of educational qualifications (Bhopal, 1997). For the more Westernised middle class professional South Asian women, seeking to break away from the cultural restrictions, their British upbringing encourages notions of individuality and independence, and convinces them that they have the ability to earn a living. Even for them the notion of filial duty is difficult to shed except in forms of vulnerability and guilt (Afsar, 1989).

Whilst most women subscribe strongly to the centrality of the family, it is clear that they follow very different routes through the life-course from their mothers. By contrast with their mothers' generation, younger women who have been educated in Britain see paid work as a means to independence and self-esteem. Women with higher level qualifications have shown considerable determination in managing to combine paid work and child-care. Increasing numbers of younger Muslim women are entering the labour market. As a result, religious differences between South Asian women in terms of employment participation and career advancement are gradually being reduced. (Ahmad and Modood, 2003; Dale et al., 2003).

However, fundamentalism is having an adverse effect on women because it attacks them in the demand for a return to the traditional family and its values (Siddiqui, 1995). For example, in the majority culture, the state privileges Christianity through its talk about family values and 'back to basics', whilst within the minority culture the Rushdie affair became a symbol of changing identities in terms of a move away from racial or ethnic to religious identities. Within minority communities, young men in particular have taken on new identities associated with fundamentalism and it is these religious identities that are currently being treated as racial identities. Again, women are on the receiving end of these developments since they have been primarily victims of fundamentalist politics (Sahgal and Yuval-Davis, 1992). Nevertheless, many women joined fundamentalist movements and gained a sense of empowerment despite being the movement's victims. Women Against Fundamentalism (WAF) was organised in London in the wake of the Rushdie Affair with the aim of campaigning against fundamentalist leaderships of all religions and racism (Yuval-Davis, 1992). Women activists within WAF felt that the rights gained over the last decade for South Asian women and other ethnic groupings were increasingly under threat. Indeed, the organisation included women of all religions whose campaigning included issues relating to state religious education and women's reproductive rights.

The problems facing these women lie with the lack of resources and in the ignorance of their needs. Organisations which have been formed on religious, caste and cultural bases – for example, Hindu and Islamic associations – have been formed in the sphere of race relations with regard to local state politics. Whilst such associations are male dominated, when the local or the national state seeks an ethnic opinion, they go to these organisations. These are biased in their opinions, simply because they are not representative of their communities, yet they act as a buffer between the state and the community (Trivedi, 1984). Women continue to fight against such organisations asserting autonomy and independence by setting up their own refuges for South Asian women.

Conclusion

The value of the term diaspora increases as its symbolic character is understood by the majority culture, in terms of individual, literary, scientific, and social contributions to society. However, this points to the fact that there cannot be a pure, uncontaminated or essential South Asian culture. It is changing, and this change is inevitable. The first generation articulates Asianness as a homogeneous condition and has a dubious comfort in the belief of an eternal ethnic identity which is fixed. They are trying to create and harness a sense of sameness that does not exist, despite their attempts to manufacture it through notions of unity, and often by imposing this unity on their children. However, these changes in the South Asian community's self-understanding affect the formation, reproduction, dissemination and use of their expressive cultures in very important ways.

The differences lie in an exploration of the idea of Asianness in relation to the idea of Britishness. This South Asian identity, whilst it may be the primary identity, is influenced greatly by the majority culture. Rationalising culture and identity as growing out of communicative webs linking several national states creates problems when theorising about the diaspora. The idea of a common, invariant racial identity, that is capable of linking divergent South Asian experiences across different spaces and times, has been undermined. Nationalism and racism can become so closely identified that to speak of the nation is to speak in racially exclusive terms; for example, speaking of English or British people is to speak of White people (Gilroy, 1993). So called 'Blackness' and Englishness are constructed as incompatible, mutually exclusive identities, hence the vocal factions within the minority communities who seek to emphasise the cultural incompatibility of African–Caribbean and South Asian settlers with Britain and Britishness.

Chapter 3

Black British Feminism and the Birth of South Asian Women's Writing

Introduction

The current situation of South Asian women in Britain as expressed in their cultural creativity reflects and includes an important legacy from the past. These women were offered a sisterhood which first found its expression in the Black feminist movement. South Asian women initially published alongside other 'Black' women writers, in particular during the 1970s and most of the 1980s. This was at a time when the term Black was created as a new collective boundary in the light of racism; it defined a group of people campaigning on all levels against the existing establishment (Hussain, 2004).

Black feminism theorised the interconnection of class, gender and race as it occurred within women's lives. Black women's critique of history evolved very much like White feminism, coming to terms with absences within history and outrage at the images in which Black women have been depicted. Black women succeeded in defining a feminism that was significantly different to the general trends in the women's liberation movement, by analysing the triple oppression of gender, race and class, and how these determine the lives of Black women. Furthermore, in defining the boundaries of Black feminism from White feminism, Black women were critical not only of White feminists' theories but also of their practice (Amos and Parmar, 1984). These women have recently been split into their own ethnic categories, for instance of 'African' and 'South Asian', so they can claim a place in the South Asian tradition or the African Caribbean tradition.

The dynamics within Black women's imaginative writing were intricately connected with the development of British Black feminism. Consequently, the works of 'Black' authors, whether from the African Caribbean, the South Asian, or other minority diasporas, were enriched by an awareness of the social context within which it has emerged. The content of the writing generally produced by these women explored the soul of its authors. The women mirrored their social and personal grievances, within their literary work, and discussed their experiences of living in Britain.

Collections of stories and poems in anthologies were typical of the way in which Black British discourse has been gathered in the post war period. It was symptomatic of a publishing industry that is reluctant to commit itself financially to minority authors (Procter, 2000). Anthologies such as *Charting the Journey:*

Writings by Black and Third World Women (1988) edited by Grewal et al. and *Watchers and Seekers, Creative Writing by Black Women in Britain* (1987) edited by Cobham and Collins, became important outlets for these women to publish their work. These anthologies recognised the diverse diasporic conditions under which Black British cultural production took place, whether African, Caribbean, or South Asian, yet they all signal the hyphenated, the cross-cultural (Hussain, 2004).

Irrespective of the cultural, ethnic and religious identities constituting the Black identity, the creative writing by Black and South Asian women as a collective revealed no major difference in the ideological perspectives that were represented within them. The label 'Black' became representative of a body of literature which provided evidence of economic, social and cultural oppression in any minority framework and within a British context.

These authors articulated a perspective within their texts that mirrored their collectively experienced grievances. Bringing together these disparate voices in a common forum was to some extent a polemical act. Many writers explored the workings of a 'Black' identity which was, at the same time, imposed and embracing. However, after setting out on a collective basis, the women have recently split off in their specific groups having established relative success within the publishing industry. The first part of this chapter addresses Black women and feminism, whilst the second part examines Black women and creative writing.

Ethnicity, Women and Empowerment

Certain projects have resulted in the construction of new collective boundaries. For instance, the concept 'South Asian' includes those from Pakistan, India and Bangladesh who are in conflict in the subcontinent, but within the context of Britain, become amalgamated in the light of racism. This points to multiple identities that are constantly shifting, variable and renegotiable. The inability of 'particular' women to integrate within mainstream feminism forced the construction of a new collective boundary, under 'Black'.

But the label of Black is contradictory in its conceptualisation because its expression is defined in terms of colour, yet it is an idea that transcends colour. Women who were not 'Black' were integrated within the concept. Black feminism provided a space and a framework for the diversity of women from different ethnicities, classes and sexualities (Parmar, 1982). Cultures designated as minorities have certain shared experiences through their similar antagonistic relationship to the dominant culture, which seeks to marginalise them all. This unification strengthened similarities through differences in historical common origins and experiences. The common interest of the women had its roots in the struggle for freedom and equality as well as in women's general struggle for self-definition and personal respect. 'Papering' over the differences not only provided a broad platform for shared campaigns but also encouraged the emergence of many individual activists. Furthermore, their collective identity was based on a political analysis of common economic, social and cultural oppressions (Davis and

Ogundipe-Leslie, 1995). It was founded on the assumption of shared subjectivities in the ways in which Black women, irrespective of ethnicities, class and sexuality are shaped by common objective factors, including racism and sexual exploitation (Parmar, 1982). Consequently, these women found a sense of self by reconstructing a feminism which included their experiences. Therefore bringing together these disparate voices in a common forum is a political act.

However, the transformation of identities, whether intentional or not, also indicated the shift in the boundaries of racism (Bhavnani and Phoenix, 1994). By using the term Black to embrace those from South Asian and African Caribbean origin in Britain, racist definitions of Black, aimed at dividing these populations, were weakened. To assert an individual and collective identity as Black women becomes both an empowering and strengthening process. The unity of African Caribbean and South Asian communities and other ethnic minority women became a mark of rising strength and confidence to evolve common political strategies and face institutionalised racism and right-wing attacks (Trivedi, 1984).

The material substance of this 'idea' of Blackness was the arrival and creation of diasporic life in this country (Grewal et al., 1988). The arrival was due to the economic and/or political effects of colonial subjugation, and therefore escaping from poverty or political torture, whilst others came in search of educational or cultural sustenance in Britain. Settling in Britain involved transforming ways of being, seeing and living, involving opposition and struggle. As women and as feminists, Black women militantly campaigned on a whole range of issues, from health and fertility rights to anti-deportation campaigns and education issues. But the unity between these women redefined the very ideas of Blackness and Black womanhood in Britain as a united force. This idea of Blackness, although inadequately defined, proceeded along its path in both real social life and the collective awareness of many of its subjects, as also seen through the Black feminist movement (Grewal et al., 1988).

Consequently, the collectivity 'Black feminists' has entailed the development of Black women's groups in Britain, seeking changes in the status quo of their lives. Notably these Black feminists campaigned collectively in solidarity with each other forming their own political agendas and arguing on their own terms about how to proceed, developing networks, newsletters, national conferences and campaigns on a variety of issues. The essence of this collectivisation of the Black women's movement was the exchange of experiences, drawing on their politics as a potentially liberating task (Grewal et al., 1988). Whilst the collectivisation of experiences enhanced the chances for the harmonisation of diverse struggles on issues of gender and race, this collective identity gave way to more particular identities in the mid 1980s, as campaigns were organised in their respective communities. Wider struggles were eclipsed by more localised, communal ones. South Asian and African Caribbean women came to the forefront of the initiatives to develop African-Asian unity struggles in opposition to the common enemy of racism in Britain.

Nevertheless, just as the discrimination and disadvantage experienced in the 1970s signalled the emergence of the Black community on the social and political fronts, a literary Black collective also emerged. Writers from minority cultures began to express their creative talents in various forms. However the writers' failure to fit into the indigenous literary mainstream meant that they were marginalised and categorised as 'Black', regardless of whether their ethnic categorisation fitted the term or not. This 'boundary', which initially served to contain Black women's creativity, became a focal point for discussions about being 'Black' within contemporary Britain. Consequently, whilst the linguistic expression of Black was defined in terms of colour, it became an idea transcendent of colour. Black women's writing was established as a heterogeneous phenomenon, and diverse in the positions from which it approached its subjects. However, as with political activism, the coalescence within the literary field primarily worked to give expression to the shared concerns of these women. The literature contains contributions from women speaking about their many experiences as Black women in Britain, dealing with questions of speech and creativity. What these women do is to celebrate resilience in their writings, showing that they want to escape from silence and be heard in their own voices.

Exclusion, Ethnocentricity and Racism

The women's liberation movement in the 1960s and 1970s raised the question of the subordination of women and brought it to the forefront of theoretical and political debate. The universal category of 'woman' as utilised by mainstream feminism failed to relate to Black women and White working class women. White feminism constituted an area of support for White women, but failed to provide the same for Black women (Anderson and Buckley, 1988) The movement was built upon a notion of common oppression, which ignored Black women's subordination, thus rendering Black women invisible (Bailey, 1990).

Black women and Black feminists in the early 1980s became conscious of their inability to articulate these experiences within the framework of feminist theory because it had failed to develop a politics that addressed them (Bhavnani and Coulson, 1986; Bryan et al., 1985). On closer inspection, supposedly universal interests turned out to be those of a particular group. This began a critical dialogue with mainstream White feminism. Black women galvanised Black female scholars to make visible the social and political conditions of Black women in Britain.

Black writers emphasised the importance of understanding that Black and White women have different histories, but made this a defining factor of their positioning within society (Carby, 1997; Amos and Parmar, 1984; Hooks, 1982). It has been shown how 'race' significantly affects women's experiences of, and their treatment in, areas such as education, the health service and the labour market (Brah, 1992). The influence of race on Black women who are represented within popular culture and the mass media has also been demonstrated (Modleski, 1986). Consequently, Black women's critique of history not only involved them bridging the gaps within mainstream feminism but expressing their outrage at the way in which their invisibility has been historically reproduced.

This debate, pitching 'Black' as an alternative to 'White' mainstream feminism, had already began in North America in the late 1960s, but in Britain, it did not take place until the mid 1970s (Bailey, 1990). The progressive nature of the movement within the United States was embedded in historical differences. America had a civil rights movement that instigated the debate, yet regardless of this, much of the material advanced by American Black feminists is applicable to the British context. Black feminists revealed two concerns: first, exclusion and ethnocentricity within White feminist scholarship whereby texts that dealt with the women's movement failed to take account of the 'specificity' of Black women's experience, nor did they acknowledge racism to be indicative of the oppression of Black women. This debate took shape around a critical exchange on the centrality of the family and the definition of patriarchy within other cultural contexts from those of White feminists (Mirza, 1997). Secondly, whilst the discourse attempted to speak to the experiences of Black women, it was often from a racist perspective and reasoning, for instance with reference to arranged marriage.

There was little doubt of the validity of Black feminist claims that mainstream feminist theory is ethnocentric. Research into the lives of Black women with regard to the issues specific to them was non-existent, as the experiences of African Caribbean and South Asian women were largely ignored. In fact, the published material reflected a White middle class perspective, which is hardly surprising as the pioneers both in North America and in Britain of the women's liberation movement were predominantly middle class women (Bailey, 1990). These women had the advantages of access to academic institutions, the media and the publishing houses. Nevertheless, the absence of research and published material meant little was known of the commonalties and differences between Black women and White women. These differences were imperative in terms of appropriate care and social policy, as the needs of women differed according to their own background and their own experiences.

The failure of mainstream feminist discourse to consider sufficiently the elements of race and class became problematic. Three concepts that are central to feminist theory became issues of contention in their application to Black women's lives: the centrality of family, the definition of patriarchy and reproduction. When these ideas were used, they were placed within the context of a White 'herstory' that was frequently middle class. Consequently, their application to the lives and experiences of Black women, and even working class women, became contradictory. The issues of family, patriarchy and reproduction highlighted the different concerns of Black and White women, as each issue has different meanings within different cultural contexts (Carby, 1997).

The women's movement identified the family as the main source of oppression since it immersed women within the arena of domesticity and motherhood (Mitchell, 1971; Barrett, 1980). Feminists argued that the dependency of women on the 'breadwinner' provided the link between the material organisation of the household and the ideology of femininity. But this ideological framework of the family was not applicable to Black families, where the male was more likely to be unemployed, or to single parent families, whether Black or White, where the woman is the head of the household. Black women were in many instances heads of households because of an economic system that results in high Black male unemployment, so women were not financially dependent upon a Black man but frequently went out to work themselves.

The role of the family also functioned differently within the context of a non-white middle class family framework. In particular, the African Caribbean family functioned as a primary source of resistance to oppression. There is insufficient recognition that in a racially-ordered society such as Britain, the family became an important site of resistance and struggle. Black women had a shared political interest with Black men in fighting institutionalised racism and violence of the state. Even during slavery and colonialism the Black family was a site of political and cultural resistance to racism (Carby, 1997). Furthermore, within the context of South Asian families, immigration restrictions led to the separation of family members.

Even the concept of patriarchy within mainstream feminist discourse became problematic in its application to Black women. White feminists argued that reproductive controls, the family and legal inequalities are major features of patriarchy, but Black male dominance does not exist in the same form as White male dominance. Patriarchal hierarchies place men of different backgrounds on different levels. The patriarchal assumption that men have a shared dominance over women was contradicted during times of slavery, when Black men were denied control over White women, although in personal relationships, individual Black men may have power over individual White women (Joseph, 1981).

The differences between Black and White men extend across all areas of life. Discrimination within employment, for instance, suggests that Black men have not enjoyed the same benefits of White patriarchy in terms of recruitment and promotion. Racism has therefore ensured that Black men do not have the same relations to patriarchal, capitalist hierarchies as White men. They lack social power and, in this respect, they are in a different category from White men. It therefore becomes insufficient to talk about patriarchy without reference to racism. This ultimately means Black women have been dominated by men in different ways from White women.

Whilst Black women's relationship to Black men is unexplainable within feminist discourse, their interaction and relationships with men differ in many ways from those of White women, due to racism (Joseph and Lewis, 1981). For African Caribbean women, an integral part of their history is what happened to their foremothers under slavery, in which the struggle against racism has often assumed priority within their work (Davis, 1983; Hooks, 1982). Black women during slavery were social equals within the slave community. They suffered the same oppression as the men and also resisted slavery with a passion that was equal to the men's (Davis, 1983). The slave system ultimately both created the background in which they were to assert their equality through their social relations and its expression through acts of resistance. This unity of purpose has been visible on the political agenda within Britain in the form of the anti-racist movements.

Black women's critique of White feminism has not only involved coming to terms with the absence from the 'herstory' of middle class feminism, but anger at the ways in which its writers have chosen to view them (Carby, 1997). Stereotypes and pathological constructs have been presented when Black experience has been included; this succeeded in further marginalising Black women by oppressing them (Carby, 1997). The suppression of Black differences is achieved through the representation of Black as equating to deviance, so that when these women are depicted it is as the exception. Furthermore, White feminist writers have tended to problematise the ways in which Black women differ from White feminists' standards, portraying them as victims of primitive societies (Aziz, 1997).

The model of the Western nuclear family and related ideologies of romantic love are set within frameworks that are rigid and portrayed as more progressive than Black family structures, in particular those in South Asian families. Feminism failed to acknowledge the existence of other forms of familial relations and anything different from the model used was criticised. South Asian women were seen as passive, submissive and subject to the practices of arranged marriage and dowry. Literature on the restrictions and enclosure of South Asian girls and women focused on experiences of settling down after migration and pointed to cultural and religious norms as restricting women (Dahya, 1966; Khan, 1976). However, these sociological studies were distorted by feminism. Feminists resorted to ethnocentric arguments on the basis of protecting South Asian girls from the 'horrors' of the arranged marriage system (Amos and Parmar, 1984). The feminist version of the marriage system being practised within South Asian cultures presents South Asian women as in need of liberating, but within the social norms and customs of the West. This campaign for liberating young women led to more strict immigration controls on partners joining women in the UK. This was eventually overthrown as a result of campaigning by Black feminists who argued that it was depriving individuals of freedom of choice. The lack of support from White feminists within such campaigns was important to their assessment of it. Black feminists acknowledged the existence of racism as a structuring feature of Black women's relationship with White women, as the experiences and struggles of Black women had been ignored by White feminists.

Even in the area of sexuality, black women campaigned for rights over their own sexuality. Black women continue to be portrayed as licentious, ready for any sexual encounter; this construct has its origin during slavery, when rape became institutionalised, thus symbolising White male ownership and domination (Bailey, 1990). No protection was given to Black women, in fact White men were seen to 'possess an incontestable right of access to Black women's bodies' (Davis, 1982, p. 175). White women in contrast had protection, as they were seen as vulnerable and in need of protection from the sexual appetites of Black men and were thus protected in the USA by the White Women's Protection Ordinance which introduced the death penalty for the rape or attempted rape of any European female (Amos and Parmar, 1984, p. 14).

It is within this historical context that the struggle has to be located against coercive birth control in the form of forced sterilisation and the Depo-Provera campaign (Bailey, 1990). Black women argued the need to campaign around control over reproductive rights and to gain control over their own sexuality within the UK. These struggles, because they are structured by racism, were again different to those of White women. Whilst patriarchal explanations of their own sexuality were confronted, so too are the issues of birth control with regard to the experimentation with the contraceptive Depo-Provera and enforced sterilisation (OWAAD, 1979). Black women campaigned against forced sterilisation and the use of the contraceptive drug Depo-Provera. This is a long-acting injectable contraceptive banned in the United States because of disturbing side effects. It was tried out on, amongst others, women in Jamaica and working class women in Scotland, and has continued to be used extensively on Black and working class women (Lewis, 1983).

White feminism was regarded as racist since it failed to take into account the anti-racist struggle (Anthias and Yuval-Davis, 1992). The feminist movement was concerned with the ways in which women have been oppressed, whilst racism was one form of oppression experienced by Black women. The failure to recognise race, and consequently the invisibility of Black women, and the failure to take a stance against racism, were seen by Black feminist writers as products of the racism of White feminism.

Furthermore, the specific oppression which women experience also relates to their position within a class-based society (Anderson, 1988). It was argued that the women's liberation movement developed in relation to the experience and needs of White middle class women, which also served to keep White working class women at a distance. Yet ironically White working class women have been an important part of the historical struggles within the women's liberation movement (Liddington and Norris, 1978). As feminism failed to take into consideration the element of class, there has consequently been some acknowledgement by Black women that White working class women have also been marginalised in the feminist movement (Amos and Parmar, 1984). Whilst the effect on the White working class was evident, the effect on Black women was even more profound. Current theory remained predominately the 'herstory' of White middle class women, with certain notable exceptions, for example Coote and Campbell (1982).

Whilst most of the feminist literature was criticised for being derogatory, emphasising the 'invisibility' of their 'Black sisters' (Bailey, 1990), the simultaneous reluctance of Black women to express solidarity with White feminists was also recognised as racist since it masked Black female rage towards White women (Hooks, 1982; Rodgers-Rose, 1980). Black women's consciousness was led by internalised racism and has its roots in the historical servant/served relationship during slavery, where White women used power to dominate, exploit and oppress. Therefore, detachment and criticism was a means through which Black women asserted their own individuality. Whilst White feminists were criticised for failing to integrate Black women within their work, the difference in concerns of White and Black women was also focused in critiques of White feminist discourse (Anderson, 1988). White women were making different demands from those of Black women. Whilst White women were attempting to get out of the home and into employment, Black women were doing the contrary, having gained access within employment, they were seeking to get out of the labour force and back into the home (Anderson, 1988).

Ultimately the women's liberation movement failed for Black women and for working class women by making assumptions about all women. The way the gender of Black women is constructed differs from the construction of White femininity because it is subjected to the simultaneous oppression of patriarchy, class and race (Carby, 1997). Thus, because of the omissions of class and race, it became a middle class White women's movement. More specifically, Black and White women have different 'herstories'; the effect of this is a different approach and relationship to the issues that are affective of the groups involved (Anderson, 1988). Black feminists demanded that feminism needed to be transformed in order to address Black women, rather than have them integrated within it in a tokenist manner. They demanded that the existence of racism must be acknowledged as a structuring feature of Black women's lives and also seen as a feature of their relationship with White women (Carby, 1997).

This critique reached a peak during the 1980s where the failure of White feminist discourse to take into consideration such differences led to a disassociation of Black feminists from the mainstream and a shift towards a more focused campaign orientated towards their needs. Black women organised their feminism outside the women's movement (Bryan et al., 1997). Furthermore, because Black feminism theorised the connection of class, gender and race, its participants encompassed ethnic minority women irrespective of religious and cultural backgrounds. Black women began to articulate their demands as an organised body and participated in the formation of a number of women's organisations which addressed issues of exploitation and oppression both within and outside their communities (Bryan et al., 1997).

The Organisation Of Women Of Asian And African Descent (OWAAD) was one of the examples of this mutual solidarity, influencing Black women's politics in Britain. Although OWAAD's lifetime spanned only five years (1978-1983) it succeeded in bringing Black women together, through conferences, day schools, special project committees and its newsletter *FOWAAD*, to add a new dimension to the Black struggle of the 1980s. Similar movements included the Birmingham Black Sisters, the Brixton Black Women's Group and Southall Black Sisters. The Southall Black Sisters Group was founded in 1979 and embodied a feminist activism in its work on domestic violence and other issues relevant to women's rights, in particular regarding the South Asian communities surrounding Southall (Griffin, 1995). Whilst OWAAD, the Birmingham Black Sisters, the Southall Black Sisters and the Brixton Women's Group expressed their experience in political organisations, the creation of groups and centres orientated towards particular factions of the Black community was the product of Black women organising autonomously, within their communities. Organising from outside and within the communities establishes a positive shift in focus within the Black feminist movement, in that it shows these women building bases in all areas of their lives as opposed to the defensive modes of organising that were prevalent previously (Trivedi, 1984).

Black Women and the Publishing Industry

The feminist movement focused its attention not only on social policy and political rights, but also on literature and, in particular, the publishing industry. The refusal of major publishing houses to publish work written by women heralded the arrival of a number of feminist presses, including Women's Press and Virago, whose focus was on the material by and for women. As in the campaigns around social issues, the mainstream feminist movement failed to address the way gender processes related to those of different races, and consistently ignored the manner in which gender and class processes affect women from different ethnic and racialised social groups.

Groups such as *Black Women Talk* were set up to campaign against the perceived bias within mainstream publishers. Consequently, separate entities within the publishing industry were set up which dealt primarily with Black authors to fill the void left by the inadequacies not only of mainstream publishing but also of the women's presses. Sheba Feminist Press was the first feminist publishing house to take up the cause of Black women writers in Britain, involving them in its editorial decision-making as well as in its published catalogue. However, the problem with the smaller and more radical publishing houses like Sheba and Only Women Press remains that they can veer towards exploitation and self-exploitation in order to bring out the literature in which they so passionately believe.

Black women experienced racism within the publishing industry and often put these experiences down on paper in the form of autobiographies. Buchi Emecheta in *Head Over Water* (1986) details her treatment by her first publisher whose constant derogatory references to herself as 'that intelligent African girl with little self-control' (Emecheta, 1986, p. 111), forced her to leave and seek other publishers. Her time at Allison and Busby publishers was again marked by their racist attitude. Emecheta discusses the extent to which she was controlled. The cover of the novel featured Emecheta and her two daughters, Alice and Christy, like 'the caricature of Black and White minstrels' (Emecheta, 1986, p. 184).

However, their treatment by Black publishing houses is further loaded with controversy. The Black publishing houses – New Beacon Books, Karnak House, Akira And Karia – are relatively few in comparison to the feminist publishing houses and the distribution of their books is through alternative bookshops. Even so, the presses' treatment of their Black writers is still loaded with controversy. Bailey (1990) presents the case of Maud Sulter. Her suggestions for the cover of her collection of poems entitled *As a Black Woman* (1985) were rejected by her publishers, Akira Press, in favour of stereotyped images of a Black woman. Due to such treatment, individual writers have been forced to set up their own publishing companies. Writers including Buchi Emecheta and Iyamide Hazeley have done so, as has the group Black Women Talk. This means that Black women have control over the entire publishing process (Choong et al., 1987, p. 7).

Nevertheless, a process of incorporation has begun with an increasing number of Black authors being integrated within both mainstream and feminist publishing houses. Since the mid 1980s, Women's Press and Virago have taken up the cause of Black women and published their work. This according to Lauretta Ngcobo is due to the impact of American Black women's writing: 'it has taken the literary cloud burst of Black women's writing from North America to force Britain's feminist press to look nearer home for Black talent' (Ngcobo, 1988, p. 17). The American Alice Walker is the largest earner for the Women's Press, just as Maya Angelou is for Virago, along with the British authors, Joan Riley, and Merle Collins who are also commercially successful.

Black British Feminism and Writing – Literary Unification

One area which Black women organised was recognition within the literary field. Black women aimed to rectify the omissions within the literary field by offering new categories of thought, through discussing and relating their own experiences in various creative forms including literature, drama, film and art (Anthias and Yuval-Davis, 1992). The growing ethnic-feminist consciousness during the Black women's movement made women more confident of writing about themselves, relating their identities to their conditions within Britain as they explored their positioning both outside and within 'South Asian' and 'Black' culture. Literature, whether creative or analytical, became integral to other social activities as it provided a space in which the Black and South Asian standpoint can be defined. However, the move from silence and absence into speech-reflected presence was a revolutionary gesture. In the process of collectivisation, writing in all its forms (poems, short stories, essays, autobiographical and critical) became both an expression and an act of resistance. Writing became an empowering act and a political gesture that challenged the politics of domination that rendered these women nameless and voiceless. These women created an awareness of the ways in which racism empowered others, and focused on the interlocking systems of domination including race, gender and class, as typified in the works of Hooks (1982), Carby (1982), Anthias and Yuval-Davis (1991), Phizaclea (1983), Amos and Parmar (1984), Yuval-Davis and Anthias (1989) and Spelman (1988).

There was an insistence on finding one voice, one definitive style of writing that fitted into the notion of self and identity. Black women's fiction focuses on shared narratives and rhetorical strategies as much as themes. As a unified body of literature the 'Black women' label put across the notion of similarity. The core theme of this Black feminist writing in Britain, as in America, was a shared history of struggle, the construction of theory from everyday actions and experience together with the sense that community is not a fragile concept but a source of care and emotional strength (Humm, 1992). More importantly, it reproduced the views of Black women at the core of Black feminist theory, an acknowledgement of the diversity and complexity of female experience and the relationship to power and domination in both creative and analytical writings. The women preserved, extended and redefined themselves in order to create a situation in which 'Blackness', as it was commonly understood, had a social meaning by writers insisting on defining their own name and their own space through their writings.

Consequently, Black writing became a label which the women made their own, but which was also frequently changing as it reflected the different facets of reality experienced (Grewal, 1988).

The development of these writings, in terms of content and volume, became a metaphor for self-transformation as it established both in fiction and in non-fiction the changes occurring within these women's lives. Works published by and about Black women in Britain, since the early 1980s, have included not only a significant body of creative writing but also many theoretical and critical essays. Whilst the creative writings will be discussed in detail later, the theoretical writings raised awareness amongst intellectuals at least of the position of Black women in British society. The topics that preoccupied the women, both socially and politically, emerged within their texts, largely in the form of grievances expressed at White feminism. Many of the authors used their writings to criticise European and American feminist theory, for example Carby (1982) or Amos and Parmar (1984), by demonstrating the failings of the concept of capitalist patriarchy which presupposed a unified female subject. These writers criticised the image of unification, which the political movement consistently stressed, by documenting the forms and the extent of the sexual and racial discrimination in education, employment and the health service (Bryan 1985).

Besides criticising European and American feminist theorists, for failing to accommodate Black women within their analysis, their ability to do so was also questioned. Black women have written extensively on a writer's ability to write about a group to which they do not belong and, in particular, stress the need to consider whether their work will be used to reinforce and perpetuate domination (Hooks, 1989). The African-American writer Mary Helen Washington, argues that scholars who discuss an ethnic group outside of their own rarely explore the ethical issues of their race, privilege, and motivation or why they feel their perspective is important. 'What is important about the Black woman writer is her special and unique vision of the Black woman' (Washington, 1975, p. 10). As the women make their position explicit, the literary establishment has been criticised for its long-defined critical practice of having rendered Black women and their writing mute, cheapening and discrediting the achievements of non-mainstream writers by either ignoring or overemphasising their racial and sexual attributes (Wall, 1989). Black women argued the politics of authorship asserting individuals had the right to define their own reality, establish their own identities and name their history. They realised the process was not as simple as this: 'given the politics of domination in terms of race, sex and class oppression, the tendency...is to place more value on what White people are writing about Black people' (Hooks, 1989, p. 43).

The most important aspect of this literary renaissance is not how these Black women writers were received within the literary establishment, but the changes the writers themselves made to the way Black women are represented in literature. Over the last two decades Black women have written themselves into the national consciousness, sharing an awareness of themselves as Black people and as women that informs their relationship to their art and their societies (Cobham and Collins, 1987).

The creative writing by Black and South Asian women as a collective reveals no major difference in the ideological perspectives that are represented within them. Bringing together these disparate voices in a common forum therefore is a polemical act. The canon of 'Black women's literature' within Britain provides a body of evidence of economic, social and cultural oppression. The significance of such novels is that they produce portraits of individual personal experiences. When the experience of the single character is placed alongside that of other characters it creates an overall picture of Black women's lives in Britain (Bailey, 1990).

Whilst the connection between what Gayatri Spivak (1988) calls the 'verbal text' and 'social text' allows us to connect real lives with the fictional world of their texts, to read the literature as mimetic representation or sociology is to misread it. It would be reductive to treat the verbal text as though it merely mirrored the social text, yet to read Black writing as if it had no relation to political reality is to vitiate its power (Spivak, 1988). Therefore, as in texts about migration, or in the range of research into migrant reactions, a cross-disciplinary collaboration between the humanities and social sciences becomes an important way of extending research into Black women's lives in Britain.

Nevertheless, within the body of writings by Black and South Asian women, it is possible to focus and modulate the critical perspective these women bring to their work by looking at several of the shared thematic concerns and characteristics of Black literature. Black women's literature is strongly marked by the encounter of two or more contrasting cultures and their interaction within the diasporic communities. These literary texts explore the intersections of race, gender, class, ethnicity and generation in different discourses, practices and political contexts which become defining features of experience.

Literary Representation

Much of the published writing by Black women is contained within anthologies, whether in poetry or in the form of the short story. Whilst Black women writers have at least gained some exposure in this way, the chief appeal of the anthology format from the perspective of the publishing houses is the cost; writers in anthologies require only a single payment (Bailey, 1990). There are two main categories of literary representation of Black women: oral history works, where authors themselves write personal accounts of their lives, and general fiction which directly and indirectly reflects on their own lives.

Amrit Wilson's *Finding a Voice* (1984, first published 1979) and *The Heart of the Race* (Bryan et al., 1985), acted as sociological texts. The first contained interviews with South Asian women living in Britain during the 1970s. South Asian women were interviewed about their lives with respect to marriage, family, love and friendships. *The Heart of the Race* contained essays written by Black women about their experiences; inequalities within housing, education, law, immigration policy and health are discussed. Both Bryan et al. (1985) and Wilson (1984) deal with first generation women and the issues of inequalities with respect to gender and race. The women talked about cultural factors such as marriage and the family, and the impact these have on their lives. These texts were significant in that they documented the forms and extent of racial and sexual discrimination, and the expectations the women had are contrasted with the reality of the life they have experienced in Britain. Second and third generation young South Asian women were interviewed about their perspectives regarding marriage, family and education in Wade and Souter (1992), *Continuing To Think: The British Asian Girl*. This revealed concerns of hybridity and identity as central to the lives of young women with many of the views echoing those of Wilson's respondents. Anthologies like *Charting the Journey* (Grewal et al., 1988) typically included short autobiographical pieces such as Leena Dhingra's *Breaking Out of Labels*, immersed in a larger body of poetry and short stories. Furthermore, the anthologies also included photographs and visual representations, as well as social writing, poems and narrative fiction (Sulter, 1990).

Autobiographical material was also published in periodicals including *Spare Rib* and *Feminist Review*. The former made a positive attempt to include Black women's contributions ranging over a variety of issues and in different forms as it presented essays, articles and pieces of fictional text, but the initiative was discontinued at the end of 1987 (Bailey, 1990). Less autobiographical material has been included within *Feminist Review*, except for interviews with Diane Abbott (Segal, 1987) and Angela Davis (Bhavnani, 1989). Issue 17 of *Feminist Review* was an exception; this included a variety of materials about and by Black women. The collective gave editorial responsibility to a group of Black feminists including Valerie Amos, Pratibha Parmar, Amina Mama and Parita Trivedi (Bailey, 1990).

Whilst many of the women used writing as a form of autobiography, the linear narrative story became easier to write, because it was more acceptable to the reading public. Black women began telling 'their story' in a more conventional way by inputting their own selves within their stories in the role of the protagonist, so that their own reality found expression in a slightly fictionalised form (Hooks, 1989). This mode of writing was exemplified by writers including Buchi Emecheta in *Second Class Citizen* (1988, first published 1977), Joan Riley in *The Unbelonging* and Meena Syal in *Anita and Me* (1996). These authors put across their experiences and thoughts, by fictionalising themselves within the role of the protagonists. Emecheta represents herself in the character of Adah, Riley in the character Hyacinth and Syal in the character of Meena.

Within the creative literature that has emerged, the issue of racism becomes a key factor that emerges out of the writings by Black women. The women depict the way in which racism pervades their lives, in particular within the school environment in which the process of 'growing up' is embroiled with turmoil with respect to identity. Seni Seneviratane's poem, *Just Jealous* and Sandra Agrad's *The Blackbird*, showed racism as experienced by children. Racial identity is focused upon and makes the individual as self-conscious of her own identity. Subsequently, the school environment not only defines physical difference, but generates a hostile environment.

Ethnicity is interwoven within the work produced by these women and celebrated. For writers like Grace Nichols, Nefertiti Gayle, Merle Collins, Amryl Johnson and Valerie Bloom, whose formative years were spent in Guyana, Granada, Trinidad and Jamaica, there are similarities between their works as they experiment with Caribbean Creoles in which the rhythms of reggae have left their mark. For instance, in Nefertiti Gayle's poem *Black Woman out Dere* (Gayle, 1987), it is obvious in the dialect that is used. Whilst dialect is adopted by African Caribbean writers, the integration of untranslated words is also used within the work produced by South Asian women writers. This literature integrates words in Urdu and Punjabi into the mainly English text, but these are not translated, so that it works as a force which reminds the reader of the ethnicity of its content.

Many writers explore the workings of a 'Black' identity which is, at the same time, imposed and embracing. Contemplation and compassion sets the tone in Leena Dhingra's essay, *Breaking Out Of Labels* (Dhingra, 1987). Dhingra provides a brief narration of what she terms 'the label-fitting-fighting game' (Dhingra, 1987, p. 105), as she describes the labels of identity imposed on her and the subsequent racism she encounters: 'a girl from India, an Indian girl, a coloured, a Paki, a Black, a wog, an Asian, and recently graduated to becoming a member of an ethnic minority' (Dhingra, 1987, p. 103). Other authors also wrote of the difficulties of imposed identities. Jackie Kay's poem *So You Think I'm a Mule?* (Kay in Burford et al., 1985, pp. 53-4), centres on a discussion the writer has with a 'White face' person and whose opening line sets the tone and nature of the poem as they ask: 'where do you come from?' The respondent, not happy with 'Glasgow and Fife', continues to pry asserting, 'but you are not pure'. This instigates the fury within the poem as Kay launches her attack, and starts off by asserting, 'I'm Black' and glorifies her physical features, 'you see that fine African nose of mine, my lips, my hair'. Kay, like other Black writers, centres on her ability to find beauty in herself in the face of negative stereotyping. Written at a time when the slogan 'Black is beautiful' became the vogue, poems like the above reaffirmed the need to reject the obsolete images of White and instead enjoy the flexibility of self-definition (Macauley, 1996).

Writers such as Chatterjee, Nichols, Dhingra, Riley and many more who have spent their formative years in the Indian subcontinent, Africa or in the Caribbean, remind the reader that their access to their ancestral homelands' cultures has been strengthened and given direction by their understanding of themselves as part of a wider Black community (Dhingra, 1987). History becomes guarded in the collective memory, and is used by these women to place themselves within their own groups and in the wider world as they use their literature to discover forms of Black reality and their South Asian and African Caribbean roots (Kenyon, 1991). Immigration and its consequences become an important issue within the writings as they document their own lives. They have been displaced and longing is evoked through memories. South Asian women write about the Indian subcontinent as African-Caribbean women write about Africa and the Caribbean. These writers recapture and energise themselves with the strength embodied in their heritage to celebrate self-ownership, a sense of being wanted and strong. However, recollections of the past often break the barrier of nostalgia to the point of indulgence. The homeland becomes invested with promises of fulfilment but the issue of return is profoundly complex. For instance, in Leena Dhingra's novel *Amritvela*, Meena remembers nostalgically the India she leaves behind as a child, romanticising it to the point of exaggeration. The India Meena desires is a mythical place within her imagination, mediated by memories of what she left behind. 'It was like a wonderful cake full of layers, colours, aromas, flavours, soft and light and rich with infinite possibilities' (Dhingra, 1988, p. 153). It is significant in that in these writings there is a stark contrast between the country they leave behind and the one they enter. In Debjani Chatterjee's *The Question* (1989) the poem highlights the structural differences encountered. No longer in India with its 'throbbing bazaars' in which a great sense of fullness, activity and noise is evoked, Chatterjee presents the experience of women suddenly engulfed in a world 'amid skyscraper towers of silence'.

In Joan Riley's novel, *The Unbelonging* (1985), Hyacinth, like Meena, keeps her Caribbean memory alive through her dreams. These recollections are suffused with warmth, colour and caring, similar to Meena's memories of 'her India'. The novel opens with her dream as she remembers the 'warm glow of contentment' in the 'sweet scented bushes' (Riley, 1985, p. 9) where she would play, and the vibrancy and colour around her: 'the long-stemmed hibiscus and yellow trumpet flowers and humming with insect activity'. This image of Jamaica is in contrast to the cold of Britain, 'the biting cold' and the 'cutting wind' (Riley, 1985, pp. 14-15) she encounters when she awakes.

Whilst the encounter between the two cultures is an important aspect of the works of African-Caribbean writers, a theme which also pervades their work is the feeling of exile, and the yearning for a sense of belonging. The writing not only evokes the experience of hostility within Britain, but also the feeling of no longer belonging to the country of origin. Within this literature what there is, is a movement away from the country of origin and a concern with the difficulties in attempting to return. So that in Riley's and Dhingra's texts, for those who have lived in a new country, returning 'home' is problematic. Meena in *Amritvela* returns to India to discover a different India from the one she had long cherished in her imagination. In *The Unbelonging*, Hyacinth is also confronted with this. The poverty and the pain that she finds during her visit as she surveys the 'tangled mess of shacks' which makes 'her stomach turned, the dirt making her shake her head in horror and dismay' and even 'the smells was like a physical blow' (Riley, 1985, p. 137). The horror at her re-visit affects Hyacinth negatively as opposed to the positive emotions she anticipated feeling: 'she felt rejected, unbelonging. Where was the acceptance she had dreamt about, the going home in triumph to a loving indulgent aunt?' (Riley, 1985, p. 142).

Many of the novels concern women struggling to take control over their lives. In *The Romance*, the author Joan Riley focuses on three female characters, Desiree, her sister Verona and Mara, Desiree's friend. Desiree's grandmother informs them that 'there's nothing to liberate yourself from but yourself' (Riley, 1988, p. 226). The women challenge racism and confront patriarchy as they attempt to gain autonomy. Whilst the protagonists in Riley's novel are successful, the issue of gaining an autonomous identity is treated as far more problematic by the South Asian writers. Whilst racism remains as a subtext throughout their writing, for the South Asian women characters, their experiences are rooted in a specific domestic and cultural background (Milloy and O'Rourke, 1991). Ravinder Randhawa's *A Wicked Old Woman* (1987) focuses on Kulwant who challenges patriarchy by detaching herself from the cultural notions of identity. Divorced from her husband, disowned by her own sons and disliked by their wives, she describes herself using the image of a 'gorgeous, multi-coloured bird, soaring through the sky, swooping to the ground, iridescent with each wing shake or bright gaudy in the sunlight' (Randhawa, 1987, p. 118). But the protagonist realises her autonomy is at the expense of her happiness. Kulwant finds herself like a bird, 'grounded, its wings clipped, left to fight for survival in the cold climes and grey world of England' (Randhawa, 1987, p. 118). Her rebellion is thus quashed as she reverts back to the state that is expected of her.

The Emergence of 'British South Asian' Women's Writing

The need to develop political unity by minimising the differences between different groups of Black women on both a cultural and tactical level began to be an issue during the 1980s, especially within literature. Writers wrote encouragingly about the unification of Black women as a collective. However, a gulf appeared between those South Asian women who considered themselves part of the wider Black feminist movement, accepting the description of Black as opposed to South Asian, and the vast majority of South Asian women on whose behalf these individuals campaigned.

It is also noteworthy that anthologies of Black women's writing tend to feature many more African-Caribbean than South Asian writers. The anthology *Watchers and Seekers* (Cobham and Collins, 1987) is a perfect example; out of the 179 pieces of text, less than five are written by women of South Asian descent. This discrepancy may be partly due to linguistic heritages: English is likely to be the home language of the descendants of African Caribbean immigrants in Britain, whereas those of South Asian heritage are less likely to use English as the medium of their intimacy.

Whilst the alignment with others as part of the Black literary movement continued for a while, South Asian writers felt they were being 'squeezed' out of Black women's writing groups where the women were predominantly African Caribbean (Ahmad, 1988). The presence of large numbers of Black African Caribbean women significantly outweighed South Asian women. Some activists held that the term 'Black' belonged to African Caribbeans and not to South Asians. In order to encourage young South Asian women's writing, South Asian writers felt the need to assert their own collective identity. Moreover, South Asian women's writing was particularly concerned with exploring and expressing cultural differences, to the extent that their emphasis was on the assertion rather than the suppression of ethnic identity (Ahmad, 1988).

In 1984, the creation of the Asian Women Writers Workshop, later called the Asian Women Writers Collective, saw a shift away from the universality of the Black literary movement (Ahmad, 1988). The group was the first of its kind for South Asian women writers in Britain and heralded the arrival of a new literary movement. It played an important role in encouraging writing by South Asian women through a supportive environment. Members met to discuss each other's writings, and also attended workshops by more experienced authors (Nivien, 2003). Again the anthologisation is telling in this context as women began publishing collectively. *Right of Way* was the first anthology of poetry and prose the Collective published through The Women's Press in 1989. The anthology includes writings by, among others, Ravinder Randhawa, Leena Dhingra, Rahila Gupta and Rukhsana Ahmad. This was followed by the anthology *Flaming Spirit: Stories from the South Asian Women Writers Collective* (1994) edited by Rukhsana Ahmad and Rahila Gupta. They explored issues around identity, racism and feminism, and their projection of themselves as 'South Asian women writers' was significant in a society that was often perceived to deny South Asian women the opportunity for cultural expression (Nivien, 2003).

Whilst the women separated from Black women's groups within the literary field, Black women continued to organise in a number of ways around a variety of issues. Separating from other women within Black feminism gave the South Asian women's literary scene credibility and access to institutions, publishers and other groups within the community. Consequently, South Asian women's literature within Britain has evolved in its own right without being subsumed under 'Black' writing. A consciousness has emerged that continues to connect writing and politics. Although the literary criteria are still not defined, what is slowly emerging is a set of literary commonalties. Short stories, for instance, predominantly have abrupt endings; this marked ambiguity at the end of the short story is common to the British South Asian literary tradition. Other stylistic features commonly include prose that is short, direct, rhetorical, dramatic and punchy (Ahmad, 1988). Drama, compactness and directness have emerged with the evolution of the writing of prose and poetry as performance pieces.

Whilst single-issue campaigns have made women more aware of the nature of social conflicts, these women also questioned aspects of South Asian cultures within their literature. The 1980s and 1990s saw individuals from the South Asian communities writing not only as South Asian women within Britain but autobiographically dealing with issues within their own respective communities. For example, Sharan Jeet Shan in her autobiography, *In My Own Name* (1985), recalled her experience of domestic violence and cultural restraint within communities with respect to 'izzat'. Her act of defiance meant rejection and isolation from the community, whilst she also faced racial discrimination from the indigenous population.

Conclusion

The re-negotiation of identity has become fundamental to Black women's lives in Britain. The construction of female subjectivity through literary and cultural contexts is located within the sites of convergence where the negotiation and re-negotiation of identities take place. Black women's writing is located within a variety of geographical diasporas which generate different styles and techniques. Much of the fiction by Black writers in America, including Alice Walker, Toni Morrison, Zora Neale Hurston, Toni Cade Bambara, Gloria Naylor and Paule Marshall, centres on specific areas of the Black community: concerns with the relationship between men and women, family relationships and those within the community (Milloy, 1991). However, British Black women's writing often centres on the dichotomy between the ethnic minority and majority cultures.

Despite these differences, there are literary constituencies which relay connections. The issues of migration, race and gender are fundamental to the minority experiences, as they are specific to diasporic communities. Black women's subjectivity as a migratory phenomenon exists in multiple locations, and in adopting such a stance we can see how their presence traverses geographical and national boundaries. Therefore, Black women's writing should be seen as crossing boundaries, and not as fixed within ethnically-bound categories, redefining identities against the exclusion and marginality constructed by mainstream discourses (Davies, 1994).

Even within the publishing scene, the likelihood of lesbian writers succeeding in mainstream houses seems remote. They represent a subversion, perhaps more threatening than even the writings of Black authors. Feminist publishers therefore do still have a crucial role to play, not only in promoting minority women's fictions but also that of women who fail to fit into the mainstream due to their sexuality, which is often explicit within their work.

In Britain, and although South Asian women's writing increasingly considers religious identity in a period characterised by the growth of fundamentalism, the political message of unity is still conveyed by the emphasis placed on the marginal position of non-white women within British society. Furthermore, the publishing of Black women became an issue as White women writers' groups failed to integrate non-White women. So whilst the re-defining of Black identities as culturally plural significantly enhanced the recognition of Black women within the social and political spheres, their political unity was maintained and developed in the need to make changes within the publishing industry. Differences were minimised between the minority groups, in particular South Asian and African Caribbean women; this proved to be significant not only within the publishing industry, but also in the creative writings of the respective groups

During the 1990s the Black women's movement as a collective identity has failed to grow, because of the internal contradictions that emerged (Grewal et al., 1988). Autonomy has created a migration from past social norms, from different realities and past selves, forward to a state where women no longer succumb to notions of unity that are based on conservative or reactionary ideas. Whilst this may be a natural progression, inevitably the absence of the collective life is visible. Gaps exist from the absence of a Black women's movement; issues that still demand campaigning include cinema, mental illness and reproductive rights. Developments within these areas consequently remain slow.

Chapter 4

The New Woman in South Asian and Diasporic Literature

Introduction

South Asian women writers are largely categorised as those who are either 'indigenous' to India, Pakistan, Bangladeshi, Sri Lanka and those who are of South Asian descent but reside in the diasporas. The fiction these women write differs from that of their male counterparts in several ways, including their depiction of female characters (Sathupati, 1995). Whilst there are differences between British South Asian and Indian literature, the writings transcend barriers of nationality and culture by focusing on the awareness and awakening amongst their female protagonists. The writers assert their own definitions of femininity through the female protagonist and more specifically through the representation of the New Woman.

Within Britain, the New Woman as a term emerged in the 1880s and 1890s and depicted the changing image of women from the established and accepted role-model to a more radical figure. Initially the 'newness' of the New Woman marked her as a modern figure, committed to change and therefore the label was applied to women writers in literature and, in particular, proto-feminists. Writers in the nineteenth century including George Eliot could be incorporated into the study of the New Woman, for example through the characterisation of Dorothea Brooke in *Middlemarch*; however, mainstream English novelists such as Bennett, Wells, Conrad, Lawrence and Woolf and dramatists such as Bernard Shaw, wrote about the New Woman and her concerns in the early part of the twentieth century. The New Woman became a product of discourse manifested in various guises in both fiction and the periodical press throughout the nineteenth and twentieth centuries. She was variously characterised in the form of the 'the wild woman', 'glorified spinster', 'advanced woman' and the 'modern woman'.

There was a relationship between the textual configuration of the New Woman and the beliefs and practices of feminist women. For a large body of feminists, the New Woman was a literary means of highlighting specific issues (Ledger, 1997). Novelists considered the rise of the New Woman in her relationship with other social and cultural movements of the period. Therefore, textual configurations of women in history became a political agent. The way in which the New Woman was constructed as a product of discourse became as real and historically significant as she actually was.

Whilst the New Woman was a modern figure, who was regarded as being a force for change, for the latter part of the nineteenth century the term New Woman continued to be used as a term of reference. Women continue to interrogate their own lives with respect to cultural norms. Her categorisation as sexually transgressive, politically astute and determined to claim educational and employment rights had considerable relevance for the women's movement in the late twentieth century as these concerns have resonance with those of the nineteenth century. Thus, the New Woman continues to make an important contribution, and indeed is central to the shaping of the cultural landscape of Britain (Ledger, 1997).

Nevertheless, the definition of the category remains as ambiguous and unstable as it was a century ago. The confusion surrounding the term arises from the role of gender itself. Gender has been, and is currently, a site of conflict and therefore the New Woman, whoever she may be, generates differences in interpretation and thus creates instability. But the New Woman continues to be a defining category on a geographical level, where it means different things to writers in different locations (Ledger, 1997).

The New Woman within the South Asian communities was expressed through feminism within South Asia and the Black feminist movement within the UK. These women collectively dismissed traditional notions of womanhood and asserted a strong and confident image in their creativity. The New Woman within these movements, and consequently the writing, has become the embodiment of escape, from restrictions within the home and questions of marriage and instead resurrects a belief in education allowing women to lead financially independent and fulfilling lives. Furthermore, this New Woman acquires and establishes for herself a distinct identity in the traditionally male-dominated society in which she lives.

In criticising traditional forms of cultural practice, including patriarchal societies, or religious and ethnic groupings, these women are often attacked for not fitting into the colonial nationalist project. The whole question of setting up a woman's critique of patriarchal systems is something that becomes very problematic for women writers, they are seen as allying themselves with so-called White feminism (Hai, 2004). So when for example British South Asians were asserting their rights as women they often campaigned alongside White women. The changes in the depiction of women within South Asian and diasporic literature are related to changes that have occurred within society at large. Education in particular has brought about changes, empowering women and changing attitudes. Consequently, women from South Asian groups expect satisfaction from life, as opposed to readily accepting a life which may not offer none.

The protagonists within these novels are New Women because they recognise themselves as individuals, and choose a strategy, no matter what the outcome, to overcome the pressure to conform to the role or category others want to see them enact (Hussain, 2004). The strategy used by the New Woman within the texts involves a journey into her self, within both a psychological and a geographical context, questioning convention and tradition. This process forces her to display characteristics that show an obvious shift from the ideal traditional woman that is desired to the one which is criticised and rejected. The theme of journey had previously structured the literature written by immigrants as the writers recounted the transformation of migration, its effects and problems. This continues to be central to South Asian women's writing, it gives structure and pattern to the narrative, but changes occur in its use. The journey of immigration has been closely followed by the journey into settlement and now the journey into self.

The female protagonists show an assertion of their rights as human beings and fight for equal treatment. Women writers either writing in English in India, or writing in the British diaspora, present with insight the dilemmas women are facing. Liberal and unconventional ways of life are desired to avoid those problems within traditional society where self-willed and individualistic women often face suffering caused by broken relationships. Whilst there is much evidence of the alienation of vision and crisis of self-image, there is also an emphasis on an essential self. The characters possess a strong sense of self identity.

By juxtaposing such disparate texts, both South Asian and diasporic, in this chapter the aim is to illustrate the antagonism and similarities between the images of the New Woman within and between these two canons of literature. The significance of this is primarily geographical. In other circumstances both literatures may have been able to form a productive strategic alliance, but within these parallel contexts a New Woman emerges who is not necessarily a revolutionary transformation of the conventional, but who nevertheless gives literary expression to changes and challenges arising in the 'real' social world. The following analysis considers the changing image of women within the texts of two bodies of writing, that of the South Asian within the Indian subcontinent and that within the British South Asian diaspora.

The 'New Woman': Indian Women Novelists

Literature in South Asia has long been criticised by the perpetuation of the traditional 'Sita Savitri' stereotype. The Hindu goddesses Sita and Savitri were powerful cultural ideals of women in South Asia, which were projected as ideal images for women to emulate. Women were encouraged to devote themselves to their husbands through loyalty, and self-sacrifice (Landow, 1989). This led to a body of literature written not only by Hindu women but by South Asian women in general whose very presence in the literary field contradicts these very images (Hai, 2004). Within these writings the image of women in South Asian novels has moved away from the traditional self-sacrificing woman toward characters searching for identity. The interests of women writers have changed within South Asian society and its relationship with the West (Landow, 1989).

Women are often projected in Indian women's fiction as trapped in the categories of wife, mother and daughter. These women are usually depicted as victims of social and political injustice, cruelty and exploitation. The 'New Indian woman' also features strongly in the works of Indian writers abroad. Writers including Kamala Markanday, Anita Desai and Nayantara Sahgal have documented dissatisfaction with the cultural and sexual roles assigned to Indian women through the issues raised in their stories and the protagonists' characteristics, evoking their internal psychic turmoil. The New Women in their writings are not elevated on a pedestal as goddesses, but are depicted with their human flaws. Their predicaments are shown as a rite of passage as they pass through processes that symbolise transformations from weakness to strength and from restriction to freedom.

Two types of women are presented within Indian women's fiction, the conventional and the unconventional. Both suffer from either conforming or choosing not to conform. Firstly, the conventional woman suffers within the constraints of traditional culture. She addresses herself to the task of making others happy and upholds traditions and conventions. Living with her parents initially, marriage merely transfers her from one family to the other, from the father to the husband. We are presented with conflict, between the traditional woman and the image of modernity. This conflict dominates Indian women's literature as well as the British-Indian diasporic literature (Dhawan, 1993).

Secondly, unconventional images of female roles in Indian women's literature are represented by the images of suffering of women who violate and question the accepted norms of society. Alienation from family, the community and discontentment with their own lives together with problems with husbands and fathers dominate their lives. These experiences of suffering teach them to subdue their individuality in favour of traditional ways. Moreover, death is presented as the ultimate freedom from such suffering (Dhawan, 1993).

Hence, the unorthodox suffer for their rejection of accepted social norms whilst the conventional suffer by satisfying the demands of a patriarchal culture. Writers use different strategies for liberating these women from tradition or conventions. For instance, Shashi Deshpande uses the format of a travelogue, whilst Anita Desai employs psychological approaches in which the protagonist goes into withdrawal or suffers from alienation. Other strategies adopted include abduction or exile as methods of freeing women from such roles (Dhawan, 1993).

Shashi Deshpande, Anita Desai and Rama Mehta

Shashi Deshpande primarily addresses issues of conflict within the social environment and the minds of the protagonists. In *Roots and Shadows* (1983) and *The Dark Holds No Terrors* (1980), the identities of the protagonists, Indu and Saru, are overwhelmingly influenced by, and contained within, tradition. However, as each novel establishes tradition to be cramping the lives of women, it also depicts the character's struggle to release herself from a tradition-bound society in order to gain an independent identity. Indu and Saru rebel against the traditional parental family and hope to discover themselves by embarking on journeys, both geographical and spiritual into their own selves.

Preconceived notions of gendered identities are the main cause of antagonism for the protagonists. Here the concept of 'woman' signifies certain roles and behaviour and thus the protagonists find their lives dictated by such gender identification. This generates the overwhelming frustration and dissatisfaction which dominate both novels. In *Roots and Shadows*, the protagonist's disgust at the positioning of women within Indian society is clear. Indu expresses outrage at the lack of identification women have except in relation to men: 'a woman who sheds her 'I', loses her identity in her husband's' (Deshpande, 1983, p. 54). And even in the novel *The Dark Holds No Terrors* (1980), Saru observes how differently her mother responds to her brother, Dhruva compared to herself. Disgusted with the outside world and desiring self ownership, the women become isolated. Education becomes the first step towards autonomy and a means through which the women are able to realise their inner potential. It becomes a route to emancipation and creates career opportunities and economic independence. Saru initially travels to Bombay and studies for a medical degree, and Indu, already educated, leaves home to pursue employment (Dhawan, 1993).

Both women also embark on marriage as a means of detaching themselves from their families. For Saru and Indu, marriage is a means of establishing their individuality and rejecting tradition, Saru marries Manu and Indu marries Jayant, who are beneath them in terms of caste and status. Their marriages become symbolic of rebellion against the traditional standards their mothers adhered to in the form of an arranged marriage. Marriage ends up being a downfall for both women; it diminishes their independence and instead ties them down to tradition. As their husbands fail to match their expectations and begin to manifest a lack of sympathy with their wives, Saru and Indu journey back home or to the past to try to create a redefinition of the present by confronting the issues that previously troubled them. They conform to the roles that are expected of them (Dhawan, 1993).

Both texts attempt to offer a chronicle of the women's suffering as they shift from being controlled through tradition to asserting independence. However, as this New Woman makes her way through her crisis of identity, she takes one step back through adopting the traditional roles that are assigned to her. Saru, for instance, emerges as a whole woman who appears economically independent through her profession. However, Deshpande ends by asserting that an existence in isolation, without any relationship to society, is not a life. Saru gains an 'awareness' that she was somehow to blame for Manu attacking and raping her. She says she has murdered him: 'I destroyed his manhood' (Deshpande, 1983, p. 217). Even Indu ultimately submits to society's traditional and conventional demands having become the pillar of the household and therefore achieved her ultimate aim of gaining control of her life. Indu and Saru become the embodiment of the new educated woman seeking relative freedom. Their deviation from the traditional way of life is seen as a phase, such that the protagonists remain intrinsically Indian at the end (Dhawan, 1993).

There is a sense in which the modern history of India is echoed in the trials faced by Desphande's women. Autonomy is one of the key aspects of the novels, which the protagonists experience through rebellion. Ironically, they discover their identities in resistance to oppressive tradition, but then revert back to this tradition. The characters, irrespective of their reversion, are nevertheless New Women because they recognise themselves as individuals. Both women choose a strategy that marks them out as New Women whatever the context and outcome (Dhawan, 1993).

The changing role of women is also explored in the novels of Anita Desai and Rama Mehta. Whilst Desphande's characters externalise their thoughts through taking control of their lives, Desai's and Mehta's protagonists internalise them. Although Desai and Mehta explore the internal mental lives of the protagonists, they also offer an insight into their social experiences. The characters nevertheless represent the New Woman, because they interrogate their own lives, especially with respect to the impact of tradition. The outcome of such reflection is often dire as the protagonist may resort to suicide as a form of release from her present conflict.

In the novels, Desai's *Where Shall We Go This Summer* (1975), and *Voices In The City* (1965), and Mehta's *Inside the Haveli* (1977), an overwhelming sense of suffocation is conveyed as the proganists, Sita, Monisha and Geeta, reveal the turmoil of existence in a male-dominated society that is pervaded by conservative values. Conflict arises because the protagonists' own thoughts contradict the norms dictated by society and therefore the women address questions which they might have been expected conventionally to ignore. This process of self-evaluation dominates all three novels and is contained within narrative modes and techniques that portray the inner reality of the protagonists through intense emotions, feelings and sentiments. What is significant about these novels is that the protagonists seek answers to the problems and dilemmas facing them. The women are dissatisfied with their present situation, and in particular the roles that have been prescribed for them. During their interrogation of their selves; the past, the present and the future become important. Thinking of the past allows the women to escape in fantasy and nostalgia. The present is dominated by fear, uncertainty and confusion whilst the future becomes daunting (Dhawan, 1993).

In her novel *Where Shall We Go This Summer?* (1975), Desai depicts the tensions within the novel's protagonist, Sita. She feels herself trapped in the 'dull sterile world' of the present, which offers her little hope of happiness and contentment within the conventional roles she has been forced to adopt as wife and mother. Sita escapes the reality of her existence, her husband Raman, her four children and the monotony of her life to seek peace in her childhood home on the island of Manori. However, this eludes her and consequently her stay at the island represents a pilgrimage into the development of her own self-identity.

Sita withdraws into nostalgia during her stay on the island, as she re-evaluates the past from the perspective of her present circumstances. Melancholy is the predominant emotion during this as feelings of alienation and estrangement are interwoven with an unfulfilled yearning to be recognised as an individual. The themes of dispossession and alienation become central to the novel and are reinforced by images of death, sterility and disease. Sita describes herself as a 'grey dull-lit empty shell' (Desai, 1975, p. 39), as she feels enriched by the beauty that surrounds her. She feels restricted and imprisoned in contrast to the freedom she envisages within the water. Sita also longs for something different that would: 'proclaim her still alive, not quite drowned and dead' (Desai, 1975, p. 39) and waits 'for the two halves of this grey egg-world to fall apart and burst into fireworks' (Desai, 1975, p. 39).

The very fact that Sita has such thoughts casts her as a New Woman who interrogates her life and becomes frustrated with it. But Sita also finds herself confused; despite her questioning attitude, and finds herself having no other option, saying, 'only if I could paint or sing or play the sitar well, really well. I should have grown into a sensible woman instead of being what I am!' (Desai, 1975, p. 81). She adds: 'I should have known how to channel my thoughts and feelings and put them to use' (Desai, 1975, p. 82). But whilst Sita attempts to find a means to assert her own identity and her feelings of 'choking' and 'enslavement', she realises: 'life must be continued, and all its businesses' (Desai, 1975, p. 111). Ultimately Sita, typical of Deshpande's women, reverts back to tradition rather than taking control of her own life (Dhawan, 1993).

The novels *Voices in the City* and *Inside the Haveli*, explore feelings of alienation and dispossession through the protagonists Monisha and Geeta. Feelings of suffocation and imprisonment are again characteristic of the novels. Both protagonists are educated, upper class and move into their husband's homes after marriage. The novels are thus preoccupied with the women's search for self-identity and their attempt for self autonomy in the face of the constraints of marriage. Whilst Geeta, like Sita, finds herself becoming reconciled her circumstances, Monisha's search for herself culminates in self-destruction.

The role that is imposed upon them is the main cause of antagonism for the protagonists. Education has allowed them to move towards autonomy and realise their inner potential, thus allowing them to question themselves and others. However, after marriage, Monisha and Geeta's husbands and their families impose a role which the women refuse to acknowledge. This conventional role of a wife is determined through tradition, whereby she is placed in a subservient role towards elders and her husband. This concept of 'woman' within the marital home signifies specific roles and behaviour, which fail to correspond to Monisha's and Geeta's own personal identities but overwhelm them on first entering the marital house. The New Woman within both novels desires privacy, contrary to the communalism which is characteristic of South Asian life. Geeta longs for privacy; 'oh the lonely luxury of being alone' (Mehta, 1977, p. 4) and Monisha desiring privacy, goes on to the terrace for the 'splendour of stars and solitude' (Desai, 1965, p. 18).

Whilst both Monisha and Geeta re-assess their own lives, this self-awareness takes different forms. For Geeta, her interrogation of her life began as an awareness of 'the value of kinship and wanted to preserve the ancestral dignity of the Haveli' (Mehta, 1977, p. 142). Whilst Geeta realises the importance of tradition and becomes close to the members of her family, for Monisha the situation is quite the reverse. She experiences a loss of identity and self-confidence as she questions her life. Monisha continues to feel totally alienated and chooses to take her own life rather than submit to a life with which she does not want to identify. Desai explores the loneliness of the individual and shows the New Woman to be different from previous women. Rather than living the way they do, they are attempting to find a way out, even if it means the ultimate – death (Dhawan, 1993).

The ending for Monisha is typical of the novels written by Desai. For example, in *Cry The Peacock* (1963), the conclusion consists of the protagonist killing her husband and then herself. Desai's protagonists feel extremely alienated from the society in which they live. They find family and traditions both alien and claustrophobic. Their refusal to conform to tradition and convention instigates their choice to take their own lives. The New Woman of Desai's novels fails to find the meaning that she sought; she fails in her quest, but rather than accept the situation, rebels again by taking her own life.

The New Woman in Diasporic Literature

Just as the women within South Asian women's literature question their identity, this self-evaluation is a major preoccupation for British South Asian women writers, but written in a different context with rather different conclusions. What comes out of their writing is a combination of concerns with migration and diaspora for the New Woman.

Evaluating identity largely takes the form of a concern with place and displacement as the novels' protagonists discuss their diasporic identities, being South Asian in Britain, and the relevance of British and South Asian cultures to their lives. Conflict between individualism and communalism is thus at the heart of their creativity, as the women struggle for independence and self-reliance as well as clinging to the traditional requirements of the minority culture. The strategy used by the New Woman within these diasporic texts involves a journey similar to the South Asian writers' questioning of conventional and traditional assumptions. Journey as a metaphor is evident within the context of diasporic writing as writers recounted the transformations of migration, its effects and problems, thus the journey of immigration has been closely followed by the journey into settlement and now the journey into self. Writers treat journey as a means of self-knowledge, not only through re-entry into a collective historical experience, but also through an exploration or rediscovery of personal experience.

Looking at South Asian women's writing as a global phenomenon, the South Asian diaspora spans the world; communities are located in Africa, the Middle East, England, North and South America and the Caribbean. They often write about how enabling it can be for women to be in a different kind of community. For example, Bharati Mukherjee describes women emigrating to the US or Canada and being able to construct a new selfbyself-invention. But at the same time, that separation from community can also be very traumatic (Hai, 2004). These women authors incorporate their experience in both worlds in an attempt to make a new, empowering image for women.

The novels considered here, like those in the previous section, begin with their main protagonists embarking on a journey, thus establishing immediately each novel's preoccupation with place and displacement. But South Asian women writers, like Black African-Caribbean women within the diaspora, use a journey to explore a growth of consciousness, where voyages over geographical space become a metaphor for the journey into the self. The journeys, whether real or imaginary, may enact the retrieval of the collective past, but are essentially about the exploration and discovery of the self. The novels succeed in documenting this process, and trace the self-discovery of their main protagonists; in essence, the emphasis is on story telling as a means of fixing identity. Hence the protagonists can be seen as diasporic 'New Women'.

This process of self-evaluation has been inappropriately yet widely described as a 'crisis of identity'. This derives from the development of an affective relationship between self-identity and place. This self-identity is the offspring of the immigrant and the place is Britain. Unlike post-colonial literature, which explores the active sense of self eroded by dislocation, resulting from migration, the literature written by British South Asians establishes the inhibition of an active sense of self from both the cultures into which they are born and a desire for location within both. In short, this literature is an expression of hybridised identities.

Ravinder Randhawa, Farhana Sheikh and Leena Dhingra

As with the Indian novelists, preconceived notions of gendered identities are the main cause of antagonism for the female protagonist within diasporic texts. The concept of 'woman' signifies certain roles and behaviour. This generates the overwhelming sense of frustration and dissatisfaction which dominates all three novels. However, a further layer of meaning is laid on to the category of New Woman in these diasporic writings, as the characters are depicted as 'cultural navigators' negotiating their way between the traditional culture of 'home' and the 'freedoms' of White British society. In this way, the diasporic women's writings that represent British South Asian New Woman are forms of cultural hybridisation that reflect the experiences and social positioning of the authors themselves, who have been born or brought up within Britain.

For all three protagonists in these novels their self-evaluation spans generations of history; they are frequently lifted out of the present and forced to confront their past. Each of the characters explores the identities thrust upon her, whether from within her own culture or through racial and sexual oppression. The first-person narrative reveals a consciousness frustrated at the link between culture and personal identity, and where gender plays an important role within 'acceptable' social behaviour, as one is immersed in to the other. What annoys these characters is the control they are subject to from the larger community, so this sense of community is often registered in negative terms and evokes an atmosphere of claustrophobia.

This conflict between individualism and communalism is at the heart of all three novels. Ravinder Randhawa's *A Wicked Old Woman* (1987) primarily deals with Kuli, 'a shabby-looking woman' who resorts to wearing clothes from Oxfam and controls her life by choosing to live this way. However, the criticism vented upon her by others, in particular her sons, forces her into self-evaluation and she finally adopts the conventional roles she has spent all of her life rejecting. The novel examines how asserting personal autonomy and identity conflicts with cultural prescriptions. Kuli discovers and begins to assert her own identity despite this oppressive traditional environment and ultimately because of it. She becomes a New Woman because she recognises herself as an individual and interrogates her heritage even if she ends up accepting it. Kuli's interrogation of her role and her life stems from her desire to choose, and the lack of 'real' choice due to the discrimination she experiences both within and outside of the community. The restrictions and inhibitions from within the minority culture force her to be part of it but Kuli 'wanted to be Indian and English: wanted to choose for herself what she wanted out of both' (Randhawa, 1987, p. 29). She initially wants to be part of the indigenous British culture from which her family desperately want to protect her, even 'when being the same meant having a boyfriend' (Randhawa, 1987, p. 6) and thus take control of her life.

Kuli's attempt to navigate between the ethnic colony and the indigenous population is successful to an extent. Her family fails to find out about her relationship with her White friend Michael. However, Kuli's cultural restrictions have an impact on this relationship. The emotional repercussions of rebelling and engaging in activities she knows are unacceptable also remain strong, despite her attempt to control her life. The turmoil in her mind is strongly conveyed as she describes herself 'as a newly emergent Machiavelli ... skilled in circumventing the protective barriers of parents and community, lying with ease to cover her tracks' (Randhawa, 1987, p. 6). Kuli finds herself in conflict with the inner Indian voice that is still entwined within tradition, therefore emerging and judging her, and it evokes a sense of uneasiness. During her time with Michael, she continues to interrogate her life, 'what was wrong with living a nice, ordinary, Indian-girl type life? Millions did. Why couldn't she?' (Randhawa, 1987, p. 22). Kuli is sitting in a women's centre when the issue of belonging is raised as another South Asian woman says, 'we have to leave a legacy for the future, for the children to whom India will be just another country. Immigration part of their history. They'll be British by birth, but never by colour' (Randhawa, 1987, p. 144). The conversation upsets Kuli to the extent that she leaves and does not return to the centre despite being invited back.

Having incorporated aspects of both the minority and the indigenous culture within her behaviour, Kuli soon realises that the combination is not sustainable and her choices are, in reality, limited. Declaring herself an outcast within British culture she announces, 'no more trying to walk in the middle, there were too many pot holes she was a like a blind woman without a stick' (Randhawa, 1987, p. 29). She attempts to revert back fully to the Indian part of her identity whilst significantly remaining in control of her own life. Kuli forces her parents to arrange a marriage for her. The marriage fails because her husband has problems with her asserting her independence and her failure to fulfil the role prescribed for her as a wife.

Kuli is a New Woman because she recognises herself as an individual and chooses different strategies to overcome the pressure to act in the role or category others want to see. Contrasted with the sari-clad typically Indian wives with a fixed image of life, Kuli is a middle-aged shabby-looking woman. The conflict between personal identity and culture remains a powerful hindrance to her progress. Kuli suffers from asserting her own identity as she appears a misfit, in sharp contrast to the sari-clad women she encounters on the roadside at the opening. Her physical appearance and her attitude alienate her children from herself. She also experiences discrimination from both within and outside the South Asian community.

Significantly, Kuli is a 'cripple', not physically but emotionally. The arguments and her assertion of her identity have made her unable to stand on her own two legs; she symbolically makes herself into a 'cripple' by using the stick, which becomes a metaphor for her life. Not fitting into either of the two cultures fully she remains disabled, loaded down with the comments those around her make. Her walk becomes a metaphor for dependence. 'She walks ritually over every grating' (Randhawa, 1987, p. 30) deliberately, although she knows that she could have a much easier time by conforming.

Kuli's initial pain derives from her failure to understand her life, and it is her interaction with others that provides understanding. She becomes aware of the image others see and comes to realise it contradicts the image they longed for. Kuli comes to recognise her situation as that of a misfit. Accused of thinking like the English by her ex-husband (Randhawa, 1987, p. 132), she thinks 'she was. And she wasn't. Never could be English' (Randhawa, 1987, p. 133). But at the same time, she finds herself rejected by the South Asian community. She is also mistaken for being English, laughed at by 'two nice ladies in silken saris' from whom she 'hears a sentence from one to other how the English folk go funny in the head' (Randhawa, 1987, p. 51). She realises her detachment is due to her not conforming to traditional norms of how someone her age should act.

It is the reaction of her children which pushes her into self-analysis. Confronted by Pavan's accusation that she is dividing the family and that only she can bring about reconciliation, Kuli's immediate reaction is one of anger. Her reaction and thoughts afterwards symbolise her first step upon her journey into self-consciousness. What unfolds in the novel are experiences and memories, heavily embroiled within cultural ties and religion. Kuli's journey involves the reopening of old wounds as she ponders on feelings of resentment, anger and frustration by those close to her and comes to understand them. Her meetings with Shirley and her son Arvind are a classic example of how disassociated she is from the minority culture. She does not call her own son Arvind and anglicises his name to Arnold, yet his own English wife refers to him as Arvind and corrects Kuli (Randhawa, 1987, p. 91). Her own son is embarrassed by being related to her: when she walks in to see him he says, 'mother. You look like a …!' (Randhawa, 1987, p. 96), leaving the sentence unfinished.

Only by fully understanding the past can Kuli redefine the future in which she has a positive and active role within her family. This revaluation of history is marked by the 'stick-leg-shuffle-leg-shuffle. Stick-leg-shuffle-leg-shuffle' that recurs through her journey. Her stick-led gait symbolises the soul-purging process taking place within Kuli as she thrashes out her life with her rejection of the stick at the end establishing the completion of her quest. She talks to Caroline about her most personal thoughts, describing herself using the image of a:

> Gorgeous, multi-coloured bird, soaring through the sky, swooping to the ground, Iridescent with each wing shake or bright gay in the sunlight … by a cruel twist of fate, this flamboyant rover of the skies had been grounded, its wings clipped, left to fight for survival in the cold chimes and grey world of England. (Randhawa, 1987, p. 118)

She ends by saying, 'No wonder it had lost its colours, shed its feathers, lost its way, become one among the soulless throng' (Randhawa, 1987, p. 118). Kuli describes herself in terms of imprisonment and disillusionment, irrespective of having taken control of her own life. Whilst she acknowledges her past and takes responsibility for her decisions, there is a general sense of frustration, which is due largely to her determination to control her own life.

However, Kuli as a New Woman merely conforms to the South Asian woman stereotype at the end, simply because of her acknowledgement of isolation from the family. Only by reverting back to the traditional image that others want to see is she able to integrate and interact within the South Asian community. The character, irrespective of her reversion to traditional norms, is a New Woman; she recognises herself as an individual and attempts to overcome the pressure to be a role or category.

The Red Box by Farhana Sheikh, features Raisa, an MA student who interviews two fifteen-year-old girls, Nasreen and Tahira, for a project. On the outside, Raisa projects an image of being New Woman. She lives alone, has a career, is embarking on education and is unmarried, yet in reality the identity of the protagonist Raisa is overwhelmingly influenced by, and contained within, tradition. The novel depicts her struggle to release herself from a tradition-bound society in order to gain an independent identity as she journeys into her own identity.

One of the steps Raisa undertakes to have autonomy is her decision to live alone. Whilst this strategy theoretically allows her independence, her father and sister both have keys to the flat; it is 'family property'. She also receives daily phone calls from them. The novel is centred on her parents' attempts to make Raisa's behaviour conform with that of a 'traditional' daughter – she is told, 'You can't just ignore accepted codes of behaviour' (Shekh, 1991, p. 4). The pressure to conform to the role of daughter causes Raisa discomfort, as she abides by her father's request.

When Raisa interviews Tahira and Nasreen her thoughts are dominated by hoping to be accepted and deciding which aspects of her true self she should make visible, and which others she should conceal, in order to conform to their cultural expectations. Her preoccupation with being accepted by others is an important element in the novel. On the one hand, Raisa appears to be strong, independent and self-reliant; at other times she is weak, dependent on others and reliant on their approval. In her interaction with the two girls, her strong obsessive need for this approval is strongly evoked. We learn of Raisa's concern with how they perceive her: 'how would the girls receive her? As a teacher, a fellow Pakistani? Would they approve of her?' (Shekh, 1991, p. 18). The image that other people have of her provokes criticism of her supposed lifestyle. Tahira, for example, points out Raisa's difference: 'you ain't even lived like us. You've never worried about half the things we worry about. Where you live, the people you meet, it's all different' (Shekh, 1991, p. 189).

These conversations with Nasreen and Tahira and their families become a catalyst for Raisa as she begins to question herself, her past, and the relationship with her mother. Raisa's ability to understand critically the way her life had been dominated by attempts to impose roles and categories becomes important in her assessment of her own identity. Her re-evaluation of her life before her mother's death stresses her self-determination and her need to establish her identity as distinct from others.

Ultimately, whilst it is evident that Raisa seeks an autonomous lifestyle, there are indications that complete independence is neither desired by her nor permitted by others. Whilst she takes herself out of her community's culture during her youth, it is clear that Raisa seeks more integration within her community through Nasreen and Tahira. She accepts her own family's lifestyle to an extent, but her isolation and loneliness is highlighted within the text, which establishes self-rejection, or the lack of community support that she seeks with the girls. Only by coming to terms with her past, her rebellious stage, her mother and her life can she emerge as an active self, prepared to re-define the future.

Leena Dhingra's *Amritvela* (1988) is a novel about the protagonist's journey back to India after years of living in England. The novel deals with the social and cultural aspects of Meena's stay in India, as she seriously entertains the idea of migrating back to settle there. The return to India brings about a wave of emotions for the protagonist ranging from comfort and frustration to familiarity and bewilderment. Life in Britain is depicted negatively, and the process of adaptation within the diasporic communities is rendered problematic and lonely, a feature of diasporic New Womanhood. The conclusion of the novel is an awareness of the protagonist's failure to fit into the country she left behind and the knowledge that not only has she changed, but so has the mother country where she wants to fit in. The New Woman in this text is one who seeks to integrate aspects of her Indian culture with aspects of the White British culture that she was immersed in as she was growing up. She attempts to do this by travelling from England to India, therefore her presence in India takes the form of a search for her 'authentic' ethnic identity.

The differences between the cultures are highlighted when Meena arrives in India. The issue of identity is central to the novel and is the preoccupation with which the narrative opens. Suspended in the air halfway to India, Meena connects this physical state to her own self, to her dual identity. 'I feel myself to be suspended between two cultures. This is where I belong, the halfway mark. Here in the middle of nowhere' (Dhingra, 1988, p. 1). The metaphor evokes the overwhelming sense of confusion central to the image of the diasporic New Woman.

Typically, the problems of 'home' and 'belonging' are represented as integral to the diasporic condition within the text. The issue is addressed largely in terms of exclusion, when cultural identification with Indian society is the most important criterion for the protagonist. Meena's account of her life before her journey 'back home' evokes a sense of rootlessness: 'from my first journey at the age of five and the countless ones in between, I have always been on my way' (Dhingra, 1988, p. 2). Her awareness of being cut off from a sense of community and society evokes feelings of isolation and loneliness such that there is a strong desire for a sense of worth and belonging, 'I need to get a sense of what life would be like' (Dhingra, 1988, p. 38), knowing 'there is something I need to integrate and fit together again' (Dhingra, 1988, p. 37). Meena's personal odyssey initially takes the form of a geographical journey as she travels to India to re-discover aspects of herself. Whilst she questions herself at the beginning, 'what am I doing? Who knows!', she strongly believes the answers are embodied in India; as she says on arrival, 'over the next few weeks, I'm sure that some clarity will emerge' (Dhingra, 1988, p. 38).

Cultural identification with India is by far the most important element for Meena as it represents home. Theoretically, home is a site of everyday lived experience, where the discourse of locality and feelings of belonging are continually reproduced in daily practice (Brah, 1996), but for Meena, India represents a mythical place of desire in her diasporic imagination, the home of her soul; 'when I came to India, it was like magic. So full of promise and possibilities and idealism. It was like a wonderful cake full of layers, colours, aromas, flavours, soft and light and rich with infinite possibilities' (Dhingra, 1988, p. 153). She connects the notion of home with India because it signifies the social and psychic geography of space that is ordinarily experienced in terms of a hometown; 'my connection to India was through my parents, now I must make it myself' (Dhingra, 1988, p. 39). Her India connotes the network of family, kin, friends and 'significant others' which generates shared human warmth. This home is a place with which Meena remains intimate even in moments of intense alienation from it.

However, when Meena arrives in India, the conflict between 'East' and 'West' within her are explored as she confronts unfamiliar norms and customs. Meena finds herself in unexpected predicaments; the simple chore of posting a parcel becomes a complex ritual that has to be learnt and performed in the time-honoured Indian way. Bringing her parcel, neatly wrapped in brown paper and ready to post she inadvertently causes a sensation in the post office, because, as Bibiji later confides 'in India parcels have to be wrapped in cloth' (Dhingra, 1988, p. 24).

Meena sets about trying to fit into Indian culture. On the first morning she arrives in India, finding the table set with 'the toast rack, egg cup and the other superfluities belonging to the English breakfast' (Dhingra, 1988, p. 8), she asks instead for a traditional Indian breakfast 'roti' because it is what the other members of the family had. Meena further asserts her Indian identity by using her maiden name, identifying herself as Meena Sahgal, which naturally 'slips out' (Dhingra, 1988, p. 43), as opposed to using her husband's surname.

Despite her attempts to integrate within India her differences are too obvious. The way she responds to others reveals her Englishness. Her manner of saying thank you is immediately picked up by others including Bibiji who says: 'What is this "please, sorry, thank you" business?' (Dhingra, 1988, p. 9). She reprimands her by saying, 'you're not in England now. You're in India and there's no need for any 'please, sorry, thank you' business here!' (Dhingra, 1988, p. 9). Meena's English characteristics are constantly highlighted against the backdrop of Indian characteristics, and established as more pronounced, thus accentuating her difference from the indigenous population. She soon realises the inappropriateness of her Western shoes, 'my high heels sink into the dust on the pavement' (Dhingra, 1988, p. 44) and decides to buy some chappals (sandals). This is not just a practical act but a cultural concession, rich in metaphor; Meena's East-West encounter is a step-by-step journey and her adaptation, if she is to feel at home in India, involves inescapable realities including the ground under her feet.

However, there are occasions when Meena deliberately allows her Englishness to supersede her Indianness. On the first morning she wakes up in India, she asks the untouchable servant, Minoo, to prepare some tea for her. Meena is conscious that her assertion of Englishness is inappropriate, believing the women will talk about her eating food prepared by an untouchable: 'these western ways! She sleeps until nine and then drinks tea from the hands of an untouchable' (Dhingra, 1988, p. 4), but she does so regardless, reflecting her status as a New Woman.

Meena tells Usha of her experience of living in Britain, full of pain and disillusionment: 'it's a tearing apart. Both ways from here from there ...' (Dhingra, 1988, p. 50). She stresses the alienation and the isolation she feels: 'In London, I am a stranger and constantly feel a stranger. It's very lonely and I seem to have lost my way' (Dhingra, 1988, p. 72). Meena behaves like an expatriate. She still considers India to be her home, so that when Usha asks her 'no place like home eh?' (Dhingra, 1988, p. 48) Meena instinctively associates home with India: 'I suppose so. Yes. Though it would be nice to be at home longer, or to live ... at home' (Dhingra, 1988, p. 48). She overlooks the fact that by 'home', Usha means England.

As a diasporic New Woman Meena's disillusionment with her marriage and her life in Britain develops into a yearning for the past, hence her journey to India, the ancestral home and evolution of memories and experiences. However, Meena has an exaggerated feeling of affinity with India because it signifies something that western culture does not. Images of unity and the extended family are stressed throughout the text with reference to India, and this is contrasted to the real life of her family in Britain. Meena's own family lacks unity; her husband has left her. Home for Meena becomes a mythical desire to fit into India because it is seen as a place of 'origin'. Meena appears to have built some form of cocoon around herself, a refuge from the alienation and coldness she experiences in her life in Britain. She clings to her ethnic identity, envisaging her life in India as being fulfilling and true. She tells Sita, 'you're still in India! ... The sounds, the smells, the life, the fascination of the place. It's still where you belong' (Dhingra, 1988, p. 72). She seeks integration within that culture, believing spiritual India holds the answers to all her questions and her confusion. The image Meena has of India is nostalgic and exotic; it is the image of a tourist India. To her, India is a country of colour, warmth and moonlit nights, and the image connotes an essentially romantic image of India as opposed to the perception of someone who lives there. Even the dust feels exotic to her: 'The sun, the sounds, the light, the heat, the smells – all seem to combine to create a special kind of ... what is it? An effect? ... a feeling? A sensation, tactile almost – something which touches but cannot be grasped' (Dhingra, 1988, p. 127).

During the course of her stay and irrespective of her attempts to integrate, Meena encounters the difference between 'feeling at home' and laying a claim to a place as her own and comes to realise that they are incompatible. The experience of social exclusion prevents her from proclaiming India as home, and she acknowledges the inaccuracy with which she remembers India. The India that she desires is a mythical place within her imagination, mediated by memories of what she left behind, the experiences of disruption and displacements. She is able to see the difference between what she expected, hoped and desired of India, and what she actually experiences on arrival. Such is her disappointment at the real India she is forced to confront that she says, 'I don't understand India anymore ... It's as though the idealism and promise has just ... dissolved into the dust!'(Dhingra, 1988, p. 153).

After this physical and mental battle, Meena emerges acknowledging that India is no longer her real home; although it remains a part of her, she cannot live there again. But as a New Woman who is able to enjoy the India around her and feel a part of it, she feels that 'I have shed a weight. I realised it after the fever had left, but now my whole being confirms it – as if a whole new and clear space had been created within me' (Dhingra, 1988, p. 167). Appropriate to the title of the novel, *Amritvela*, which translates as the coming of light after the dark, or the beginning of the new day, Meena's stay in India also sheds a new perspective on her life. She initially views the journey as a realisation that India was no longer the dream image she carried with her. During the course of her stay Meena sheds the negative feeling of being caught in a flux between cultures and moves towards an appreciation of both. The New Woman who emerges at the end has developed from a total identification with India to the acceptance of both India and Britain as her home. She even becomes capable of questioning the Indian part of her identity. When she is given a shawl from her aunt Daya as a leaving gift, Meena protests claiming, 'it's like inheriting the mantle of a tradition from which I am uprooted and of which I know nothing' (Dhingra, 1988, p. 173). However, she has to recognise that she has her place in Indian culture and acknowledges this by keeping the scarf, which symbolises a new beginning.

Meena gains the support and the sense of belonging she did not previously possess and emerges as a strong and confident woman in touch with her true self as she acknowledges the importance of East and West to her identity. Symbolically she asks her aunt to throw the books in which she recorded her thoughts during her stay in India into the river Ganga. The ashes of the dead are scattered here, symbolising new beginnings. She sheds the old Meena and embarks on the journey back to Britain. Meena realises the double-placeness of 'home' as she fails to feel anchored in India or in Britain and that her identity is not continuous, uninterrupted, unchanging and stable but instead plural and in process. Awakening in this new light (Amritvela), Meena is not so much a tourist as an explorer, discovering her 'home' within herself, within her multi-dimensional experience of life. Her Indian ethnicity is one dimension of her person, but her search for wholeness and authenticity leads her to an awareness that she has an individuality which resists being reduced to the ethnic or cultural categories thrust upon her by India or Britain. She went to India to find what she felt she knew, and instead found what she did not know: herself. Like every human being, she is ultimately her own mother country.

Conclusion

The New Woman who emerged from the tide of feminism in the 1960s is supposed to be radically different from her traditional counterpart (Chandra, 1995). This is established in both sets of literature, diasporic and South Asian. However, there are notable differences between the two genres in regard to the emergence of the New

Woman. In the diasporic literature, she shows an inexorable awakening of identity in relation to Western values of individuality and independence. In South Asia, her emergence largely expresses a growing awareness of patriarchy and its demands on women and the desire to move from tradition to modernity. The evolution of the latter is somewhat natural as opposed to the imposed development for the diasporic canon of literature.

Both sets of literature demonstrate how the female characters conform to the postulate of the New Woman. They are shown to have the strength to assert their identity and self amidst conflict and their predicaments. In depicting this, the writers address the social and cultural modes and values that have defined the preconceived notions of women and what womanhood constitutes.

Whilst the New Women in both sets of literature discover their identities because of oppressive tradition, they revert back to it. The ways in which the New Woman deals with her awareness of her new identity are different. The New Woman in South Asian fiction fails to go on with her journey but takes a step back and conforms to the old image, so that no change really occurs. But within the diasporic literature, they go on to assert and explore their own identity, even when it reverts back to traditional concepts. The women's fate when they assert their identity leaves them outside the community to which they belong. Feelings of isolation, frustration and anger therefore pull them back. The women are cast in the mould of the New Woman; however, in the course of the novels they establish themselves not as autonomous but as depending on others for their survival.

The characters, irrespective of their reversion, are nevertheless New Women because they recognise themselves as individuals with the power to choose. The assertion of identity, the struggle for independence and self-reliance is echoed in the trials faced by the women discussed in this chapter. Self-determination and autonomy are the key aspects of the novels, which the protagonists express through their rebellion. Each woman in her own way interrogates her life and attempts to overcome the pressure to be only a role, or a category. Both sets of New Women choose a strategy, which makes them 'New' whatever the context and outcome. Although each woman has thought about self and culture as disparate ideas, they all focus on issues of culture and personal identity to the point of re-defining the self and deciding how much they should surrender to their husbands and to the surrounding culture.

Chapter 5

Bhaji on the Beach and *Bend it like Beckham*: Gurinder Chadha and the 'Desification' of British Cinema

Introduction

As the first British South Asian woman to direct feature films, Gurinder Chadha occupies an important role as spokesperson for South Asian women as well as being in a position to challenge the misrepresentation of South Asian women within mainstream film. She succeeds in re-defining British identities as culturally plural rather than fixed around some national, ethnic, racial or other absolute boundary and hence also explores ideas of diaspora, hybridity and cultural syncretism. Her work reveals the similarities between the individuals across cultures and tries to communicate the Englishness of her South Asian characters.

According to Chadha she uses the camera to educate her audience, 'I wanted to use the camera which is so powerful to change the way that people are portrayed' (Chadha quoted in Fuchs, 2004). She has made a conscious decision to operate in the mainstream thus presenting images that are normally invisible in mainstream. What she does succeed in doing is showing the characters in her film not as isolated individuals, but as socially located within the wider family and community framework. Consequently, the characters are more rounded, the viewer is able to have some sense of their personality, and their background together with their family and community. It is argued here that these films involve the 'desification' of British cinema. 'Desi' means authentically South Asian, but it also entails a deeper meaning of being rooted in the South Asian community carrying with it connotations of pride and self-worth. For example, when Gurinder Chadha's films 'desify' British cinema, the themes, music and language of British film is transformed through the introduction of South Asian elements, so that the result is a specifically British South Asian form of cultural hybridisation. Chadha's feature films thus have a distinctive mise-en-scene characterised by their expression of cultural hybridity.

Born in Kenya, and brought up in the UK, Gurinder Chadha began her career as a news reporter with BBC Radio, directed several award winning documentaries for the BBC, and then worked for the BFI and Channel Four, where she produced the documentary, *I'm English But ...* (1989). This film followed young British South Asians and discussed generational differences between them and their parents. In 1990, Chadha set up her own production company; Umbi Films. Her first dramatic film short was the 11-minute *Nice Arrangement* (1991) about a British South Asian wedding. Chadha's feature directorial debut, *Bhaji on the Beach* (1993) traced the adventures of three generations of British South Asian women on a day trip to Blackpool. After *Bhaji*, Chadha directed a two-part drama *Rich Deceiver* (1995), for the BBC, and continued to work on documentaries. She followed up her previous cult hit with *What's Cooking* (2000), the story of four Los Angeles families on Thanksgiving weekend. *Bend it like Beckham* (2002) is Chadha's most commercial film to date about a teenage South Asian girl who longs to play football while trying to balance it with her parents' demands.

Both the films *Bhaji on the Beach* and *Bend it like Beckham* discussed in this chapter raise general issues of concern to South Asian communities in Britain, in particular generational differences. In both films, Chadha shows the parents fearful of the future and desperate to protect their 'Indianness'. Chadha explores the 'fossilised' values of the 1960s including commitment, duty, honour, sacrifice – perpetuated over the years as she sharply contrasts these attitudes with those of the second and subsequent generations. Even in *Bhaji on the Beach* these old ideas are contrasted with the visiting Bombay relative, clad in Western attire, revealing cleavage and leg in contrast to the older women in their drab saris that cover their bodies completely. Rekha, like Jess's cousins in *Bend it like Beckham*, represent the new liberated woman, where the body is now flaunted, in the form of short skirts and low-cleavage blouses.

Both films become representative of the lives of South Asian women living in England. The films not only examine the cross-cultural conflicts but also aspirations and dilemmas of a generation of Indian-born South Asians who find themselves teetering between two cultures, that of India and of their adopted homeland and their children born in the UK. Chadha decides to opt for discussing issues of identity due to the personal nature of the topic 'I grew-up in an environment where my family wanted me to be Indian while I was inclined to adopt a British way of life. So I've experienced the dilemma faced by thousands of Asians born in the West. When I decided to make a film the issue which was closest to my heart came first in mind,' (Chadha quoted in Sehgal, 2003). Identity overwhelms both films as she chooses to focus on that which is absent in mainstream.

Both films show either the 'Indianising' of Britain, or the 'hybridising of Britain' (Chadha in Bailey, 2003). In both films, individuals juggle different traditions, different languages, and therefore know what it means to be bicultural. 'it's the nuts-and-bolts of integration or immigration or diversity or multiculturalism or whatever you want to call it. It actually shows that process at work, how it happens and what are the very personal decisions that people make. That's a cultural paradigm that we don't often see expressed, but you'd be surprised how many of us live and breathe it around the world.' (Chadha in Bailey, 2003).

It is important to understand that Chadha attacks and dissects the dominant ideologies that shape the identities of South Asian women within a diasporic context, and yet that she is doing so to a certain extent from within that cultural framework. Chadha's discussion of the South Asian community as it acts within the diaspora raises problems in itself, as she has been influenced by the fact that she herself is, to a certain extent, caught up in the community she examines. Her own positioning as a South Asian woman has a great deal to do with her articulation as a British citizen exploring Indian identity within an English context, or the positioning of minority culture or diaspora within the context of a majority culture. Her upbringing gives her a unique viewpoint, and it is this viewpoint that she captures when she directs her films.

Both films are thought provoking, but ultimately flawed in various ways. Chadha succeeds in illustrating the effects and development of an identity that has been inextricably bound up with the process of understanding one's own self, in which the pretence of a common purpose is linked to, and expressed by, means of control and nationalism. Perhaps the films' main deficiencies are their attempts to handle too wide a variety of issues in great depth.

Despite the criticism, both films have been successes. *Bend it like Beckham*'s success came from its timing. The film was released when football fever was reaching its pitch because of the forthcoming FIFA World Cup in June 2002. Gurinder readily agrees that she decided the release date with the Cup in mind 'Football is like religion in England ... I wanted to cash on this hysteria which sweeps both British and Asian fans,' (Chadha quoted in Sehgal, 2003). Another unique feature of the film is that many relatives of Chadha have done cameos in the film. Explains the filmmaker, 'It is very difficult to find extras in England so I asked my aunts and uncles to play the roles of members of an extended Punjabi family. The whole thing turned out to be one big family picnic of sorts. We thoroughly enjoyed it' (Chadha quoted in Sehgal, 2003). *Bend it like Beckham* became a smash hit and one of the highest grossing home-produced films of 2002 in Britain (Bagguley and Hussain, 2003). *Bhaji on the Beach* was also a surprise commercial and critical hit (Bhattacharyya and Gabriel, 1994). It gained numerous international awards, was nominated for a Bafta and won Chadha the Evening Standard Award for 'Newcomer to British Cinema'. *Bhaji on the Beach* was a lower budget film in comparison to *Bend it like Beckham*, and was also different in that the women were seemingly running away form their problems instead of confronting them like the women in *Bend it like Beckham*. Yet, in *Bhaji on the Beach,* the journey becomes a search into new possibilities, the trip to Blackpool becomes a journey of self-discovery. However, in both films Chadha explores the ways in which South Asians are marginalised in western cultures as well as considering the internal dynamics of South Asian diasporic communities.

'England' in *Bhaji on the Beach*

The England represented in *Bhaji on the Beach*, is multicultural. The film relates concepts of 'essential' English characteristics to the positioning of the South Asian community within England together with the wider cultural implications of these ideologies. It shows how one has to learn to be both British and South Asian, and where identity is grounded and energised by both the minority culture as well as the British culture. What Chadha attempts to do is construct diasporic space within the framework of Englishness, which combines those from different localities, in essence a hybrid space. Yet within this space Chadha reinforces the complexities and intersections of cultural difference and identity. She incorporates issues of home, hybridity, identity and belonging within the three generations of South Asian women.

Bhaji on the Beach is a story of a group of South Asian women who go on a day trip to Blackpool. The day trip has been organised by Simi who works for the Saheli Asian Women's Centre. Among the day-trippers are Ginder, a young women who has taken sanctuary, along with her son Amrik, in Simi's shelter, after being physically abused by her husband Ranjit. Hashida, a student about to start medical school, is pregnant, the father of her baby being Oliver, an African Caribbean art student. Included also is Asha, a middle aged newsagent who feels neglected by her family; Pushpa, an elderly Indian grocer; Rekha, a visitor from Bombay, Bina, a shop assistant from Marks & Spencer's, and Ladhu and Madhu, a pair of teenagers. Ranjit follows Ginder to Blackpool, forced by his parents to do so. What follows is a chain of events leading to the discovery of the violence and abuse suffered by Ginder at the hands of Ranjit. Oliver too follows Hashida, and the issues of interracial relationships, abortion and community support are raised with respect to this. The conclusion is a dramatic confrontation between Ginder and Ranjit.

When it was first released, *Bhaji on the Beach* was defined as an 'English' film. Primarily, it stands as a representative of a genre that can itself be seen as a form of culture essentially English in nature. This genre comprises the seaside trip, a setting representative of classical Englishness, reflecting a tradition of family life. Chadha used a backdrop outside of the 'inner city' to discuss contemporary issues facing South Asian women. She attempts this by setting her film at the seaside as opposed to a rural or urban environment, yet uses the same characteristics inherent in the pastoral ideology. Social change is underlined by locating the drama within a seaside resort that becomes representative of the rest of England, an England that becomes defined as much by what it excludes as by what it contains.

Blackpool is widely regarded in dominant culture as a White working-class holiday resort, but in *Bhaji* its promenade, tower, pier, fish and chips and souvenir shops, together with the pleasure beach, are acknowledged as legitimate objects of fantasy and nostalgia for British Asians; as Rekha, a woman visiting from India, on seeing Blackpool for the first time, exclaims 'Bombay!' Chadha does away with archetypes that portray the English family spending a day at the seaside. The family unit is replaced with single women choosing to break away from their families. They travel to the seaside to get away from chaotic lives, yet in an ironic twist, find their problems have followed them, despite their attempts to break free. The seaside becomes a platform for their grievances to be discussed.

On arrival, the hospitality received by the women is overshadowed by criticism vented by the White inhabitants of Blackpool that is manifested predominantly in the form of racist comments. The women serving food in the café pass remarks as Pushpa and her friend bring out their own food; 'bloody heathens! ... No manners!

... they ought to send them all back ... they breed like rabbits you know' (Chadha, 1992). The comments appear as a casual exchange of thoughts; both women reciprocate the other's idea of non-Whites and these thoughts are expressed in a way that is free from any inhibitions. The South Asian women are denied their own identity, but one is imposed on them, and a demeaning one at that. Cultural dominance is absolute with the assumption that Englishness itself is superior to any other culture, furthermore, it is actually obliterating alternative cultures with the element of control. In contrast, the exchange between the two women has an arrogant tone, which is established as patronising outrage as they question the audacity of the two South Asian women, representing the embodiment of English racism. At the core of their criticism is Englishness with passion vented on the South Asian women whom they see as 'colonising and corrupting English life'. They go against the traditionally English ideal of café behaviour by consuming their own food. The seaside atmosphere, upon closer inspection, is found not to be one of sun and sand, but dull and cloudy, typical of British weather, thereby destroying the idealised image for one that is closer to reality.

Chadha then sets about stripping away the myth that Indianness is necessarily positive; for example, when Ginder is frequently attacked for destroying the family unit. Chadha attempts to put across Ginder's perspective and, to a certain degree, is successful in this. As observers, we are able to sympathise with her, especially when we witness the violence of Balbir destroying the women's refuge where Ginder is staying.

However, as the other women on the day trip talk more about her situation it becomes apparent that Ginder is destroying the family unit by separating from Ranjit. They criticise Ginder's Englishness, since being in England has allowed her the strength to be independent and this contradicts her Indian ethnicity, which favours a more submissive image of women. Ginder feels the consequences of this as her Englishness isolates her from the other women, she is placed on what she herself refers to as the 'social rejects bench' (Chadha 1992). Ginder essentially rejects the Indian, as well as the English ideal of the family. In turn, the other women's reactions to this become an example of how it is celebrated. They criticise her for leaving Ranjit and use this to justify South Asian men embarking on relationships with English women. The very fact that Ginder suffers is because her marriage with Ranjit is a love marriage. So while Chadha is highlighting and criticising attitudes and behaviour towards love marriages, she is also displaying another characteristic in her own criticism. She is reinforcing the concept that the arranged marriage is necessarily a good thing and that young people are incapable of looking for an ideal partner. Chadha is part of the dominant 'Indian' ideology, she has been immersed in it all her life and it is difficult for her to escape it (Chadha, 1994).

Racism and Social Darwinism

The racial attitudes Chadha is presenting and criticising through the film can be seen as related to theories of social Darwinism. In this form of racism, race represents a stage in the evolutionary process of mankind, with the White being the most highly evolved race and the Black race being at the bottom of the evolutionary ladder. Central to this concept is the notion of the English being 'civilised', which the Black races are not: the film launches into this in its very opening. The film commences with the headline of the newspaper reading 'they curried my budgie', which carries connotations of the 'savagery' of the 'non-Whites'. The budgie in the cage, which represents a symbol of the urban working class, is taken out of its English context and defined in a term exclusive to South Asians, 'curried'. Here the media are seen as a means for expressing racist ideas. Although it explores an Englishness that takes into account multicultural identities as it acknowledges the presence of ethnic minorities, the integration of these people is established to be solely used as a means of mockery.

As already suggested, Chadha successfully highlights those elements of English culture that define 'Englishness', and shows how they are celebrated, but then she sets about stripping away the myth that they are necessarily positive. On the way to Blackpool, Chadha explores just how 'highly evolved' the English race is, the reaction of the White youths at the service station contests the very meaning of civilised. Sexism and racism are established at the core of the men's Englishness, which exhibit characteristics of imperialism. Simi becomes relegated to the position of a sexual object and faces abuse and violence for rejecting their advances. The arrogance and abuse of the man who is rejected spreads to the others, working as metaphor, which represents the parasitical nature of their White youth behaviour and their disintegrating morality. He becomes the unrestrained image of Englishness, where his arrogance and cruelty at its prime has, as Chadha suggests, no social and legal framework to control them. This notion is highlighted also by the film's opening when the supermarket is fortified with heavy metal grilles suggesting violence and attacks. Chadha emphasises the cruelty and arrogance of the men to connote the assumed authority imperialists have over non-White races. However, Chadha's film fails to allow the men to take control: instead, it is the women who gain control, subverting imperialistic notions of Englishness.

Chadha also highlights the tensions between African Caribbean and South Asian communities. This is explored with her use of a sub-plot involving a cross-cultural love story between an African-Caribbean man and a South Asian woman to explore the prejudices that exist within the South Asian community against Blacks. Even with similar histories, the prejudices between the two communities manifest themselves aggressively when sexual relationships come into play. Hashida's involvement with Oliver is seen as the ultimate taboo by the South Asian community and elicits reactionary responses by the women. Hashida is depicted as more of a rebel, the potential good doctor and 'beti' and 'Little miss perfect' (p. 29) becomes a 'jaktee, junglee! jamardani!' (Chadha, 1992, p. 46) as the women discover her pregnancy. But Hashida's non-conformity is presented primarily in terms of sexual transgression and becomes the focus for a wide-ranging critique of her culture's racism and sexism. Her Indian identity comes to be questioned as her Englishness is attacked; the ultimate response is expulsion from the Indian community.

Representing Hybridity

Different expressions of hybridity and ethnic identity are abundant in Chadha's film, especially concerning dress, food and music. What becomes central to the film is the discussion of a dual identity. Although they live in Britain, Chadha shows that her characters are not concerned with fitting into one identity or another, it does not mean being Western or being South Asian, but being both. The music incorporated in the film provides an ideal expression of this, for instance, she uses bhangra music as a backdrop to explore questions of identity and belonging amongst a group of British-born Asians in the mid-1990s (Bennett, 2000). The use of Punjabi and English music expresses features specific to the British experience of these South Asian women.

The film frequently bursts into bhangra music, mainly that by the British South Asian bhangra group *Ajuba*. Furthermore, the insertion of Punjabi lyrics into Cliff Richard's *Summer Holiday* transforms something essentially English into something new. Although translations of lyrics are routine, the context of the translation in this film has a quite different effect. Even the women themselves replicate this sense of hybridised identities, showing comfort in several different cultures, as they slip from one language to another within the same sentence without noticing and dip their onion bhajis in tomato ketchup and sprinkle chilli powder on fish and chips (Bhattacharyya and Gabriel, 1994). Simi, the coach driver, appears the most balanced of all, comfortable with both her British and Indian cultures. Her visual image projects her comfort as her shalwaar/kameez work as a backdrop for her bomber jacket. She is always trying to combine the two polarities in terms of dress and language, speaking Punjabi and English and comfortable with both the younger and older generations. Here, Chadha captures a sense of English identity and Indian ethnicity in one person; there is no identity crisis, she is not torn between two cultures. She has wholeness, a sense of belonging to both worlds rather than being comfortable in neither.

The older generation of the South Asian community display an understandable tendency to return to the security of the traditional way of life and consistently romanticise a past age in which they were morally stable and self-confident. They consistently talk about the effects of British life and reaffirm the basic values of their Indian origins, as the values and ideals by which they have been taught to live no longer carry their traditional authority. 'This country has cost us our children', laments Pushpa. According to these women, this England presents an image of people living in an age of dissolving moral community. However, the film contradicts this in other ways. For example, the woman visiting from India, Rekha, shows the most obvious signs of Westernisation through her clothes, mannerisms and the reaction she provokes in others, especially the older generation.

Characterisation

In choosing to explore her feelings about England, Chadha addresses mythical notions of Englishness through the character of the English gentleman, Ambrose. He represents the old Englishness – he is the perfect gentleman, hospitable and chivalrous. But despite this, the world of *Bhaji on the Beach* is the present, an England of social disharmony and religious decline. Its disintegration is confirmed by the fact that those characters that stand for civilised values such as Ambrose are marginalised. Ambrose undertakes to show the women around Blackpool because he is an outsider, with no role in society he becomes a one-dimensional caricature of Englishness.

Even Chadha's representation of the South Asian women is one dimensional, Ginder and Hashida become mere symbols rather than characters – the woman suffering abuse at the hands of her husband and the pregnant teenager. Both women fall into the stereotype of the South Asian woman who defies their families by either breaking their marriage vows or having secret relationships with unsuitable suitors and subsequently becoming pregnant out of wedlock. There are the traditional roles associated with South Asians represented in the film; the shop keepers, Asha the newsagent, and Pushpa who runs the supermarket, roles that connote the business-orientated South Asian. Many wear traditional dress such as saris or shalwaar kameez. The third generation are represented through the adolescents Madhu and Ladhu – overtly western through dress and behaviour, as their main objective is teenage romance. They become visually integrated into British White culture. The second and third generation women, Hashida, Ginder, Simi and the two teenagers are presented as finding it easier to manoeuvre between British culture and the minority culture.

In exploring Asha's discontentment with life through the medium of day dreaming, which Asha frequently slips into, Chadha also highlights the difficulty in distinguishing between art and life in South Asian society. Reality and fiction no longer imitate each other but appear to have merged. Rekha Tandon, the visitor from Bombay, emerges as an important figure as her money pays for repairs to the women's centre roof. Given that her name exhibits the glamour of the Bollywood industry as it is recognisable as a combined version of the real Indian actresses Raveena Tandon and Rekha, one cannot help wondering whether this is used as a deliberate tool by Chadha to target her South Asian audience. Although the film is intended as an English film, there is a layer of private meaning and jokes for South Asians. For instance, Asha is played by Lalita Ahmed who is best known for her appearance in the *Tilda Basmati Rice* commercials. To South Asians she has become 'Miss Tilda'. At one point in the film, Chadha shows her reading a magazine with an advertisement for Tilda rice prominently on the back cover, this being one of the many little asides planted for the South Asian community.

In using references to Indian cinema, Chadha explores differences in perceptions of Indian identity. The images of women that Asha recalls in her daydreams are those of the older Bollywood films, where the ideal woman not only represented beauty and chastity, but was also obedient and pious. Rekha represents the new liberated woman, where the body is now an essential expression of self-identity, in the form of short skirts and low-cleavage blouses. She becomes the personification of the glamour sought by many South Asians who watch Bollywood films, and she is the personification of the kind of escapism that Asha seeks. Rekha's visual image is as equally Western as her attitude. She displays more western characteristics than her British South Asian counterparts. Ironically, the women who have lived in Britain for most of their lives are more concerned about preserving the traditional Indian culture and perpetuating their images of India, which are rendolent of the country in the 1950s. Rekha, who represents contemporary India, is equally eager to distance herself from such images. Hence, ultimately Rekha appears more English than the rest of them.

Bend it like Beckham

Bend it like Beckham was the surprise hit in British cinemas in the spring of 2002 having reached number one in its first weekend of distribution taking over £2 million at the box office (Bagguley and Hussain, 2003). The film itself is in the same mould as director Gurinder Chadha's earlier ventures *Bhaji on the Beach* and *What's Cooking?* The protagonists in all three films are characters divided between the traditionalism of the ethnic culture largely in the form of the previous generation and the 'modernisations' of the present generation.

Chadha focuses on football as a culture and the significance of ideology and consciousness within it. She does this by exploring the relationship that football has with cultural formations of gender and race, by examining questions of agency and social constraints. More specifically, the film is a story of two young women, Jules (Keira Knightley) and Jessminder Bhamra (Parminder Nagra), confronting family resistance to them playing football. Their love of football is what connects them, and they are shown to bond very quickly, so swiftly it never seems real; Jess's scenes with her friend Tony (Ameet Chana) seem much more authentic than the bonding she has with Jules. The issue that tests their friendship is a man in the shape of their coach Joe (Jonathan Rhys Myers), to whom Jules and Jess both are attracted. He captures the hearts of both girls, so that the relationship between the two young women, both on and off the field, comes under strain at the most crucial time. Mixed into this is Jess's tenuous relationship with her family, as they prepare for the wedding of their other daughter Pinky (Archie Panjabi) – another plot device to put into jeopardy Jess's dream of playing professional soccer.

Director Gurinder Chadha explores the articulation of racial, ethnic, religious and gendered identities through these two principal characters and the problems that they overcome. The use of White and Sikh families underlines the contrasting relationships the two girls have with their parents as they embark on playing football. However, for the Sikh girl, the ramifications of this extend beyond the family and into the sphere of the wider South Asian community. The film explores how ethnicity acts as a prism through which gendered identities are lived, contested and re-made. Chadha, in interviews about the film, has emphasised the double-coding of the title – bending the ball is analogous to bending the rules of one's culture to achieve your aims. She explores the development of both girls within the realm of football, an essentially masculine sport, and the ramifications this has within their respective communities. Consequently, the film works on two different levels. On one level it is about football and the other is the problems an Indian girl has at home with her family.

Family

The dynamics within the family as well as their contact with each other are used within the film as an important interplay of differences. Both families are presented functioning within their own ethnic frameworks, but are exaggerated and stereotyped, so that the Indian family is excessively Indian and the English family excessively English. The Indian ethnicity within the family framework is shown through the maintenance of traditional values, the wearing of traditional dress, and the consumption of popular culture in Punjabi, whilst the Englishness is expressed though the portrayal of a white middle class family. They have afternoon tea in the garden and Jules' mother adopts a hat more suitable for an English wedding to wear to a football match. Within the Bhamra household, cooking, dress, and attitudes all indicate an environment that is expressive of their ethnicity.

However, there are differences in the representation of the two families. The Paxtons are presented comically, yet in contrast the Indian family is presented in more serious terms. The only real concerns for Jules' family are their questions about their daughter's sexuality, but this is handled in the film in a flippant manner. Because the audience knows 'the truth' of her sexuality – it provides a comical element to the film. The White family becomes a parody of a television sitcom stereotype. But within the Indian family the concerns are seen to be more serious, an engagement is broken off as Jess supposedly kisses a boy in the street. This indicates that marriages are not only unions between two people, but also between families conscious of their 'standing' or 'honour' within their community.

The adults in the film, in particular the mothers – Juliet Stevenson who plays Jules' mother and Shaheen Khan who plays Jess's mother – are caricatured as dithery and hysterical, in some instances too absurd to be taken seriously. It sometimes appears as though there is a clear separation of the sequences between the insane mothers of the girls, who boss around their husbands and the girls themselves who appear more adult than their mothers. The women panic about what others think and the loss of their reputation – Jules' mother cringes when she sees two girls hugging on the pitch and Jess's mother, who is concerned about appearances, tells her daughter to cover the burn on her leg. It is the fathers who are 'normal', they are the ones who act rationally, they calm their wives and negotiate between their wives and daughters. There are touching father–daughter moments between the characters in both the South Asian and the English families.

Both girls come from two completely different families, ethnically and religiously, yet the similarities between the two young women are so striking that Chadha wants to draw on similarities as opposed to differences. Even the names start with J! Both Jess and Jules live in semi-detached middle class suburbia and not in inner city areas. Chadha's decision to present her Indian family within suburbia challenges the stereotype of the South Asian from the inner city. *Bend it like Beckham* works on the basis that suburban people can 'identify' with the movie. However, in doing so it also attempts to show middle class consumers themselves refusing to engage seriously with issues such as racism or sexism. Instead they tend to fit themselves into a multicultural mosaic (McNeil, 2003). The film deals with a variety of issues, including gender, sexuality, cultural identity and Britishness, but it does not develop any of these tensions in sufficient detail due to the proliferation of sub-plots. The film touches on issues of homosexuality as Tony reveals his homosexuality to Jess, an issue with which Chadha refuses to engage. Even the religious hostilities existing within the South Asian categories are aired but not developed. As William Brown comments, *Bend it like Beckham* 'does not make a big deal of any of the possible tensions in the film – be it racial, gender, generational, sexual ... It gets on with telling the story' (http://www.honestdog.com/may2002/films3.shtml). But in failing to develop such issues, *Bend it like Beckham* represents middle class disengagement for some, leaving working class ethnic minority communities to 'fend for themselves' (McNeil, 2003).

In Chadha's world, we find the new lower middle class in England comprising well-educated minorities which the Bhamras represent, they live in suburbia, and drive an (old) Mercedes – a symbol of wealth and status in South Asian communities. Chadha shows a new society through the family which can reap economic rewards. Non-white 'achievers' can even afford to buy a Mercedes and shop at trendy outlets such as *Daminis*. Consequently, for the film to be accepted as a truly national film, it had to assume that 'suburban south-east England = Britain, and that middle class suburbia = the West' (McNeil, 2003). The cultural landscapes of the working class communities of Northern England may also provide the opportunity to learn about cultural and ideological diversity, as seen in films such as *East is East*, but this is not the case with *Bend it like Beckham*.

In promoting *Bend it like Beckham*, according to Chadha 'the film celebrates the processes of cultural change, the experience of living in a diverse environment from one generation to another and not only the difficulties involved but also the pleasures in becoming more integrated' (Nayman, 2003). The integration displayed in the film fails to be applied to the white family next door to the Bhamras, who continue to live in blissful ignorance of the party going on next door. There is no contact, where interracial alliances are shown. Furthermore, Jules' mother emulates racial ignorance when she talks to Jessminder (refusing to call her by her anglicised Jess) referring to her as Jules' 'Indian friend' saying that her parents will be setting her up 'with a nice Indian boy' and claiming she 'made a lovely curry the other day'.

The difference between the girls lies in the boundaries they have to negotiate – Jules does not really have to negotiate any boundaries. However, Jess has to navigate the boundary between her home life and the outside world. She has to negotiate a careful path between the traditional views of her family and those of the younger women in her football team. Her covert joining a women's football club is not seriously damaging, yet the family must not learn of her misdemeanour, and Jess goes to considerable lengths to prevent her secret from being discovered, hiding her kit in the bushes and lying about a job. In this respect she works effectively as a cultural navigator. According to Ballard, 'if parents are not prepared not to ask too searching questions and their offspring are prepared to do their code switching well out of sight of their elders, some wide contradictions can be bridged with surprising ease' (Hall, 1994, p. 33). Jess's team does well and, not surprisingly, Jess is the star. Her tribulations with her family continue against the backdrop of her sister's proposed marriage and the eventual climax of the tournament and wedding. Pinky's relationship with Teetu is performed effectively without confrontation, although her mother reveals her knowledge of the relationship. In contrast Jess's secret is out and although she battles her way to playing football, Jess eventually toes the parental line and give up playing in the cup final to attend her sister's wedding. The day is saved when her father permits her to go and play. Jess has to negotiate a careful path between the traditional views of her parents, the repercussions of her actions on her older sister and her own interests.

Religion is an added dimension for the Indian family as they place the portrait of the Sikh God respectfully over fire place, a focal point of the living room and also of their lives. The film often shifts to the image of the guru which stands above the fireplace, as the family, especially Jess's mother, look up to the image and engage in a dialogue with it. Mirroring this image, within Jess's bedroom a poster of David Beckham occupies a central position in her room, with whom she also converses and confides in privately. David Beckham is established as Jess's God. In contrast, Jules' English family seems devoid of religion.

Cultural Hybridity

Chadha's work also explores the formation of a diasporic space – in essence a hybrid space in which her characters learn to be both British and Indian. What becomes central to the film is its discussion of the dual identity of second-generation South Asians living in Britain. Chadha shows that her characters are not concerned with fitting into one identity or the other. It does not mean being Western or being South Asian, but being both. The presentation of Southall in all its 'traditional' South Asian glory is a perfect illustration of the way that Chadha has explored how Britain absorbs and adapts external influences. Southall is represented as a 'little India' with roadside food stalls, and traditionally dressed South Asian women out shopping. However, the film focuses most of all on hybridity and its role within the life of Jess. The film follows Jess who negotiates between her ethnic minority familial background and her ambitions and desires fuelled by Western popular culture, in particular the fascination with David Beckham.

What the film does is establish Jess as a cultural navigator, it shows the movement of Jess from her minority group and into the majority culture and vice versa. She is able to make the shift from one environment into another, from that of the home into the football team or with the boys in the park. The film deals with two forms of negotiation that take place. Firstly, Jess changes her external characteristics to fit into the surrounding culture. This involves modifiable characteristics that can be changed, including linguistic and cultural features. Within the home she conforms to the roles required, adopts traditional dress at particular functions, speaks Punjabi and functions within the home environment in a culturally acceptable way. Yet outside of that environment, she seeks to become indistinguishable from members of the majority culture. Jess wears English clothes, speaks English and becomes Jess instead of Jessminder – to compensate for the inability of non-Indians to accurately pronounce her name.

Secondly, un-modifiable dimensions such as race and sex are represented. Both of which becomes focal points for others. Jess's gender is an area of tension for her family and her race becomes focused upon on the pitch where she gets called a 'Paki'. Although she has no problems in shifting between one domain and into another, other people do have problems with her attempts to navigate across boundaries. Everyone else points out the level of difference, yet it is the player on the football pitch who defines her as a 'Paki' not just as a label, but with all the weight of racist negativity that is associated with it. Even when she visits Jules' home, her mother defines Jess according to her ethnicity and states 'I hope you can teach my daughter a bit about your culture, including respecting your elders and the like' and assumes 'I expect your parents will be fixing you up with a nice handsome doctor soon'.

Although the film can be seen as 'English', there is a layer of 'private meaning' for South Asian audiences. The dialogues in Punjabi are not translated with subtitles, they remain as features that could only be appreciated by those sections of the audience from the South Asian community. Similarly, there are actors, often in minor supporting roles, who would only be known to South Asian audiences. For instance, Bollywood's Anupam Kher who plays Pinky's and Jess's father, as well as the bhangra group B21. Yet others would be known to British audiences more widely such as Kulwinder Ghir and Nina Wadia of *Goodness Gracious Me*. This invites the South Asian audience to engage in the game of 'star spotting', which is seen initially in the wedding scene, and reaches its most explicit and self-referential at the close of the movie with David and Victoria Beckham seen walking through the airport when everyone White and South Asian can join in the game. These and other aspects of the film can only be understood by particular sections of the audience depending on their cultural background.

The soundtrack to *Bend it like Beckham* closely reflects the film's narrative content and themes by combining British pop acts such as Melanie C and Victoria Beckham, with fusion bhangra tracks by artists such as Bally Sagoo, Malkit Singh, *Partners in Rhyme*, and ghazals by Nusrat Fateh Khan. In the scenes with football, Chadha uses English music such as Victoria Beckham, Mel C, etc, underlining football's 'Englishness' and the space of the football pitch as an English location. But for the scenes involving the family and the wider Indian community, the director inserts South Asian music – specifically as a backdrop to explore questions of identity and belonging amongst a group of British born Asians in the mid-1990s. This stylistically underlines their hybridity and difference. Here the music is again tightly linked to the social context, where the use of Punjabi lyrics and western rhythms represent hybridisation. The growth of this music at social occasions such as weddings has been integrated to the development of British Asian music. It is the South Asian community itself that has encouraged bhangra groups to perform at weddings. Significantly, in the wedding scene the film uses old bhangra, whilst when the crowd are performing the conga the language used in bhangra is cultural, singing in Punjabi – reaffirming the language and the ethnicity of the family. Contemporary British bhangra largely stems from a specifically British South Asian experience. Is not a case of these artists returning to their roots but actually asserting the Britishness of diasporic Asian music (Sharma, 2004). Bhangra is seen as expressive of the local cultures from within which it develops, and its influences are taken from within the subculture of Britain. The music shows neither integration within Western society nor a disassociation from traditional themes, but represents the blending of both cultures, the construction of new collective ethnic identities of second generation South Asians through a process of hybridisation.

Gender and Football

The film explores and critiques conventional ideas about sport, and about the nature of masculine and feminine identities. Discussions of gender are utilised within the film as an organising principle, images of masculinity and femininity are presented through the ways in which the characters perpetuate dominant gender ideologies. For example, the film examines the ways in which conventional gender identities are reproduced through Pinky (Jess's sister) and Jules' mother. Both look outwardly feminine, and the film shows how these gendered conventions are contested through Jess and Jules.

Chadha shows the development of both girls within the realm of football, an essentially masculine sport, and the ramifications this has for how they are seen within their respective communities. She breaks down the barrier between masculinity and femininity so that women invade an area associated with men. It is inevitable that the two women will have problems as they contest socially constraining gender identities that close relatives seek to impose upon them. The shifting nature of gender relations is ignored by privileging a view of gender relations as fixed and determined by tradition.

Jess's intervention in football is a political act, and more disruptive than Jules', as it brings women's role in sports within the South Asian community onto the agenda. The issue of women's marginalisation within the realm of football is discussed through the problems the women face taking their football careers further. They both have to leave for America. In numerous scenes we are shown a plane flying over the houses – is this symbol of freedom? Or does the aeroplane flying over become a symbol of the necessity of migration?

The film shows the importance of using gender as a fundamental category for analysis and to explore some of its complexities with regard to identity, family and society. The discussion of gender and football takes place on two levels. Firstly, the playing of football in the park 'with the boys', outside of the formal arena of the Hounslow women's team, the league and the 'real' football pitch. In the informal arena there is a recognition that the problem of male power is fundamental, the boys in the park laugh at Jess's attempts to play football, and even on the pitch the women are still controlled by men via the male coach. However, having a male coach is a protective mechanism that allows women to play football professionally. Whilst the film shows that football does not produce a straightforward system of domination of men over women in the way it uses Jess as a female character playing good football and being more skilful than the men, it contradicts this by placing her within a formal environment where she continues to be controlled by men. The film does seek to represent the changes that have occurred with the acceptance of female footballers and the integration of women within the professional game. The integration of Jess in particular also relates to changes in the patterns of consumption and leisure within British South Asian culture.

By exploring the relations between the sexes, it brings to prominence the values and norms that are given to the body within both the minority and majority cultural contexts. In order for the girls to be successful at playing football they have to become masculine to an extent. Historically, women within sports have been defined as unfeminine (Hargreaves, 1994). Within the context of the film this is also the case. Their attitudes to things feminine, like boys, clothes, make up, etc – essentially female symbols – are balanced by them wearing tracksuit bottoms and disregarding their femininity, thus boosting their masculinity. Both sets of parents cannot accept their daughters' tomboy personas.

For Jules' and Jess's families, their daughters' love of football is incomprehensible. They find it difficult to transcend traditional assumptions about masculine sports and the natural order of things. They find their daughters' behaviour inappropriate for their gender. It is the tension and conflict between generations with opposing interests, which is maximized, to the point where Jules' mother defines her as being sexually deviant – a lesbian. Both sets of families fail to comprehend the significance playing football has for the girls and this creates friction within both households as they both 'act like boys' – this is at the core of their families' disillusionment with them. In the film we see scenes where their families are encouraging them towards more acceptable versions of femininity, but these sometimes have different meanings within the two different cultural contexts. For both girls, femininity is equated with physical appearances. For Jules, the white girl, her mother – disillusioned with her flat-chested daughter and her interest in wearing jogging pants – encourages her towards wearing a wonder bra to emphasise her chest and 'pretty' dresses – archetypes of White heterosexual English femininity. The concept of femininity within the English family is explored through her mother's 'gentle' persuasion of her daughter to wear feminine clothes and behave in a more feminine way than kicking around a football. For Jess, the tomboy in the Punjabi family, it is again the mother who wants her daughter to be more outwardly feminine, as she similarly despairs in her daughter's desire to kick around a football. In one scene Jess's mother wants to emphasise her daughter's chest, to transform the 'mosquito bites' into 'juicy mangoes', so instructs the seamstress to tighten the area around the chest. Becoming overtly fuller in the chest has the underlying objective of becoming more feminine in order to express their authentic femininity, thus finding a prospective partner. As Jules mother states 'there is a reason why Sporty Spice is without a fella!'

Whilst there are overlaps across ethnicity, the image of femininity is also contained within an ethnic framework. Here, the image of femininity is related to appearance, but is even more significantly related to domesticity. Being feminine for Jess means to be able to cook 'aloo ghobee' (cauliflower and potatoes). Here, the image of femininity is embedded within cultural norms and values. Making the perfect chapattis and being able to cook are symbols of femininity. Jess's parents want her to be a nice Indian girl, to study law, learn to cook and find a suitable boy to marry. But Jess has different ideas. Growing up in the shadow of Heathrow, she wants to be a footballer and dreams of playing football like her hero David Beckham. The film shows how culture and ethnicity are entwined with gender. It shows Jess's relative lack of power and control within her cultural context, but also illustrates similar struggles within the surrounding White English context.

One of the main themes within the film is conformity. The film explicitly shows how one has to conform to the predisposed ideas contained within society and conform to society's regulations. Within the ethnic environment of the home we are presented with numerous examples of conformity to both gender and ethnic expectations. To some extent, sport symbolizes freedom and liberation for Jess – it allows her to do what she wants. But even in the context of football we learn of the conformity required within it. It is significant that within the sporting environment there is pressure for Jess to integrate with others through dress, she is forced to wear shorts even though she expresses her discomfort in showing her scarred leg. She has to conform in order to be able to play, and thus ends up wearing clothes similar to the other women. This becomes a mechanism of control, a uniform. It is also within this environment that the other girls attempt to feminize Jess into their own cultural framework. She is dressed up by them in what they regard as fashionable and attractive clothes, so that she can integrate within their social sphere without any problems. They re-style her hair so she looks like the others, so that she now fits in. It is also within this environment of the women's football team that they question ideas contained within her South Asian culture. The dialogue in the changing room is significant in this context, as Jess changes herself out of one image and adopts another and walks onto the pitch. On finishing the game, she changes back into the image which is acceptable for her family – those who are significant for her.

These ethnically specific regimes of gender identity are also explored through Jess's relationships with the other female footballers. For instance, Jess's sister is having a love marriage as opposed to an arranged marriage. To her this is a major issue for her family, but to the White and African-Caribbean English girls in the dressing room its significance is puzzling. The other girls cannot understand how

South Asian girls juggle both parental expectations against their own desire to choose what they want. These differences from the other girls are not always highlighted in this way. For the most part, Jules is focus of the narrative, so that she becomes the embodiment of the other non-Sikh girls. This implies that her experiences are deemed to be similar to the others, so that she becomes the principal contrast to Jess. Jules becomes the embodiment of the social backgrounds that are representative of the others in the team.

Significantly, there are two sisters but no son in the South Asian family. Pinky is overtly feminine, wearing clothes that are elegant and sophisticated – she is representative of one particular mode of British South Asian femininity, interested in shopping, clothes and men. Similarly, Jess's 'tarty' cousins are clad in short skirts and low cleavage tops, sit in the park eyeing up the boys playing football and out to pull the men at Pinky's wedding. Jess in contrast resorts to wearing tracksuits, is concerned about kicking around a football and shows no interest in clothes or men.

By placing women at the centre of analysis, the men in contrast are relatively superficial characters who are not developed. By placing women at the centre of the analysis of sports and women debate, it provides an important challenge to the way in which male standards have become generalised.

Football and Ethnicity

It becomes clear that the physical body is a fundamental symbol of power relations not only between men and women but also in relationship to 'race'. Jess has to struggle against popular definitions of her role in order to participate in playing football. She exemplifies the link between other social factors, such as race, as she plays football. Jess actively shuns old restrictions and participates in football, and in this she faces harsh opposition, which results in limited opportunities, her participation in football is never without resistance.

The film raises an important issue regarding the integration of South Asians within the realm of football. The successes of Black professional players within football provided role models for Black youngsters, however, South Asians are not represented in the sport at elite levels. Traditional explanations for this focused on cultural tendencies, such as strong work and education ethics, making it less easy for talented South Asian youngsters to persuade their parents that sport is a viable career option. Irrespective of this, football promotes an identity originating from a private culture that may not be universally shared across the multicultural society. It excludes those from South Asian origin. When the first Black players began to enter first team football, and prove that they could perform, this was the catalyst for others to follow their example. For South Asian hopefuls there is a complete lack of any role models to emulate and aspire to follow. Consequently, South Asian youths have no alternative but to look up to players such as 'Mark Hughes, Romario and Ryan Giggs' as their role models, but surely the presence of an Asian player in the Premier League would achieve a huge following no matter what team he played for

(McGuire and Collins, 1998, p. 82). Jess having no South Asian role models adopts Beckham – a White male – as her role model.

Sport is a means for ethnic minorities to earn respect and acceptance in British society. The existence of sporting role models can contribute to the assertion of ethnic identity. However, the film also illustrates how sport can be a focus for perpetuating ethnic differences and as a vehicle for wider racism. Jess is called a 'Paki' on the pitch, which reiterates the racist abuse her father received when playing cricket. This kind of racist abuse is quite normal within the realm of football. Since their early appearance in the 1960s, black football players have been treated with abuse in the form of racist chants and individual barracking.

Consequently, South Asians are well represented in football and cricket at a local, amateur league level. Jess plays football with young South Asian men in the park, but they play 'for fun' not professionally. This does not yet explain their absence from the professional scene, although the cultural factors mentioned, attitudes of coaches, and a lack of role models in sports such as football may be significant. As well as the extreme lack of South Asian players, there is also a visible lack of South Asian fans attending live matches. Black and South Asian fans make up just 1 per cent of crowds. Jess's father, clad in his turban, a symbol of this religious affiliation, sits in a crowd of predominately white spectators.

The South Asian community is often accused of not helping their plight, by continuing to play in South Asian teams and tournaments. This could be interpreted as reinforcing the view that they are an insular community that only plays football in their own company (Bains and Johal, 1998, p. 56). However, the example of racism directed at South Asian players gives a clear indication of why they continue to play within this safer environment.

Jess's father experienced racism and exclusion when he wanted to join a cricket team on arriving in Britain. The experience that his daughter faces on the pitch is indicative that the situation has not changed, as she too is a victim of racism. However, the theme of racism in the film is not developed to the same extent as the themes of the negotiation of gender identities constructed in ethnically different contexts. This ethnic solidarity of father and daughter is explored at various points, by the father 'secretly' going to watch his daughter play in a key match and, on appreciating her sporting talent, he encourages her against the wishes of his wife. By the end of the film this is reinforced when we see him playing cricket with new found White and South Asian friends, with the plane flying over in the back ground as the ever present dualistic symbol of freedom and forced migration. Jess's desire and need to leave for America, echoes the South Asian communities' economically driven migrations to Britain. Only in America, where women's soccer is really appreciated, can she pursue her sporting dreams and combine this with the university education that her parents desire for her, on a sports scholarship in California.

Within both ethnic frameworks, different kinds of negotiation take place between the two girls and their parents. For Jules, her negotiations involve her dismissing her mother's feminising tactics, but for Jess the negotiations are more intense, more intricate and more complex, as she has constantly to negotiate between what she desires and what her parents will allow. Not telling her parents about joining the women's football team is done so as to protect her parents – hiding her sports clothes in the front garden is complicated, but Jess does so as a protective mechanism.

Despite this, *Bend it like Beckham* ignores the material circumstances that provide compelling reasons for overachievement in these sports. These circumstances include the availability of both role models and opportunities in such sports, and hence motivation: 'The majority of young blacks will structure their ambitions around the icons they see before them, all but deified by television culture' (Cashmore, 1982, p. 112). It must also be remembered that such sports offer substantial financial reward to a proportion of the population who often have limited social and economic opportunities.

Whilst there is an underlying solidarity between Jess and Jules based on gender and the struggle to play football, their own individual paths to realise their aims are strewn with ethnically specific obstacles. Ultimately, the film is not about football, but is about bending rules, bending cultures and transforming identities.

Conclusion

This chapter has discussed the principal themes and issues in Gurinder Chadha's two British films, *Bhaji on the Beach* and *Bend it like Beckham*. Both pieces of work are central to the desification of popular British cinema; in many respects their plots, themes, characters and style are emblematic of cultural hybridisation. Whilst they might be compared in various ways with *East is East* and *Anita and Me*, together they constitute a distinct and unique, but still problematic, body of work within British cinema. Central to both films is the theme of negotiating identities between the minority ethnic culture and the majority White culture. Both films feature as central protagonists young second-generation South Asian women who have to make critical life decisions that involve navigating between South Asian and Western cultures. Whilst they struggle with the apparent constraints of South Asian culture, they try to embrace the more individualised opportunities seemingly offered by Western culture. In the process they are confronted by the enduring racism of some sections of the dominant White British population. This involves conflict between the generations within South Asian families and communities, but this is not presented dysfunctionally, but as normal problems that can be, and are, resolved. Both films are 'coming of age' narratives, whereby the plots are resolved by the younger and older generations coming to understand each other and reconcile their differences. In this sense, the films follow the conventions of popular cinema's narrative structure. The 'coming of age' of the protagonists in some senses represents the 'coming of age' of the South Asian diaspora in Britain.

Common to both films is the concern with the dilemmas of being a South Asian woman in contemporary Britain. However, there are also stylistic features and techniques that mark them out as distinctive, especially the use of music and language. Chadha uses music transculturally to underline and emphasise ethnic difference. She draws upon both mainstream western 'pop', as well as bhangra and other South Asian genres. Western pop is used to underline the English activities and spaces, such as the football scenes in *Bend it like Beckham*, whilst bhangra and other forms of South Asian music are used to bracket the scenes focusing upon distinctly South Asian events and activities such as the wedding scenes in *Bend it like Beckham*. In yet other scenes we have western songs performed with Punjabi lyrics, as in the Punjabi rendition of Cliff Richard's 'Summer Holiday' in *Bhaji on the Beach* and Jennifer Rush/Celine Dion's 'The Power of Love' in *Bend it like Beckham*. The use of music and lyrics that are only recognisable to a South Asian audience is also reflected in Chadha's use of language. In several scenes in both films the dialogue is performed in Punjabi, without subtitles in English. In these ways the films are strictly aimed at British South Asian audiences.

The production and the success of these films, especially *Bend it like Beckham*, highlight the growth of the South Asian audience in Britain and its interest in specifically British South Asian cinema, yet the films also appeal in certain ways to White audiences. Between *Bhaji on the Beach* and *Bend it like Beckham* there has been a development in the quality of the films, especially in terms of production values. However, there are certain common technical and aesthetic weaknesses that they share. The quality of the acting in both films, but especially *Bhaji on the Beach,* is often questionable, and certain actors appear in both as well as other widely known British South Asian films and TV. This suggests that this cultural sector is rather underdeveloped. Although Chadha's central female characters are often well developed, and clearly located within their families and communities, at times there seems to be too many characters. Furthermore, within the films there seem to be too many sub-plots. For the viewer it feels there is too much happening with respect characters, motivations and actions within the single cinematic space, and this tends to undermine the verisimilitude of the films.

However, Chadha's cinema remains strikingly distinctive and popular. Thematically her work shares many of the characteristics of the literary culture considered in other chapters, as she locates her characters within the social space of the South Asian diaspora in Britain. It is a women's cinema that springs from and speaks to that diaspora.

Chapter 6

Brick Lane: Gender and Migration

Introduction

This chapter explores the themes of gender and migration in relation to Monica Ali's *Brick Lane* (2003). The novel shows Britain's Bangladeshi community through the eyes of 18 year old Nazneen who comes to live in London's East End from Bangladesh, after her marriage to 40 year old Chanu – also a recent immigrant from her country. Subsequently she has two daughters, Shahana and Bibi, and a son Raqib who dies in infancy. Monica Ali takes the experience of a relatively new immigrant community, so that her characters in the early sections of the novel live in a world sealed off from the 'host' society. Ali uses her characters to explore the positioning of Bangladeshi women within Britain, as the novel focuses on their social relations inside and outside the home.

The distinctiveness of the Bangladeshi community as compared with the other South Asian groups has been acknowledged (Ballard, 1994; Eade et al., 1996). Whilst the growth of the Bangladeshi community has been reviewed from a historical perspective in studies such as those by Adams (1987) and Choudhury (1993), differences of gender have been given less attention (Gardner and Shukur, 1994; Gardner, 2002; Phillipson et al., 2003). Kabeer's (2000) research on Bangladeshi women in Tower Hamlets records the pressure on first generation women to adjust to the different life in England. The women moving to London and Tower Hamlets in particular had to adapt from coming from a 'rural peasant society to a hostile urban culture' (Kabeer, 2000, p. 282). What *Brick Lane* does is show this transition and the impact migration has women's lives. Monica Ali's text shows how, after migration, the position of women in families and in the wider community undergoes considerable transformation (Vertovec, 2000, p. 15). What the women in the text refuse to do is to see themselves and their cultures as inferior or alien. Here ethnicity becomes a source of positive rather than stigmatised identity (Barot et al., 1999).

The women within Ali's text are shown to be a product of ideologies, social practices and social structures where race and class are key determinants. They are shown to play a distinctive role within transnational communities as the author highlights their role in strengthening kinship ties (Khanum, 1994). Ali focuses on the way they are disadvantaged in terms of limited career opportunities, greater domestic responsibilities and less freedom to pursue leisure activities. As the author explores the dynamics involved in the social constructions of identity, she also sheds light on other disadvantages inherent within the women's lives. The high rates of poverty characteristic of Bangladeshi households (Berthoud, 2000) are shown in the novel, coupled with the overwhelming sense of isolation faced by the female characters and their reliance on their male counterparts. Consequently the overall context of the novel presents a picture of deprivation and hardships for Bangladeshis in Britain.

Monica Ali was born in Dhaka, Bangladesh in 1967, and grew up in England. She was named by *Granta* as one of the twenty best young British novelists and *Brick Lane,* her first novel, was selected for the 2003 Man Booker Prize long list. Monica Ali migrated to Britain from Bangladesh as a child, albeit as the daughter of a White English woman and a relatively privileged member of the Bangladeshi intelligentsia who had to leave Bangladesh for political reasons. This experience, and her social positioning outside of the core British Bangladeshi community originating from Sylhet, colours her representation of both Bangladesh and the British Bangladeshi community.

Brick Lane has sparked controversy from within the British Bangladeshi community of East London. When the novel was published it upset some in the Bangladeshi community who referred to it as an insult to the community. The Greater Sylhet Development and Welfare Council, representing many Bangladeshis in Britain, wrote to the book's publishers Random House arguing that the book was 'shameful'. The Council complained the book treated Bangladeshis as 'economic migrants' and portrayed them as ignorant. For example, the character Chanu's comments about the Bangladeshis of Brick Lane as: 'uneducated; illiterate; closed-minded; without ambition' was cited as offensive.

This raises a critical question regarding the authenticity of the novel in comparison to the others texts and films considered in other chapters of this book. Authenticity is always a hotly contested concept in this context, as 'The discourse of authenticity has been a notable presence in ... mass marketing ... to White audiences' (Gilroy, 1993: 99). *Brick Lane* is no exception to this. In this sense its 'authenticity' as a text from within the Bangladeshi diaspora is a marketing myth. Whilst the novel shares many of the thematic concerns of the other texts, of migration, gender and generation for example, it provides an outsider's view of the Bangladeshi community and a rather negative one at that. The cultural expressions considered in other chapters have emerged from within the diaspora, although they have frequently been critical of it. Their authors have often been politically active, seeing their creative works as political acts. Although *Brick Lane* is critical of many features of the Bangladeshi community, its representation of that community seems seriously dated. To a South Asian reader in particular, the novel lacks that essential verisimilitude as a novel about a South Asian community that would authenticate it for a South Asian audience. It presents an image of Britain's Bangladeshi community which is a textbook definition and it is not a book which is written from 'within' the community it explores.

The novel is not the first about the Bangladeshi communities who live in *Brick Lane.* Syed Manzurul Islam wrote a collection of short stories in *The Mapmakers of Spitalfields* (1997) and Farrukh Dhondy, wrote *East End at Your Feet* (1976) and *Come to Mecca* (1978) – both aimed at young adults. Monica Ali's *Brick Lane* differs from the others in that not only is it written by a woman, but it is also the first novel to focus almost exclusively on the lives of Bangladeshi women in Tower Hamlets (Sandhu, 2003).

This chapter seeks to analyse some of the key themes of *Brick Lane*. Central to the novel is the emotional shock of migration and the contrasts between Bangladesh and Britain. This is initially explored by locating *Brick Lane* in the context of debates about the East-West encounter within fiction (King et al., 1995). The connection between Bangladesh and Britain is maintained through the transnational sisterhood between Nazneen and her rebellious sister Hasina. The representation of Bangladesh in the novel is then considered largely in terms of the migrant Nazneen's memories of it and her sister Hasina's negative experiences of continuing to live there, which we learn through the device of Ali presenting the reader with Hasina's letters to her sister. Thus the novel always presents Bangladesh at a distance, as either a distorted memory or through a letter in broken English, never as a direct representation in the way we read the Bangladeshi community in Britain. This leads on to an examination of how England and Nazneen's experiences of it are represented. England appears as a place of poverty and Nazneen is assailed by various images of tatty, dirty, broken people and urban landscapes, and noxious smells of rubbish and waste. However, the Bangladeshi community in Britain is presented by Ali in negative, atavistic terms. It is presented as dysfunctionally insular and traditional, riven by internal dissent and unable to organise itself even in the face of racist mobilisations. A further dimension of this internal dissent and the dysfunctionality of community atavism is explored through the gendered relationships between the generations, especially between Nazneen's daughters and her husband.

The East-West Encounter within Fiction

The theoretical frameworks that have been developed for analysing transnational movements of people consider the diversity and commonalties that link the concepts of diaspora, border and location (Brah, 1996). An extensive body of literature has been produced dealing with the social and cultural aspects of migration. Whilst the study of migration has formed an important aspect of the research agenda for social scientists, this fails to capture the emotional responses of immigrants and visitors to a new country (King et al., 1995). Social science provides statistical information and theoretical concepts of cross-cultural adaptation, but leaves a role for creative writing on migrant experiences to express, as only it uniquely can, what it is like to be a migrant.

The literary works that feature migration focus on nostalgia, exile and the restlessness generated by the migration process through giving a voice to the individual or individuals involved. There are two main categories of literary representation of the migrant experience: autobiographical works where authors themselves write personal accounts of migration, and general fiction which directly and indirectly reflects on migration. Those authors writing about migration have not necessarily directly experienced movement from one country to another, but they are in some way the product of past migrations, and hence the topic appears within their work. Expressions of ethnic and cultural identity feature heavily, particularly where their ethnic identity may have exposed them to discrimination, as is the case, for instance, within novels such as Leena Dhingra's *Amritvela* (1988), Ravinder Randhawa's *A Wicked Old Woman*, (1987) and Meena Syal's *Anita and Me* (1996), as well as texts like Amrit Wilson's *Finding a Voice* (1978) and autobiographies such as Sharan Jeet Shan's *In my Own Name* (1987). Writings dealing with migration are also to be found in abundance within the texts produced during and after the Black feminist movement, in particular the anthologies edited by Cobham and Collins, *Watchers and Seekers* (1987); Bryan et al., *The Heart of the Race: Black Women's Lives in Britain* (1985) and Grewal et al., *Charting the Journey: Writings by Black and Third World Women* (1987).

With the emergence of diasporic creative literatures a change has occurred in how the issue of migration is depicted. Whilst the authors make use of more sophisticated narratives, they do not ignore the wider histories and geography of migration and diaspora (King et al., 1996). Although migration and East-West encounter themes are prevalent within British South Asian literature, the concept has changed according to the generation of migrants, with a divergence in responses between the earlier and subsequent generations. The earlier work dealt with issues of racism and colonialism, and then began to reveal how the migrants reacted to their marginalisation according to generation, gender, race and class (Bald, 1995). In contrast, the response of the migrants and their children was constituted by the discourse of racism and colonialism and later by their location of themselves within the framework of diaspora, where issues such as gender, class, race and sexuality become defining features of experience. Ali's *Brick Lane* is but one more recent example of this phenomenon.

Whilst the diverse realities of migrant's lives have been represented in the works of British writers of South Asian descent, in the last two decades fiction authored by women has expanded our knowledge of the migration experience from a gendered perspective. These texts reveal both the role of gender as a variable in the experiences of women, whether as migrants or visitors, and how the discourse of racism also permeates their lives. The stories and novels explore the intersections of race, gender, class, ethnicity and generation in different discourses, practices and political contexts. These relationships are rarely addressed together but when they do so, these texts provide an insight into the immigrant experience as individual circumstances serve to illuminate wider issues of migration. Monica Ali's novel is no exception, and at certain junctures it seems to be preoccupied with petty class and status snobberies within the Bangladeshi diaspora in Britain.

Undoubtedly, *Brick Lane* works well as a migrant text. It explores immigration, the shock of arrival and the subsequent problems involved in the transition from one country to another. The emotional impact of migration is further discussed through the excitement, trauma, disillusionment and disappointment arising from this. Nazneen copes with a high level of uncertainty and unfamiliarity within the new culture and also find herself facing the task of acquiring the necessary competence to function satisfactorily, even if that is only at a minimum level. Ultimately, moving to a new land prompts Nazneen, as it has other migrants, to adjust her own life and thinking to the new cultural environment

(Kabeer, 2000). During the transactions of daily rituals, the women in the novel detect similarities and differences between the surrounding environment and those that they have always known. They gradually become better acquainted with various aspects of living within Britain, becoming proficient in dealing with the situations they encounter.

The novel is interesting also in the way it evokes the emotions of the migrant by providing insights into the nature of migration as it is lived. Ali's novel focuses on nostalgia, exile and the restlessness of the migration process by giving a voice to the individual. Nazneen describes herself feeling trapped in her flat. It is a first person's narrative that is far more penetrating because it is personal; the accounts evoke a sense of rootlessness, isolation, loneliness and detachment from the wider community. What is unusual in the characterisation of Nazneen is the lack of excitement, expectation and new desires that she has as an immigrant. She fails to manifest any aspirations and ambitions. She fulfils her role as a wife as though she were in Bangladesh and becomes the dutiful wife and mother. Her horror at those who disentangle themselves from the discourse of femininity as defined through culture is evident when she initially encounters the 'librated' Mrs Azad and is critical of the changes she sees in her friend Razia who asserts her Britishness 'almost like the Queen herself' (Ali, 2003, p. 358). Through these characters, the author shows that migration has brought major new economic opportunities for women and new ways of constructing their futures.

Within the novel, as in diasporic discourse, the issue of proclaiming identity has become important. Showing Nazneen going through a self-defining analysis is thus in keeping with the concerns established within the theoretical framework. However identity is not only constructed from within the minority culture, Ali also deals with the dichotomy between the 'home' country and the 'host' community. In Britain, a racialised discourse is evident as the Bangladeshi community is constructed to be outside the nation. Racism as a theme is not focused on as a plot but becomes interspersed as part of everyday reality.

The Bangladeshi community as constructed by the individuals becomes the medium both for locating and depicting their selves. Diasporic cultural reproduction and the reconstitution of cultures assume geographical sites and points of origin as definitive in shaping diasporic cultural forms (Bhachu, 1996). *Brick Lane's* focus is on the reconstitution of a 'traditional' Bangladeshi culture – one which has existed for generations.

Gender and race become two of the concerns that underpin the debate which occur in the narrative, these differences are conceptualised in different ways, via experience and social relations, as subjectivity and as identity. It is towards the end of the novel that Nazneen shifts from complacency to questioning her positioning and role. She begins to realise her migration to Britain is initially an experience of constraint rather than opportunity as she said 'she had submitted to her father and married her husband' (Ali, 2003, p. 248). This brings about changes in her character as she begins to assert her own identity.

Ultimately, the ability of Nazneen to adapt to a multicultural context is central to the novel. The process of adapting lifestyles to the patterns of the surrounding culture takes place with respect to different axes of differentiation and social divisions. Nazneen provides a discussion about the cultural consequences of dislocation and displacement through migration, which are important to the construction of the identity of the individuals within the story.

Transnational Sisterhood

Ali uses Nazneen and her sister Hasina as two characters through which she explores two images of femininity. What is interesting is the way in which she maintains the bond between the sisters to explore their identities within their respective environments. The reader has a privileged insight into Nazneen's life through the narrative; Ali draws us into Nazneen's world, a world of regular prayer and regular housework – the regularity is emphasised through the author writing about the minute details of Nazneen's everyday life. Nazneen's life revolves around her living room, her kitchen and her occasional journeys out of the home. Hasina's story is conveyed through a series of letters, written in a rather unconvincing broken English, in which she reports her tragic turn of fate. Hasina's life is far more dramatic. Life moves far more quickly, the narrative of the letters is more active than the mundane details of her sister's life. Hasina runs away from a violent husband, is raped, works in a factory, turns to prostitution and becomes a maid. Nazneen's only contact with Bangladesh is through the letters she exchanges with Hasina, and as both stories run parallel with each other, the reader is able to appreciate the differences and similarities between the two sisters' lives.

Nazneen has been the 'good daughter' in her family, the daughter who accepted an arranged marriage, yet her younger sister Hasina was the 'bad daughter', who eloped in a 'love marriage', and was consequently disowned by her father (Whipple, 2003). Nazneen accepts her fate yet Hasina rebelled to create her own. Hasina's Western-style attempt at romantic freedom, contradicts the traditional structures of Bangladeshi society within which she lives and within which her sister is immersed in the diaspora. Both sisters have problems settling with their husbands, and ultimately both have relationships with younger men. Nazneen is plain 'not beautiful, but not so ugly either' (Ali, 2003, p. 17), yet in contrast her sister Hasina is beautiful and feisty. Hasina defines herself in contrast to the activities around her and Nazneen defines herself against the talkativeness of her husband. Through these transnational links, Nazneen and Hasina become embodiments of womanhood in two very different but connected locations.

Both women are 'Bangladeshi'; one is contained within the physical environment of Bangladesh whilst the other migrates to the diaspora. The sisters embody femininity within these two different contexts. Both sisters initially are equally confined by their circumstances, by the traditions that silence women and constrict them within an oppressive system of honour and shame. Hasina writes about her beatings from her husband, blaming herself '[My husband] is a good man and very patient'. Hasina writes that: 'Sometimes I make him lose patience without I mean to' (Ali, 2003, p. 37). Both women accept Hasina's subsequent beatings as normal; even Nazneen accepts the beatings her children receive from their father as normal. But it is Hasina who shows more signs of change and westernisation. Her decision to leave her husband as a result of his beatings is frowned upon, as the landlady reiterates 'it is better get beaten by own husband' (Ali, 2003, p. 46).

The author explores the impact of migration and the pressure to maintain ethnicity within a diasporic context for those within the Bangladeshi diaspora, an experience which social researchers have confirmed (Adams, 1987; Choudhury, 1993; Eade, 1989). Within the context of diaspora it appears the women are more Bangladeshi than the Bangladeshis in Bangladesh. They perpetuate the tradition of assistance and try to replicate this within the area where they live. We learn how those in Britain replicate the social practices and norms of Bangladesh so that the culture also migrates to Britain with the people ... 'through the open window, drifted wafts of music and snatches of curry ... main meals were cooked at all times of the day or night' (Ali, 2003, p. 189). Yet in contrast, those who remain in Bangladesh are adapting to the changes occurring in society. Hasina acts as if she was the person who has shifted geographically to another country, she appears more modern in her thinking in contrast to her sister, who appears more traditional. The two women placed within the two different localities also enable Ali to show how social practices and social relations change in the two locations. Within the context of Britain, Nazneen witnesses changes in the images of Bangladeshi femininity among her friends, who become more westernised.

The passivity with which Nazneen lives her life contrasts with the activity of her sister. Nazneen appears to conform to the teachings of her mother, who instructs Nazneen that it is a woman's role to accept her suffering with indifference. Nazneen accepts this legacy of passive stoicism, just as equally as she seemingly accepts the miserably lonely existence that fate has bestowed upon her in a London council flat. She does not argue, but remains quiet. She restrains the anger inside her, just as she gives the outward appearance of passivity. However, inside her thoughts, which through the first person narration the reader is privileged to, we find a sense of determination which surfaces as the novel concludes.

Bangladesh: Warm Memories and Cold Realities

Issues of home, belonging and identity are central to *Brick Lane* as they are so important for Nazneen. Her idea of home embodies a discourse of locality, a sense of place which embraces networks of families and friends and signifies a specific space, both geographically and psychologically, that is experienced in terms of neighbourhood. The memories of Bangladesh reiterate this concept of home, and she fondly remembers her mother and her friends – they become warm memories, yet she has no recollections of her father, nor any further contact with him.

The notion of diaspora in *Brick Lane* invokes the imagery of the traumas of separation, dislocation and adaptation that are central to the experiences of migration (Adams, 1987; Ballard, 1994; Choudhury 1993; Kabeer, 2000). Throughout the book there are constant references to 'back home'. The women become defined by their history in Bangladesh – their attitude to life is entwined with the pull of 'home' (Gardner, 2002). The novel shows the ways in which the

Bangladeshi diaspora feeds back economically into the homeland through remittances often to the detriment of the family (Khanum, 1994; Westwood and Phizacklea, 2000). Razia's husband sends money to Bangladesh to build a mosque, whilst his family suffers economically, forced to shop for second-hand clothes. She finds her husband's decision to send money back to Bangladesh tiresome: 'all the money goes back home'. Whereas within Britain 'If the children need toothbrushes, I have to beg, I have to get everything second hand' (Ali, 2003, pp. 77-78). Britain was seen as the 'promised land' in terms of economic opportunity and material advancement, allowing the Bangladeshis to save money which was sent to relatives to help their strategy of investment in land, and to escape from indebtedness (Adams, 1987; Eade, 1997).

The novel shows the ways in which social networks are generated and sustained in Britain (Phillipson et al., 2003). Brick Lane is described as clustered with shops, travel agencies, cafes, restaurants, garment factories, voluntary organisation and the London Great Mosque, which has become Bangla Town, and which attract other Bangladeshis (Eade, 1997). The activity within the novel fails to extend beyond the maintenance of the ethnic boundary constructed through community organisations, family and kinship networks, mosques and the local community centres in and around Brick Lane. Consequently, engagement with mainstream British society is lacking. The characters talk about the commonality that ties them together back to their country of origin. Even in the face of racism, it is their Bangladeshi identity which is questioned by the 'natives'.

The novel features an imminent return to Bangladesh for the main characters. Here, the immigrant experience is depicted through the women talking about Bangladesh and the sense of belonging that it evokes. There is also the diasporic sisterhood with other Bangladeshi women when individuals are thrown together, and becoming part of a larger Bangladeshi family in Britain. However, the conclusion to the novel fails to provide a solution to their sense of loss and 'homing' desires. Nothing is resolved, Ali's characters are still living in a transitory state. The placing of home for Bangladeshi has become more complicated as the relationship with the country of origin has been transformed (Eade, 1997).

The Bangladesh Nazneen refers to is different to the Bangladesh Hasina writes about in her letters. The contrasts between Tower Hamlets and Bangladesh are shown, for example by the fact that Nazneen comes from an idyllic, warm, green environment quite unlike the England of dead grass, broken paving stones and net curtains. Hasina's letters dispel the myth that Bangladesh is still rural, a paradise; it is urban and violent. A more dangerous Bangladesh with corrupt politicians dominates the letters. Hasina describes to her sister how the garment girls have become branded as sexually immoral due to their working in close proximity to men. The patriarchal world of Bangladesh mirrors the patriarchy practised within Britain, but is stronger. For example, Hasina, left without the protection of a husband, is raped, then forced to become a prostitute to survive and her friend (Monju) is murdered by her husband drenching her in acid. Whilst Hasina works within a factory as a machinist, her sister, in the liberated environment of the West, also resorts to working as a machinist, but in purdah within the home.

For Nazneen as with other first generation Bangladeshis, feelings of isolation are an important factor in the development of her concept of 'home' (Kabeer, 2000). Her existence within the home and remaining within the confines of the home, forces Nazneen to seek comfort in the past. Typical of expatriates, she nostalgically remembers her past life in Bangladesh and therefore home continues to be Bangladeshi (Gardner, 1995). However, the past becomes remoulded to be perfect, as it is the letters from her sister which depict reality instead of nostalgia. The letters from Hasina force Nazneen to realise the Bangladesh that she has left behind 'was an ugly place, full of danger' (Ali, 2003, p. 356). Even Razia has a more realistic concept of Bangladesh instead of a fictional one, and tells Nazneen, 'if everything back home is damn wonderful what are all these crazy people doing queuing for visa' (Ali, 2003, p. 357).

The Bangladesh which is reflected in British society angers Chanu, Nazneen's husband, as it perpetuates a derogatory image of Bangladesh through education. He despairs over what his children are taught about Bangladesh: 'all she knows is about flood and famine. Whole bloody country is just a bloody basket case to her' (Ali, 2003, p. 151). Even the image that Shahana has of Bangladesh is old and traditional. As she tells her sister, 'just wait until you're in Bangladesh ... you'll be married off in no time ... and your husband will keep you locked up in a little smelly room and make you weave carpets all day long' (Ali, 2003, p. 329). 'In Bangladesh you'll have to brush your teeth with a twig. They don't have toothbrushes' (Ali, 2003, p. 331).

Issues of home, belonging and identity remain important for those who have migrated because they are contested and unsettled issues. For the first generation, this home is in the country of origin, but for subsequent generations home is within the diaspora (Eade, 1994; Gardner and Shukur, 1994). As Mrs Azad says in the novel, 'we live in a Western society ... our children will act more and more like westerners' (Ali, 2003, p. 93). The construction of new ethnic hybrid identities is what the author explores with the second generation characters, in particular Shahana. This is part of a more general debate about British Bengalis and their sense of belonging (Adams, 1987; Choudhury, 1993; Eade, 1990; Hall, 1992).

England: A Grey and Noxious Land

The process of adapting lifestyles to the patterns of a foreign culture takes place with respect to the recognition of social inequalities and divisions within that particular society (Brah, 1996). Gender and race have become two of the concerns highlighted in social research as particularly significant in the migratory experience. Yet social research has been limited when dealing with Bangladeshi women; for instance, earlier oral studies such as Adams (1987) and Choudhury (1993) focused on men and although research into the Bangladeshi community in Britain has expanded in recent years, the work in relation to women continues to remain a neglected area, with the exception of Kabeer (2000) and Gardner (2002). It is interesting therefore that the novel focuses on gender and race as two key aspects of experience. By highlighting these issues, *Brick Lane* offers a particular representation of the cultural locations of Bengali women within a British context. By constructing these axes of differentiation Ali provides a discussion about the consequences of dislocation and displacement through migration and the importance of this in the construction of identity of the individuals, but in particular the women, within the story. In this respect, the novel becomes a social text in that it provides an insight into the lives of women who have migrated are learning to adapt to an alien environment.

For Nazneen, Britain is loaded with negativity: it fails to accumulate the warmth and security she experienced in Bangladesh. Whilst Bangladeshi culture is re-synthesised within Britain, the lifestyles and consumption styles of the diaspora do not reproduce its strength and support for Nazneen. Instead, loneliness and feelings of exclusion become defining features of the diasporic experience for her. Nazneen's loneliness is treated through anti-depressants, which baffles her sister; 'I do not know what kind of pill can cure disease of sadness' (Ali, 2003, p. 143). Nazneen is disappointed with Britain and recollects Bangladesh with fondness, a nostalgia that provides the framework within which the story is located.

Ali uses the cluttered room where Nazneen lives as a metaphor for her protagonist's state of mind. It becomes even more cluttered over the course of the text. When Bangladesh is presented it is done so with space; however, the restrictiveness of England is stressed through the feelings of claustrophobia. Nazneen's perception of Britain for much of the novel is not only contained within the environment of her flat, but also when she gazes out of her window. Her London is restricted to her own council estate: outside her window she sees 'dead grass and broken paving stones' (Ali, 2003, p. 12), 'cycle racks which no one was foolhardy enough to use' (Ali, 2003, p. 230), and round the corner is a playground that has shrunk to one decrepit roundabout. Nazneen evokes an image of Britain which is dark and grey and congested 'a roaring metal army tearing up the road' (Ali, 2003, p. 33).

The novel fails to discuss the relationship between the Bengalis and other migrant groups. Ironically, Tower Hamlets has a long history of immigration, shaped by periodic waves of overseas settlers starting from the French Protestants during the late seventeenth century, Jews in the nineteenth century and, more recently, Maltese, Cypriot, Somali and Bangladeshi arrivals (Samad and Eade, 2002). The book evokes an atmosphere of community that is entirely Bangladeshi and Muslim. There is an absence of the indigenous population, except for passing references, and contact between Nazneen and White Londoners is limited. No contact with the host country is sought. The English are observed, by the characters in the novel. For example, the 'tattoo lady' who lives opposite Nazneen and Chanu, but no contact develops between them. This reflects the ways in which Bangladeshi men interacted with White people in the 1980s, but their wives often did not.

The novel attempts to explore the complexity of a Bangladeshi community that has been pushed to the margins of British society. Bangladeshis have increasingly become synonymous with economic, social and political disadvantage in comparison to other ethnic minority groups (Eade, 1997; Modood et al., 1997). The poverty in Tower Hamlets is emphasised if not exaggerated by Nazneen's as she ventures out of the home, and 'stepped over an empty cigarette carton, a brick and a syringe' (Ali, 2003, p. 380). Although Nazneen's husband Chanu has a degree from Dhaka University, they live in a grotty tower block in Tower Hamlets, where the paint flakes off the 'eczema-ridden walls'. Poverty, socio-economic deprivation, dominates the social fabric of Ali's Bangladeshi society in Tower Hamlets. This deprivation is also evoked through Nazneen smelling 'the overflowing communal bins' (Ali, 2003, p. 13).

Bangladeshis suffer high rates of unemployment. Although there are no recent figures for the rate of Bangladeshi unemployment in Tower Hamlets, unemployment in this borough is very high (13.6% of the total population was unemployed in 1998, compared with the national average of 4.6%), and the Bangladeshi unemployment rate is likely to be even higher (Samad and Eade, 2002). For the younger Bangladeshis in Brick Lane, their response to the hostility and social deprivation they face is to spend more time outside their homes. Young men dominate the landscape of Brick Lane in the novel. In her attempts to depict the realities of contemporary experience of Bangladeshi youth, Ali draws upon the popular image of the Asian gang. In recent years the British media has discovered a growing youth militancy within an environment of urban deprivation and the Asian 'underclass' (Alexander, 2000). This re-imagination of Asian young men has focused on violence, drug abuse and crime, and in the novel this is set against a backdrop of cultural conflict, generational confusion and religious fundamentalism. Ali shows the extreme consequences of this of through Razia's son Tariq and his drug addiction. In the novel these men roam around, treating Brick Lane and its surrounding streets as military zones to be occupied and fortified, territories worth annexing; anxiety and resentment are in the air as they attempt to rid the estate of the racism that has infiltrated it. They are presented as merely competing for control over territory, undermining attempts to unify them.

The book presents an image of England as racist. The park situated near the estate on Whitechapel Road is named after Altab Ali who was murdered in a racist attack by three men in nearby Adler Street (Sandhu, 2003). But Ali discusses racism in the light of contemporary debates, by looking at Islamophobia in the wake of September 11. She takes the reader inside the Muslim community's response to September 11 as the characters in the novel discuss how the Muslims were blamed for the attack, the 'magic passport' of one of the hijackers having been discovered which miraculously survived the fire 'heat of over one thousand degrees Fahrenheit ... found in the rubble of the World Trade Centre' (Ali, 2003, p. 318). The characters also discuss the backlash they experienced in the wake of September 11. For example, where Nazneen recounts that her neighbour's daughter 'had her hijaab pulled off. Razia wore her union jack sweatshirt and it was spat on' (Ali, 2003, p. 328).

Diasporic cultural reproduction and the reconstitution of cultures assume that geographical sites and points of origin are definitive in shaping diasporic cultural forms (Bhachu, 1996). The novel shows the formation of Bangladeshi space. The area around Brick Lane is presented as predominantly Bengali. Curry houses, sari shops dress factories, and food shops 'stacked with kebabs, tandoori chicken, bhazis, puris, trays of rice and vegetables, milky sweets, sugar shind ladoos, the faintly sparkling jelabees' (Ali, 2003, p. 398) are described alongside the 'Sylhet Cash and Carry, the international cheap calls centre' (Ali, 2003, p. 391). The book depicts the construction of their own community on their own terms, their 'desh pardesh' as Ballard (1994) calls it. Part of the construction of the Bangladeshi desh pardesh is illustrated by the 'red and gold sari' (Ali, 2003, p. 12) hanging on the washing line, and the road sign around the towers in Bengalis 'the sign screwed to the brickwork was in stiff English capitals and the curlicues beneath were Bengali' (Ali, 2003, p. 13). We also see the way in which the religious character of the British social order has been transformed as a result of the Muslim presence. 'Men walking around in skull caps', 'white Punjabi-pyjama' (Ali, 2003, p. 13) suits dominate Nazneen's local environment (Ali, 2003, p. 81), whilst the women adopt the hijab and the burkha. Bangladeshis have created an ethnic enclave of small shops, cafes, restaurants, taxi companies and travel agencies, as other migrants to the area had done before (Samad and Eade, 2002).

The novel focuses on the reconstitution of a cultural base in the diaspora, which corresponds to the continuous reinterpretation of a 'traditional' cultural form that has existed for centuries in the country of origin. For the characters having migrated to Britain, their lives remain contained within the ideological practices inherited from Bangladesh. In fact Brick Lane, as defined by the novel, becomes representative of a holding area, a temporary zone for immigrants who have not yet fully settled in England; whose lives are defined by the past (Sandhu, 2003). The past dominates the context of novel, in the lives of all the characters. It appears as though the estate represents a mid point between Bangladesh and UK. The characters at the end of the novel either find themselves integrating into English society or have migrated elsewhere, such as Karim and Chanu.

Within the Bangladeshi community the novel illustrates the creation of an 'artificial bridari' (wider family) which Anwar (1998), Ballard (1994) and Shaw (1994), in considering British Pakistanis, discuss as a wider kinship group which encourage loyalty from individuals and also expectations of their roles. Within Brick Lane and its surrounding areas, the individuals within the novel operate within this 'bridari system' through their social contacts and relationships within the community, through visits to each other, and by offering services of assistance. Nazneen's life is initially defined by her female Bangladeshi neighbours, her close friend, Razia and Mrs. Islam. Their lives and their perceptions of the world are spun through deep channels of gossip and rumour. Social networks were vital in supporting the women within the constraints they experienced in terms of overcrowding at home, racism within the wider community and the financial pressures they experienced (Phillipson, 2003). Even the young men on the streets, despite the image of deviance they represent, are contained within the respectable roles in the novel, as when Nazneen 'passed a group of young Bangla men on the path, they parted and bowed with mock formality' (Ali, 2003, p. 117).

However, petty class and status snobberies dominate these diasporic social networks in *Brick Lane*. Those educated are presented as deliberately attempting to detach themselves from the British Bangladeshi community. This is a minority educated elite, as the major part of the population of Sylhetis in Britain are uneducated (Kershen, 2000). Chanu looks down upon the majority of Bangladeshis who are from Sylhet and who are working class. His education from the University of Dhaka marks him out as educated and middle class. Consequently, he distances himself from other fellow Bangladeshis. Commenting on the ten children playing in the courtyard of the estate Shahana observes that their 'parents don't want them all inside all the time ... they'd only get on each others nerves' (Ali, 2003, p. 272) to which Chanu replies 'Ah, its overcrowding ... overcrowding is one of the worst problems in our community. Four or five Bangladeshis to one room. That's an official council statistic' (Ali, 2003, p. 273). He sounds like an outsider commenting on the Bangladeshi community. Chanu desires integration within White society and the Bangladeshi professional class, hence his 'forced' friendship with Dr Azad. To this extent, the novel is as much about class and its petty snobberies within the Bangladeshi community as it is about ethnicity. Whilst Nazneen is discouraged from socialising with her Bangladeshi neighbours, she secretly engages with them socially much to Chanu's displeasure.

Even in the supposed homogeneity of the Bangladeshi diaspora, Ali highlights the fragmentation of this community further. *Brick Lane* shows a community divided and individuals seeking to benefit themselves. Mrs Islam is authorative, gives orders to those around her and sets herself up as the voice of moral authority, yet is ultimately revealed as corrupt and hypocritical. Her role as a money lender is justified by herself under the pretence of being a frail old widow who donates the money to Islamic charities. Nevertheless she exploits the community, taking advantage of its weakest members by charging them excessive rates of interest and using her sons as thugs. The Bangladeshi community is also shown to be one riven by gossip, largely about women who break out of traditional moulds.

Ali ultimately shows the Bangladeshi community at odds with itself. Even the community's attempt to create solidarity through the Islamic group proves unsuccessful, and results in a shambles as the men resort to squabbling between themselves. The action of Karim and the Bangladeshis in Britain mirrors the rise of fundamentalism in Bangladesh itself.

However, when analysing the social motives and behavioural patterns of the characters within the text, it is important not to assume that the community is an institution built from the culturally-determined preferences of the group concerned. Apart from the effect of internal constraints on behaviour, external influences need to be considered, especially that of racial discrimination. The emergence of a wider South Asian lifestyle, the appearance of traditional dress, the attraction to brotherhood and sisterhood cannot be understood by only looking for internal causes. They are the obvious consequences of inter-ethnic relations and symbols of separatism which serve to distinguish the 'us' from 'them'. These are cultural symbols which provoke a questioning reaction from the host country. The text therefore tells us as much about Britain as a host society, as it does about the minority people themselves. The text explores how, as ethnic consciousness grows stronger in response to growing external hostility, the individuals within this environment come closer together.

Prejudice and discrimination are illustrated through the leafleting by the far right groups in Tower Hamlets. The racism that is experienced brings with it a potential threat to the continuity of the group identity. Although a person's group identity comes under threat when a migrant changes cultures and is confronted with a minority status definition of himself or herself, the experience potentially constitutes a threat to an individual's own identity (Verma et al., 1986), because it challenges the individual's personal and social identity. Racism forces the Bangladeshi community in the novel to define and emphasise their own ethnicity, by seeking support from their own groups. The meetings of the militant groups show the assertion of their rights and their demands for equality. Ali presents a community that is attempting to be socially self-sufficient and autonomous, but is ultimately seen as being incapable of self-defence, as in the concluding 'riot' scenes where the Bengal Tigers' demonstration degenerates into fights between young Bangladeshi men. This is quite unlike the 2001 'riots' in northern England, upon which this sub-plot might be thought to be modelled, where young South Asian men overcame their differences and fought the police and white racists (Hussain and Bagguley, 2005).

Gender, Generation and Identity

Ali deconstructs the way gender becomes indicative of the experiences of the characters in everyday life. It becomes clear how circumscribed the characters' lives are by the mere fact of being a woman. Simple signifiers of clothes and mannerism become important for the social identities of gender and generation. Ali explores the changing gender identities in relationship to the first generation through Nazneen and Razia, and then with reference to the second generation through Nazneen's daughters, in particular Shahana.

Brick Lane explores the emotional conflicts of immigrants who are attracted by the possibilities of a new culture which is radically different from the culture of their past (Shaw, 1994). Nazneen's sudden, forced isolation in a culture very different from her own is central to the novel, and her reflections become the product of her alienated existence within Britain. The more Nazneen moves within her own thoughts, the more disillusioned she becomes.

The way she responds to the external reality is through an interplay of impulses, urges, deep-rooted instincts and an awareness of the existence of her femaleness, which is socially distinct from maleness, primarily in the form of restriction. As she notes at one point, she has only been out twice, the rest of the time she remains within the home, very much like a prisoner of her gender role. Her husband restrains her from going out, 'why should you go out? ... If you go out, then people will say, "I saw her walking on the street" and "I will look like a fool". Personally I don't mind you go out but these people are so ignorant' (Ali, 2003, p. 35) and continues, 'if you were in Bangladesh, you would not go out. Coming here you are not missing anything, only broadening your horizons' (Ali, 2003, p. 35). Nazneen's approach to the environment surrounding her and her memories of her past makes her turn inward. She remains confined to the four walls of her room, a setting which contrasts with the openness of the environment in Bangladesh.

Nazneen behaves exactly as she would in Bangladesh; the British environment initially has no effect on her. Her Bangladeshi roots maintain her subservience within her marriage and family as she cuts out corns from her husband feet, looks after her children, and walks a step behind her husband when out of the home. She remains contained within the domestic environment of the flat, as a form of purdah. Even her desire to pursue English classes is diminished, she is denied the right to pursue employment, and her life exists for her husband and her family. Asking Chanu if she can go to English classes with Razia his response is 'you're going to be a mother ... will that not keep you busy enough? And you can't take a baby to college ... it's not so simple as that, just to go to college, like that' (Ali, 2003, p. 62).

Doing things for herself is deemed selfish. But she gains pleasure from this 'for a moment she saw herself clearly, following her husband, head bowed, hair covered and she was pleased' (Ali, 2003, p. 210). She feels others' approval of her adopting her role, as 'everything she did, everything she had done since the day of her birth was recorded' (Ali, 2003, p. 210). Her anger at her husband's refusal to help Hasina is done so quietly, as she continues to act as the dutiful wife, continuing to cut Chanu's corns and trim his nose hair while planning mini-rebellions. For a while, she puts hot chillies in his sandwiches, and returns unwashed socks to his drawer. Nazneen also knows when her children are taking advantage of her illiteracy, as they point out the red ticks from the teacher, but she notes the red biro on their desk (Ali, 2003, p. 218).

The women discover their lives are limited by various factors in both Bangladesh and Britain, where tradition, communal politics, family loyalties and social norms and above all, sex differentiation, mean that men can enjoy the 'freedoms' of Britain, but women are restricted. Nazneen realises that adaptation is best achieved through conformity. Rebelling has served only to create new conflicts and she therefore resorts to the lifestyle around her. But in doing so, Nazneeen is not at peace with herself.

Nazneen conforms to the expected role as prescribed through generations and adheres to this for some time, she is also attracted to the possibilities of British culture. She sees others around her changing, yet is initially dismissive of this. Nazneen watches her husband consume alcohol at Dr Azads' house, and sees her friend Razia changing her dress, language and lifestyle as she begins to wear a sweatshirt emblazoned with a Union Jack. Nazneen realises England offers a more liberal culture to that of Bangladesh, although she initially disapproves of Dr Azads' wife's attire and the changes she sees in Razia. As she becomes accustomed to the culture of England she begins to slowly change. She is credited with no intelligence but is alert in her mind; perceiving the real terms of the relationship between her husband and Dr Azad. Mrs Azad appears clad in a short skirt, Ali emphasises her 'large brown thighs' (Ali, 2003, p. 88) and her 'dimpled knees' (Ali, 2003, p. 87), her purple lacquered nails and short hair 'cropped like a man ... streaked with some kind of rust coloured paint' (Ali, 2003, p. 87). Her physical attributes are defined as feminine, however her behaviour equals that of the men, her continual rebukes of her husband and Chanu and her consumption of alcohol and smoking give her masculine characteristics. She stresses her ability to change her outward appearances, with an aim to integrate. She talks about her role in Bangladesh 'when in Bangladesh, put on a sari and cover my head and all that.

But here I go out to work. I work with white girls and I'm just one of them' (Ali, 2003, p. 93). Her daughter has an even shorter skirt than her mother. The daughter's request for money to spend in the pub is done so without any attempt to hide it. She also refers to herself as being different to other women and talks about her progression, 'some women spend ten, twenty years here and they sit in the kitchen grinding spices all day and learn only two words of English. They go around covered from head to toe, in their little walking prisons' (Ali, 2003, p. 93). However, to what extent is this a true image of Bangladeshi femininity and womanhood? Would a woman who has migrated to the UK from a country as restricted as Bangladesh become so westernised so quickly?

Razia is the character who undergoes the most radical changes. Referred to by Chanu as not a 'respectable type' (Ali, 2003, p. 67), Razia, like Nazneen, finds life in Britain suffocating and unchanged. Having expected cultural changes she is disappointed and dismayed when the pattern is continuously reproduced. Razia's characterization contrasts with that of Nazneen; she is loud, vibrant and active and takes steps to improve her condition as opposed to being reconciled to her fate like the other women on the estate. Razia's decision to attend English language classes changes her radically. The more she learns the English language, the more English she becomes – her lifestyle changes radically. Furthermore, having gained citizenship she physically becomes the embodiment of her new identity. She wears western clothes and refuses to wear a sari again as it forced her to take 'little bird steps' (Ali, 2003, p. 77). Razia visually shifts so that she becomes the embodiment not just of Bangladesh but also of the new Western environment she is located within. She cuts her hair dramatically which Chanu states makes her look like a 'tramp' (Ali, 2003, p. 67) and resorts to swearing at her husband. Razia is also aware of the derogatory opinions of others, 'I hear what they are saying ... "Razia is so English. She is getting like the Queen herself ..."' (Ali, 2003, p. 188).

Rebellion is inevitable from Nazneen also who, in time, feels 'she was not the girl from the village anymore' (Ali, 2003, p. 320). The novel centres on Nazneen's passivity but also addresses a gradual metamorphosis. She begins to change in a society where individuals are allowed to exercise one's free will. The reader is witness to changes which occur in Nazneen's character. These range from the minor where Nazneen and her children start to wash their hair in shampoo rather than Fairy Liquid, to attending meetings, unaccompanied by Chanu, of a group of young activists who are trying to defend their culture from the bigotry and attacks in the wake of September 11. It is a huge decision for her. Within this public space she notes the younger second generation women who are verbally expressive, despite their traditional dress of hijab and burkha. This begins to affect her sense of identity and self to the point of fostering her defiance. Her decision to shave her legs at this point is symbolic of this change, and her attraction to another younger man, Karim, marks a significant turning point in her life. The shift in Nazneen's passivity is seen when she engages in this affair with Karim.

For Nazneen, her Bangladeshi ethnicity is but one dimension of her personality; her search for wholeness and authenticity leads her to an awareness that she has an individuality which does not resist being reduced to the cultural categories that were thrust upon her in Bangladesh. She calls into question her relationship with Chanu and thus her life in Britain. It becomes evident to Nazneen that her marriage to Chanu is not working, while such a marriage might have easily worked in Bangladesh, the same marriage stifles Nazneen in England as her daughters gets older. She changes to the extent of acknowledging that she needs a partner who is not so deeply rooted in the past, but also sees flaws in Karim. She begins to see how controlled her life is by men, Chanu and Karim become the same, Karim's self-indulgence in soliloquies are reminiscent of Chanu's rants. It dawns on Nazneen that she finds her life dictated by two men, until she decides 'I will decide what to do. I will say what happens to me. I will be the one' (Ali, 2003, p. 337). Nazneen finds herself making decisions of her own, achieving a kind of personal happiness which she does not have to share with Chanu or her daughters.

There are no direct ties to Bangladesh for Nazneen's children. Being born in the Britain, their acceptance of its culture is more enthusiastic than that of their country of origin. They are shown to be representative of both cultures: 'the girls had burgers or baked beans' (Ali, 2003, p. 321) and ate onion bhajis 'smothered in tomato ketchup' (Ali, 2003, p. 337) and 'Shahana extricated a Dairy Lea ... she rolled the cheese inside a chapatti' (Ali, 2003, p. 246). Bibi is meek and pliable, whilst the older daughter, Shahana, is impressively fierce and independent-minded, full of her own will. She embodies the classic Westernised rebellious South Asian youth engaging in a potent tug-of-war with her overbearing father. The arguments between Shahana and her father dominate the latter part of the novel.

Codes of behaviour and the acceptance of fate as advocated by the parental generation are shown to be no longer satisfactory for the younger generation. Shahana and her sister participate more actively in the wider social order than their parents; the children are constantly on the move between a variety of social arenas (Ballard, 1994). Chanu who holds onto old values forces his two daughters to memorize long passages of traditional poetry, and they have to endure his indulgences in Bangla speeches when he talks about the past grandeurs of Bangladesh, India and Muslims. He wants his daughters to show an interest in their ethnicity yet they fail to show the enthusiasm he desires. Unable to fulfil his dreams for his own life in Britain, he wants his daughters to maintain their Bangladeshi culture, the one in which he feels comfortable. Their lack of interest in Bangladesh, its customs and rituals leads to the frustration of Chanu who attempts to physically beat Bangladesh into them. For Shahana, the eldest daughter, her father's tactic of coercion and physical abuse makes her rebel even more.

These difficulties arise between Chanu and his daughters because these arenas are often organised around differing and sometimes radically contradictory moral and cultural conventions (Ballard, 1994). Within the Bangladeshi context into which Chanu and his wife have been socialised, certain gendered norms are adhered to which are contradicted by the dominant liberal Western culture in Britain. For instance, Chanu disapproves of his daughters' wearing of tight jeans and the derogatory way in which Shahana chats back to him.

At an abstract level, the two distinct cultures in the text appear contradictory. Reference is made to the host country in derogatory terms by Nazneen and her husband, yet Shahana resists the dictates of the past, moving into her own space as a daughter of both East and West. She is embarrassed by the primitiveness of her parents' ethnicity and threatens to run away. Significantly, it is through the children that Ali's work illustrates the changing femininities. It is the children who most vividly question and re-define their own roles, rather than slipping into what is prescribed for them.

Cultures are codes which individuals use to express themselves in a given context; therefore as the cultural context changes so does the code. The young girls in the novel are best understood as extremely mobile in linguistic, religious and cultural terms. Bibi is more effective as a cultural navigator; she decides how to behave within the given contexts and manoeuvres between the different communities. She is able to switch codes as appropriate (Ballard, 1994). She does not create the conflict generated by her older sister. She decides to listen to her father and adheres to the image he wishes to see of her as a young woman, however Shahana's conflict arises from her failure to behave appropriately. As Bibi effectively switches smoothly from one cultural and linguistic code to the next, her sister frequently fails.

For Shahana, the problems arise when the switch is made to a second British code that is regarded as unacceptable from the perspective of the Bangladeshi father. The systems existing in the social environment are mainly in the form of reference groups, whether these are peer or family. These systems develop when the cultural norms of the community are strengthened through the member's conformity. The ways in which an individual adapts to, and participates in, these different systems are due to social learning: the individuals learn how to behave within a specific cultural framework. The community culture of which the girls are part becomes a reference group which serves as a resource of attitudes and values, the basis for social learning.

Conclusion

As the experiences of the female characters are revealed in the novel, it is clear that masculine and feminine behaviour are subject to different social rules and operate according to different norms. The dilemmas of the protagonists are not resolved happily, but in fact their circumstances develop in ways that raise new sets of problems. However, their tentative steps are towards a new kind of reality for British Bangladeshi women, a new condition of liberation. Such liberation involves a better and deeper self-understanding. The text attempts to describe this self-realisation as the respective characters start to make choices about their futures and assert their individuality.

According to Sandhu (2003), *Brick Lane* was originally called 'Seven Seas and Thirteen Rivers', a title that alludes more generally to the distance between Sylhet and England. The decision to give it what Sandhu refers to as a 'less accurate' title was the publisher's. The title of the novel thus reflects a commercial concern to appeal to a White audience.

Furthermore, the 'social reality' of the novel appears to be more reflective of Britain in the 1970s rather than the early 21st century. It is difficult to comprehend the conclusion as a contemporary image, despite the fact that the novel attempts to convey changes between the 1970s and the 1990s. The novel ends unrealistically, with Nazneen dancing to Lulu's 'shout'. Even though the novel's marketing strength is its focus on Bangladeshi women, the characterisation of the female characters is weak, and they are overladen with stereotypes. Critically, the novel lacks a diasporic verisimilitude that undercuts its undoubted strengths. As such it stands in a contradictory cultural space on the boundary between 'commercialism' and 'authenticity'. A number of features of the novel illustrate this problem.

The text is rather weak in conveying the atmosphere and experience of Bangladeshi culture from 'within'. This is one of the strengths of some of the other books and films considered in earlier chapters. Ali describes the locations quite well, but they could easily be the perceptions of a tourist. Critically there are no community events and activities, except for the acrimonious and embarrassing defence group meetings which Nazneen attends in a local hall. She does not attend any weddings or funerals, nor are there any significant religious festivals such as Eid marked in the narrative. Such events and festivals are central to the re-affirmation of Muslim South Asian culture in the diaspora. Moreover, they are the kinds of collective rituals that provide the settings for critically important events in peoples' lives. It is as if the community is only represented 'internally' from within the characters and through moral regulation in informal and private interactions. Finally, Nazneen would have been ostracised by the community if her husband had left her in the circumstances presented in the novel.

Chapter 7

Childhood in *Anita and Me*

Introduction

This chapter seeks to explore the concept of childhood in relation to the protagonist within Meena Syal's novel, *Anita and Me* (1996). The semi-autobiographical novel presents a witty but poignant view of a young South Asian girl, Meena, growing up in an English Midlands mining village during the 1970s. Meena is the daughter of the only Indian family in the village of Tollington and the issues of difference, gender inequalities and culture are drawn out within the text. The novel is significant due to its autobiographical quality, the experiences of the main characters echoing the real experiences of the author.

It is ultimately a 'coming of age' story. Codes of behaviour and the acceptance of fate as advocated by the parental generation are further shown in the novel to be no longer satisfactory for the younger generation. The text records the consciousness of the protagonist, as she adjusts and responds to where she lives and to those around her. Meena finds her life torn between the world's attitude towards her and her own definition of her role in life. This dichotomy of difference is used as the basis for the turmoil she experiences in her life. In the novel, Meena feels smothered by her ambitious parents who tell her 'education is her passport' and aunties, who attempt to guide her towards a path of 'good girldom' (O'Sullivan, 1996); however, Meena cannot wait to grow up and wants to stray away from conventional norms and onto the path of western popular culture. Meena longs to be like her White friends, wear mini-skirts and make-up and break free from her parents. The focus of the novel is on Meena's desire for friendship with the local wild child, Anita Rutter. Anita becomes the embodiment of everything that Meena wants to be.

In novels about childhood, the child protagonist is almost always engaged in recording the impact of a particular environment or experience (Dabydeen and Wilson-Tagoe, 1997). The plot within *Anita and Me* centres around Meena's relationship with Anita Rutter as a 'rose-tinted' friendship that changes everything one summer as it transforms Meena from immaturity to a more acute awareness of society and a dawning of racial awareness.

Meena's experience is shown to be a product of social practices and social structures where race and cultural differentiation are key determinants. Besides raising questions about the construction of childhood interaction, the novel explores the interaction within the community. It deconstructs how racism impacts upon the experiences of the girl and her family in everyday life. It becomes clear how circumscribed the characters' lives are by the mere fact of being South Asian, not only in terms of actual racial abuse, but in their day-to-day social life where their race is a constant source of comment. Simple signifiers of clothes and mannerism become an important influence not only for the social identity of race but within the wider cultural implications that these ideologies have in the construction of the Meena's own identity. The terms on which Meena participates in any kind of social life are different from the terms on which her friends do so, as some social behaviour is considered appropriate and some inappropriate.

Through such codes of behaviour, double standards are represented, so that two perspectives are gained on how one should behave and what happens when one does not conform. Meena's family are acutely aware of how others perceive them. For instance, their interaction with the shopkeeper, Mr Ormerod, whose persistence in forcing Meena's father to attend the harvest festival celebrations stoops to assumptions of how race is a factor binding all non-white individuals: 'you could see it on his face, he's made the connection, Africa was abroad, we were from abroad, how could we refuse to come along and embrace Jesus for the sake of our cousins?' (Syal, 1996, p. 21). In exploring such differences, the novel notices how experiences of a lack of free choice, the social disadvantage facing the girl and the fact of being non-white seems to determine the way Meena and her family experience life.

Syal uses Meena's life to suggest a typical South Asian childhood where issues such as race and gender are an important aspect of adolescent experience. Meena's bickering with her parents is due to them feeling she is adopting the characteristics of the indigenous population, her wild behaviour as she leaves home to go to the fair and her reluctance to do as she is told. However, the transference of discourses within the minority is presented as having dire effects, as the author puts forward Meena's desire to be part of the indigenous population: 'I wanted to shed my body like a snake slithering out of its skin and emerge reborn, pink and unrecognisable' (Syal, 1996, p. 146) and her failure to acknowledge her Indian identity, 'I began avoiding mirrors, I refused to put on the Indian suits my mother laid our for me' (Syal, 1996, p. 146). But at the end she sees this as a phase as finally: 'it was time to let go and I floated back down into my body which, for the first time ever, fitted me to perfection and was all mine' (Syal, 1996, p. 326).

This chapter examines the issue of childhood in *Anita and Me*, focusing on the protagonist's identification with an older white peer group. This is related to her conflicts with her parents, but she ultimately becomes alienated from her White friends due to their unthinking racism. Differences between generations are central to the novel and are expressed through Meena's relationship with her parents and their friends. Finally, the chapter considers how the film adaptation of the novel differs as a form of representation. Ultimately it is argued that the film version is flawed in comparison to the original text of the novel. The film fails to develop the sub-plots found in the novel, which provide the contexts that enable the reader to appreciate more fully Meena's dilemmas.

The Theme of Childhood

Considered simply, the novel shows the development of social relationships in adolescence within the areas of family and peers. During the course of the text Meena moves towards greater responsibility for herself, and shifts away from parental control and supervision, becoming more intensely involved with her peer group. Her parents do not cease to play a significant role in her social life, but subtle changes occur in the nature and emphasis of parental authority within this relationship.

Meena's life is lived in two parallel worlds, which differ from each other in terms of culture, religion and her own experience: that of the surrounding indigenous British society and that of the family home. The worlds also differ from each other with regard to the participants, the demands made of her, measures of worth and levels of personal investment. Each is relatively isolated from the other, so that her parents have very little awareness of the nature of the social world in which Meena is engaged with her friends, and her peers have limited knowledge of her parents and home life. The family offers discussion and guidance concerning school and future work as well as education about cultural requirements; the peer group, on the other hand, offers opportunities for recreation and for trying out adult activities. What is important is the type of relationship that Meena has with each group. The nature of Meena's involvement with different social worlds affects ideas about herself and those around her.

At first we find that Meena has virtually no relationship with her peers. We are told of an incident at school when she is caned with a ruler in front of her classmates, of whom she says, 'I now hated without exception' (Syal, 1996, p. 22); her disappointment with the local scene is also clear as: 'in the village, I was stuck in between the various gangs, too young for Anita's consideration, too old to hang around the cloud of toddlers' (Syal, 1996, p. 25). Meena longs to be a part of Anita Rutter's gang, which also includes Fat Sally and Sherrie. Meena wants to be like Anita; in her eyes, Anita is the epitome of beauty with her blonde hair, pale skin, long legs and lip-gloss.

Her fantasy world becomes a reality after she is befriended by the 'wild Anita'. Meena's first encounter with Anita at the local shop shocks her to the extent that even before talking to Anita, 'I had instinctively stiffened … my heart unaccountably flipping like a fish' (Syal, 1996, p. 16). However, the initial encounter upsets her as the girls make fun of her. Meena's disappointment is clear to Anita who rebukes her two friends. This act of 'kindness' touches Meena to the extent that her admiration for Anita further intensifies as she notes 'Anita broke into a beam of such radiance and forgiveness that my breath caught and my throat began to ache' (Syal, 1996, p. 17). Meena's delight in Anita's reaction is uncontrollable. After procuring sweets for Anita and being invited to join her gang, Meena says, 'I was happy to follow her a respectable few paces behind knowing that I was privileged to be in her company' (Syal, 1996, p. 38).

In befriending Anita, Meena becomes engaged in a wide variety of new social contexts, which provide conflicting demands and expectations. Meena begins to experience a conflict of parental ideas, personal interests, peer attitudes and the reality of her social environment. Hence, the parents fail to learn the extent of Meena's mischievous behaviour but still attempt to curb this by restricting her going out. The very fact that she is being mischievous with her friends is appealing enough for Meena. Her delight in enjoying Anita's gang is short-lived; immediately after, she is hurt when she is not invited to dinner at Anita's. Having spent the day with Anita, having dinner at her home is not considered to be in dispute so Meena casually follows Tracy, Anita and Deirdre into their garden for some 'tea'. But her presence is hardly welcome. Meena notices the reaction from Anita's mother, 'Deirdre looked me up and down as if making a decision' (Syal, 1996, p. 55) and does so by turning her back on her and walking towards Anita. This physical gesture is understood by Anita, who informs Meena that she has to go and shuts the door. Meena blames herself for the rejection. She fails to understand that Deirdre has based her decision on Meena's physical characteristics.

This feeling of exclusion dominates the early part of the friendship. Despite such rejections, Meena overcomes this; her relationship with Anita is strengthened. Meena does her best to please her friends. The strength of their relationship is secured when Meena uses her cousin Baby as a carrier for the gang's stolen confectioneries. This act is greatly admired by Anita who states, 'Yow'm a real Wench. That was bostin' what you did' (Syal, 1996, p. 156). Her act is rewarded; Meena is given joint leadership of the gang which delights her beyond words she naively 'nodded stupidly, too overcome to speak' (Syal, 1996, p. 156). This change in status not only bridges the gap between the two girls within the gang, but also contributes to Meena's interaction with her home; Anita becomes the first White girl she invites home.

Meena becomes aware of the contrasts and the similarities between the two cultures. In one incident in which she is invited to 'tea' at Anita's house, her consumption of lard sandwiches results in her being physically sick. The lard sandwiches and fishfingers which dominate the household cuisine of Anita's home are contrasted with that of Meena's own home. Within Meena's household, the preference for fresh vegetables is highlighted irrespective of Meena's love of fishfingers: 'I loved fishfingers, we hardly ever had them at home' she highlights the difference, whereby her mother 'somehow found it quicker to make a fresh vegetable sabzi than fling something from a packet into a frying pan' (Syal, 1996, p. 54).

Meena worships Anita because she seems to be free, 'I never had to force my admiration, it flowed from every pore because Anita made me laugh like no one else, she gave voice to all the wicked things I had often thought but kept zipped inside my good girl's winter coat' (Syal, 1996, p. 138). Having previously turned to her parents, especially her father, for support and advice, she now begins to turn to Anita and her friends. Her father notes her absence as he says she no longer sits on his knee. She makes increasing use of, first, same-sex friends and then opposite-sex friends for such purposes, for instance, a boy she meets in hospital, Robert and later, Sam Lowbridge. She longs for the same attention as Anita: 'I began wondering if any boy would ever notice me, the way that they always noticed Anita' (Syal, 1996, p. 145) and writes a letter to the problem page of the girls' magazine *Jackie*.

Although Meena's parents may not be fully acquainted with many of her friends, they are acutely aware of her interaction with Anita: 'she's not picking up the right influence here. So many good children to play with and she always finds the bad ones' (Syal, 1996, p. 250). Their interpretation of Anita is made obvious to Meena as they attempt to curb their friendship by denying her time to go out with her. The past is used as a means of reference for the present; as the differences in her behaviour are highlighted and pointed out as her father reprimands her by saying, 'I have watched you change, from a sweet happy girl into some rude, sulky monster' (Syal, 1996, p. 247). This generates an air of hostility: Meena resents her parent's attempt to curb her (Syal, 1996, p. 149). The peer group becomes a dominating factor within her life and consequently her thinking.

Besides feeling restricted by her parents, Meena feels excluded by her mother particularly after the birth of Sunil (her brother) leaves Daljit (her mother) exhausted and drained (Syal, 1996, p. 135). Meena begins to draw comparisons between the mothers of her friends within her peer group, in particular Anita's mother Deirdre, and her own mother, particularly with reference to their leniency. At the local fair, whilst Meena has to sneak out, she is surprised to see Deirdre not only attending the fair but also going on the rides: Meena's feelings of exclusion by her mother disturb her. Her attempts to talk to her mother about the death of their neighbour, Mrs Christmas are received with a rebuke. Meena feels guilty as she believes herself and Anita effectively murdered Mrs Christmas by their annoying behaviour outside her home.

Whilst the exclusion and restriction succeed in creating barriers between herself and her parents, her parents' 'secret' discussions about her behaviour further generate division (Syal, 1996, p. 47). At one of the mehfils (gatherings of individuals, sharing food and conversation) organised by her parents, Meena walks in on her mother talking to her Aunty Shaila about her (Syal, 1996, pp. 117-8): 'to my mortification and in front to the rest of the Mafia, mama actually presented an entire CV of my misdemeanours, including some I'd completely forgotten about' (Syal, 1996, p. 117). Consequently Meena begins to see herself as a victim, and defines her role within the home as nothing but a slave (Syal, 1996, p. 148). She justifies spending time with her friends so that the lack of attention within the home is compensated by that she receives with her peers and therefore concludes that 'my life was outside the home, with Anita, my passport to acceptance within society' (Syal, 1996, p. 148).

Whilst Meena's conflict with her parents centres largely on her inability to control her own behaviour, her understanding of the friendship with Anita and the gang which she claims allows her to assert her individuality is misguided. Meena's involvement with the gang involves a submission to an alternative controlling influence. She looks to Anita for approval at every step. Everything is said and done with the intention of pleasing Anita.

Meena, quite naturally for someone growing up, feels her family are ignorant of the peer context from which she comes. Meena's mother only agrees to invite Anita to dinner as a humane gesture for 'that poor girl' (Syal, 1996, p. 250) whose mother ran off with another man. Meena's anxiety to please her friend is stressed through her attempts to make sure it is perfect, as she sets the table with care, instructs her mother on what to cook and also tells her of appropriate behaviour. During dinner, she has to sit down as opposed to running to and from the kitchen (Syal, 1996, p. 252). However, her friends are ignorant of the family context. The business of allowing someone to enter sacred family ground is perfectly conveyed as Meena realises that Anita was 'the first non-relative to sit and break bread with us' (Syal, 1996, p. 254) and therefore she realises the importance of the occasion: 'I had never eaten Indian food in the presence of a white person before' (Syal, 1996, p. 254). Anita's ill manners and 'her complete lack of emotion or indeed social graces' (Syal, 1996, p. 252) are continually contrasted with that of Meena's own family who do their best 'to engage her in friendly chit chat ... clear of anything that might possibly be connected to mothers' (Syal, 1996, p. 252). Again during dinner, the food and mannerisms are highlighted as Anita 'stopped in mid-chew, looking from her knife and fork to mama and papa's fingers with faint disgust' (Syal, 1996, p. 252). But the other three sit disgusted with Anita, who stares 'unaware that all of us had a great view of a lump of half masticated fishfinger sitting on her tongue' (Syal, 1996, p. 254). This incident evokes the differences between the expectations, the norms and values of those of different cultural backgrounds. Both social worlds generally do not overlap, being a group outside of home and one within the home.

The racist outburst by Sam in the village forces Meena to turn her attention away from Anita and move towards her family. Nevertheless, the detachment from Anita has a profound affect on Meena as her life that evolved around her friends no longer exists. The loneliness and hurt of being alone is strongly evoked, in particular on the next morning when she sees Anita with Fat Sally. Both walk past her house with Meena knowing, 'they did not have to walk this route to get there' (Syal, 1996, p. 197). They deliberately seek to enforce the issue of racial difference by identifying themselves as each other's best friend and thereby excluding Meena. Anita shouts out, 'Sherrie said I could tek me best friend with me – Sally' (Syal, 1996, p. 197). Meena is now seen as a non-person on a pretext of the outburst the day before and thereby her new form of categorisation within the village.

A new element emerges through the relationship Meena has with her visiting grandmother, Nanima. It is significant that Nanima arrives after the incident with Sam, hence Meena's attention is further diverted from Anita and the others to her family. The grandmother's arrival pushes Meena back towards her family. The arrival of Nanima also steers Sunil from her mother; 'Nanima had applied some ancient witchcraft to finally cut the umbilical cord that was slowly strangling both him and us' (Syal, 1996, p. 208). Meena therefore becomes more attached to Sunil and does the chores she had previously neglected. The relationship with Nanima offers Meena a safe context for self-disclosure and for developing new strategies for understanding and dealing with social difficulties. The care-giving role which involves Meena 'looking after' her grandmother and her younger brother, Sunil, is itself a form of preparation for the wider supportive roles likely to arise in adulthood. Meena is deeply affected by Nanima and her embodiment of all that represents India. Consequently she realises the importance of preserving her ethnic identity as she says, 'I desperately wanted to visit India and claim some of the magic as mine' (Syal, 1996, p. 211). Meena also realises the destructive nature of her idolisation of Anita at this point, becoming aware that she has not grasped her own identity, having previously only possessed a one-dimensional concept of her overall persona.

The novel illustrates Meena's diverse social worlds. It opens with Meena's childhood mainly controlled within the home, where social activities were likely to be focused primarily on the family and its environment, as opposed to outside the home. Within both social worlds, adult supervision and control are clearly present. Entry into adolescence leads to less direct supervision and control by adults, more involvement with peers and movement within a wider geographical and social environment (Jackson and Rodriguez-Tome, 1993). School is rarely mentioned at all within the book, as it is largely set during the summer holiday, so school is just a backdrop for the narrative.

Racism 1970s Style

The tensions between Anita and Meena, which culminate in the eventual breakdown of their friendship, are representative of the racialised social tensions within Britain during the 1970s. Syal portrays the ways in which racism constructs difference within a multicultural society. Racism becomes an important influence within the relationship, despite Meena's attempts to ignore it and her failure to see it, and ultimately it succeeds in having a profound effect on her. At first, racism is merely registered as the local shopkeeper's ignorance and tactlessness; however, by the end of the book it is personified in Sam Lowbridge, in an aggressive and overt manner.

Meena's personal and social growth is charted in a context that is at first sensitive and welcoming. Her physical differences are initially defined as exotic and different by other individuals within the village, but this disintegrates into hostility and abusiveness. When Meena gets on the bus, she encounters a barrage of comments from the other passengers that are not derogatory but complimentary: 'ooh, she's a little doll, isn't she? ... Them eyes' (Syal, 1996, p. 20). Meena notes, 'they drew energy from me like a succubus' (Syal, 1996, p. 20). Even when Meena's Nanima arrives, her first trip out into the village draws groups of women who comment on her eyes, her clothes, 'wanting to touch and feel her like an imported piece of exotica' (Syal, 1996, p. 220). It is not until the summer fete that Meena discovers race as a source of pain as opposed to amusement.

There are, however, incidents prior to the ordeal she witnesses with Sam which make Meena aware of her cultural, religious and colour differences. For instance, the local shopkeeper Mr Ormerod automatically assumes the existence of an affinity between Meena's family and people from 'abroad' due to skin colour. Meena's childhood world is confronted with the colonialist ethos of the society around her. The prevailing ideological climate in post-imperial Britain, which still exerts power in its former colonies, involves the notion of a moral duty on the part of the privileged country to assist the development of the 'other' world which happens to be differentiated by skin colour. In this discourse, values are constructed and naturalised which set civilisation and humanity against 'savagery', 'native' or 'primitive' identities as their antitheses and objects of reformation.

For example at school, when the teacher asks the class why the area they are living in was called the 'Black Country', one of the students responds 'B...b...because so m...many darkies...live here' (Syal, 1996, p. 22). This amuses everyone including Meena, who initially laughs with the crowd, only to punch the culprit in anger, 'we were the only Indians that had ever lived in Tollington and that the country looked green if anything to me' (Syal, 1996, p. 22). This incident is largely due to ignorance. Whilst racial differences are highlighted, occasional attempts are made to paper over them with comments such as, 'you're so lovely. You know, I never think of you as, you know a foreigner. You're just like one of us' (Syal, 1996, p. 29), thereby reinforcing the divisions as opposed to smoothing over them.

Despite the recurring references to colour, Meena is not crushed by feelings of alienation and disconnection, but attempts to integrate with the other villagers. The cruelty of racism hits Meena hard when she views it in the form of Sam and his outburst during a village meeting. Meena's prior meetings with Sam indicate an adolescent crush and a belief that she is the object of his attention and affection. When she feels left out as boys notice Anita, it is Sam who notices her and shows concern for her well-being as he asks: 'yow feeling alright chick? You look a bit peaky' (Syal, 1996, p. 145). Meena's concerns at that moment are not about her physical well-being, she yearns for him to kiss her: 'if only he had kissed me, he would have tasted summer strawberries on my lips' (Syal, 1996, p. 145). Meena creates a fantasy world in which she places Sam on an intimate level. However, his racist outburst collapses this make-believe world. Sam bluntly rejects the idea of sending money collected by the village to 'some darkies we've never met' (Syal, 1996, p. 193). Whilst Sam points out his objections to assisting others, he destroys the notion of superiority which is embedded within the colonial ethos: 'We don't give a toss for anybody else. This is our patch. Not some wogs' handout' (Syal, 1996, p. 193).

Sam exaggerates the uniformity within the gathered crowd by referring to 'them' and 'us'. The 'us' excludes Meena and her family as reference is made to colour in the form of the word 'darkies'. Meena is devastated, 'I felt as if I had been punched in the stomach. My legs felt watery and a hot panic softened my insides to mush. It was as if the whole crowd had turned into one huge eyeball which swivelled slowly between me and papa' (Syal, 1996, p. 193). Whilst support for Sam is shown by several of the villagers, Meena is confused. She initially wants to share with them her affinity with Sam: 'I wanted to find these people, tell them Sam Lowbridge was my mate, the boy who had taught me how to shoot a fairground rifle, who terrorised everyone else except me. I was his favourite' (Syal, 1996, p. 194). After the support and admiration for Sam is replaced by abuse, he leaves, and a crowd gathers around Meena's father as the villagers show their disgust at Sam's words, 'offering condolences and back pats like he's just come home last in the annual church egg and spoon race' (Syal, 1996, p. 194).

Meena realises there are situations when Anita cannot console her. This comfort, she realises, is provided by her family. Standing next to Anita, Meena immediately says, 'I wished I had stood next to Papa' (Syal, 1996, p. 193). She senses Anita's discomfort, and wants support at that moment, but realises this cannot be given by her friends: 'I knew she would not hold me or take my hand' (Syal, 1996, p. 193). Whilst Meena gathers her thoughts and regains control of herself to make her way to her father, Anita finally speaks her feelings in admiration and support for Sam: 'wharrabout that then! ... In't he bosting!' (Syal, 1996, p. 195). Anita's comments cause Meena frustration and hurt which culminate in a reprimand: 'Anita Rutter, yow am a bloody stupid cow sometimes' (Syal, 1996, p. 195). She then storms off to her father. Meena is thus betrayed by Anita. Her initial concept of 'us' and 'them' was defined as her peer group versus the adults of the village. She is initially blind to the racial differences between herself and her peer group. The incident forces her to reassess her identity and makes her realise the division between her friends and herself with respect to skin colour. Through this change in perception we see a growth in Meena's understanding of her world as she says, 'I did not need a bra or some blue eye-shadow to appear older, not tonight' (Syal, 1996, p. 197).

Following the incident at the fete, Meena's preoccupation with remaining entwined with the family becomes ineluctable with the arrival of Nanima, her grandmother, from India and hence her withdrawal from everyday activities with Anita. This symbolically cuts Meena off temporarily from the world in which she existed carefree with her peers and forces her back into the family world. This sense of enclosure initially succeeds in inhibiting Meena's ability to respond to the new challenge of re-assessing her identity and position within the social environment. She therefore attempts to close herself off from the outside world and seek refuge within the family.

Whilst Meena is happy at not having to confront reality, her first visit out of the home after Sam's racist outburst clearly shows a different Meena. Bitter, but strong enough to respond to the challenges of the villagers they encounter. The 'cooing' by the women at not only Sunil but also her Nanima infuriates her, as she watches them asking about everything from the teeth in her mouth to the clothes on her back. But there is uncertainty whether they are being genuine; 'I knew they were being friendly, but it was not somehow a meeting of equals, I felt like we were suddenly the entertainment' (Syal, 1996, p. 220). Furthermore, Meena refuses to go into the village shop after she recognises the old man in the shop to be one of the 'church Mafia ... phantom hecklers' (Syal, 1996, p. 223) who had encouraged Sam. Instead, she sends Nanima into collect the groceries. But her observation of the events is interesting. She is now able to put reactions and side glances within their racist context as she notes the old man giving the shopkeeper a 'mocking glance' as he stares at Nanima, but also observes Mr Ormerod's discomfort as he 'bit his lip and looked away' (Syal, 1996, p. 223).

Whilst Meena's ability to cope with the stress of the outburst is shown with her interaction with the shopkeeper, the 'phantom heckler', and the villagers, her interaction with Sam is perhaps the defining moment and demonstrative of the changes that have occurred within her. Having initially doted over Sam and stared at him at every opportunity, Meena's fascination disintegrates to the point of not wanting to look at Sam at all. She avoids his gaze as she talks to him. What is perhaps more frustrating for Meena is Sam's failure to understand the extent of the damage resulting from his outburst. He only reacts when he notices a change in Meena's behaviour towards him as he simply asks, 'are yow angry with me, Meena?' (Syal, 1996, p. 228). Meena's disappointment is further inflamed by knowing his gang 'were on the verge of having a huge laugh at Nanima's expense' (Syal, 1996, p. 228). Having witnessed her grandmother being mocked and experiencing feelings of guilt, Meena looks directly at the gang as a confrontational message; the gang responds by immediately falling silent. The ability to do this has more of a profound effect on Meena as she feels elevated and powerful. Meena emerges from the first day out after the incident as stronger and recognises herself as superior. The humiliation of the events at the fete and the subsequent feelings outweigh the insignificance of idle chit-chat. Meena begins to see herself as a victim, believing that Sam has 'taken away my innocence' (Syal, 1996, p. 227), but she also knows that 'there was nothing in the world I could do to them that would have the same impact that would affect him so deeply and for so long' (Syal, 1996, p. 227).

Even before this incident of racism, Syal illustrates the way racism affects Meena and her family, allowing the reader to grasp the political issues of which Meena is not yet conscious, yet of which she painfully becomes aware. Meena's uncles and father talk about 'Powell's Bloody River' (Syal, 1996, p. 165), the politics involved when the family first arrive to calls of 'no Irish, blacks or dogs' (Syal, 1996, p. 165) and the problems of finding a job. Even when Daljit gives birth to Sunil and complains of feeling the pain of stitches, she is dismissively told, 'oh, you Asian ladies have a very low pain threshold' (Syal, 1996, p. 132).

Meena is too immature to understand the issues, but more importantly they do not yet relate directly to her own experiences. An outing with her mother turns into a nightmare when the car begins to slide back down the hill. Meena asks the drivers behind to move their cars back. Whilst they comply, Meena notes they do so with an 'amused expression, as if my mother's driving had only confirmed some secret, long-held opinion of how people like us were coping with the complexities of the modern world' (Syal, 1996, pp. 96-7). But one lady in the queue resorts to verbal abuse 'bloody stupid wog, stupid woggy wog, stupid' (Syal, 1996, p. 97). Meena's response is horror, 'I backed off as if I had been punched' (Syal, 1996, p. 97). She feels 'hurt, angry, confused and horribly powerless because this kind of hatred could not be explained' (Syal, 1996, p. 97). While Meena wants to tell her father about it, she realises 'what had happened to me must have happened to papa countless times' (Syal, 1996, p. 98). She is therefore able to understand why, during Sam's outburst, 'papa was staring into the distance, seemingly unconcerned, gripping his bottle of whisky, like a weapon' (Syal, 1996, p. 193). Whilst the incident with the old lady upsets Meena, it is not referred to again because it does not have the same impact as the incident with Sam. Sam's outburst affects her because she knew him and felt an affinity with him, whereas the woman was a stranger, and this made the encounter less upsetting.

Constructing a Hybrid Identity

Whilst racism has a profound affect on Meena's childhood, so do both of the cultures she inhabits. Syal succeeds in presenting two different, often conflicting images of the minority and indigenous culture as she explores the life of the protagonist. Meena experiences living between the two different worlds. She spends the day outside the home at school and returns to a 'little India' in the world preserved by her parents and 'extended' family, connected not only by blood but by something stronger, by India. The novel shows how she is drawing upon both to construct a sense of her own place in the world.

The notion of community is crucial in the construction of a South Asian identity within the text. The novel asserts a mythical unity of ethnic imagined communities which divides the world between 'us' and 'them'. For instance, it examines how immigration has developed an identity politics that homogenises the 'us', for instance, the recollections of the Powell days as a shared history (Syal, 1996, p. 165) becomes acknowledged at one of the mehfils. This mythical unity also assumes all members of the group are equally positioned as they discuss the racism encountered and the issue of family in India. But this collective identity involves the construction of boundaries and differences. Thus, when Daljit is in hospital, Mrs Worrall's offer of help to set up a 'rota': 'For Mr K. Mek sure him and the littl'un eat and that' (Syal, 1996, p. 130) is rejected by Aunty Shaila who replies, 'oh don't you worry. We will see to that' (Syal, 1996, p. 130). Aunty Shaila identifies Mrs Worral as an outsider in which race plays a particularly significant part, linked to specific cultural codes. Furthermore Meena notes the deliberate exclusion of white people within their home, 'every weekend was taken up with visiting Indian families or being invaded by them' (Syal, 1996, p. 29). However 'only once had any of our neighbours been invited in further than the step of our back door' (Syal, 1996, p. 29).

Meena recognises the role of the community whereby her Aunties' role gave them the right to discipline another's child. It becomes an example of how the minority is homogeneous, speaking with a unified cultural voice, each allowed to teach anyone's children. Whilst this irritates Meena, she notes, 'Individually the aunties were a powerful force ... but together they were a formidable Mafia whose collective approval was a blessing' (Syal, 1996, p. 33). She nevertheless accepts it, but begins to realise her perception of her family is encompassed within the boundaries of the extended family which integrates the members of the community. Whilst there is annoyance expressed at the interference of the adopted aunties and uncles, Meena realises the importance of this notion of family, 'I know how intensely my parents valued these people they so readily renamed as family, faced with the loss of their own blood relations' (Syal, 1996, p. 31).

The contrasts established between the minority and indigenous cultures is an important construct within the novel. This not only defines differences but generates a form of racism whereby Meena's parents and friends discuss themselves as morally superior to the English. Comments such as, 'you're just like one of us' (Syal, 1996, p. 29) would be acknowledged politely as Meena's mother 'would smile and graciously accept this as a compliment' (Syal, 1996, p. 29). However, when Daljit is in the company of her 'own' friends, she would join them in 'gently poking fun at the habits of her English friends' (Syal, 1996, p. 29). These 'habits' include gardening, which is ridiculed and criticised and where the English are devalued and likened to dogs: 'gnomes, wells and the like was an English thing. They have to mark their territory ... like dogs' (Syal, 1996, p. 33). The practices of South Asian families are portrayed as the model of a good society, and a contrast emerges in comparison with the English family. The latter is criticised with reference to the respect denied to elders, as Meena's mother says, 'I will never understand this about the English, all this puffing up about being civilised with their cucumber sandwiches and cradle of democracy big talk and then they turn round the kick their elders in the backside' (Syal, 1996, pp. 58-9).

Snippets of conversations within Meena's home occasionally involve the women disgusted at the hygiene tactics of the indigenous populace: 'they don't like bathing, and when they do, they sit in their own dirty water instead of showering' (Syal, 1996, p. 33) and the way they wash up, 'they never rinse the soap off the dishes' (Syal, 1996, p. 33). Here these voices of the South Asian community are constructed to make themselves as distinct from the indigenous population as possible. These differences become elevated, as characteristics of the 'other', the majority indigenous culture are devalued. Therefore, the more traditional and distant from the majority culture, the more elevated the minority culture is perceived. The construction of this binary succeeds in creating a superior culture that rejects White Eurocentric culture, especially in its crudest form. This sense of elevation also has a class dimension, as Daljit criticises her daughter for not speaking and behaving properly. The South Asian community is constructed as the ideal, positive model, which claims to represent the true essence of humanistic behaviour through a collective culture with a sense of cleanliness and morality.

In fact, the tension that exists between Meena's parents and Anita arises in their disapproval of her background and antics. For instance, the naming of their dog 'nigger' outrages Daljit as she says, 'these no good ignorant English' (Syal, 1996, p. 90), as they show a lack of awareness of the insulting weight of that word. However this snobbish attitude is criticised by Deirdre who asks Daljit outright if Meena has been stopped from seeing her daughter; 'Cos we ain't good enough for yow lot, is that it?' (Syal, 1996, p. 215). When Meena is told off by Mr Christmas for making a noise outside his home she finds this shameful: 'to be told off by a white person ... that was letting down the whole Indian nation' (Syal, 1996, p. 45).

Meena finds herself torn between the 'super-civilised' world of her strict middle-class parents and the earthier lives of her White working class neighbours.

Meena's ambition in life is to be worthy of the attention of Anita Rutter but at the same time to appease her parents; the result is a clash of two cultures, Indian respectability versus western liberalism. Meena becomes the symbol of an attempt to construct a cultural hybridity in wanting to wear mini-skirts and jeans, not shalwaar kameez in garish and flamboyant colours. She wants Diwali and Christmas presents and fish and chips instead of chapati and dhal. The notion of hybridity, which is relevant to Meena, fails to have significance for others, even to Meena's cousins, Pinky and Baby. However, her family and others impose an identity on her. It takes some time for Meena to realise that a contradiction exists between parental expectations and her own lifestyle, manifested in her failure to get along with her prissy cousins and her tomboyish behaviour 'I knew I was a freak of some kind, too mouthy, clumsy and scabby to be a real Indian girl, too Indian to be a real Tollington wench' (Syal, 1996, p. 150). Nonetheless, she claims that 'living in the grey area between all categories felt increasingly like home' (Syal, 1996, p. 150). Essentially, Meena struggles to find an identity in between her South Asian tradition, her British upbringing and her own fantasy world.

Ultimately, the more time Meena spends with Anita, the more English she feels. She looks forward to spending time with Anita as it allows her free rein as opposed to being steered in the way her parents would like her to behave. Meena's parents cannot understand what has occurred in Meena after she befriends Anita. It is Meena's gender that becomes a relevant consideration in the way her parents view her behaviour. In their value system, 'nice' South Asian girls do not behave as she does. They are supposed to be feminine, like her cousins. Her mother reproaches her: 'why behave like a boy all the time. Stand with your legs together. Why don't you grow your hair, do you want to be a boy, Meena?' (Syal, 1996, p. 30). Whilst the constant rebukes by her parents gets annoying for Meena, this confrontation underlines how women are usually expected to reproduce their ethnic identity. Women not only need to bear children but need to reproduce the community's own culture. Her parents point out the roles women play in the cultural construction of collectivities, by attempting to persuade Meena to consort with Pinky and Baby as well as to adopt more feminine behaviour.

The first generation's feelings about being in Britain are different to Meena's. Meena knows of no other culture and witnesses her adopted 'extended' family despairing at their life in Britain: 'my aunties did not rage against fate or England when they swapped misery tales, they put everything down to the will of bhagwan' (Syal, 1996, p. 67). Leaving their family back in India ... 'the loss of a distant parent would be the final proof, that they had left them and would not be returning' (Syal, 1996, p. 86). Rather than changing due to influences from the indigenous population, the first generation retains its cultural identity by celebrating it through family gatherings, or mehfils. These mehfils become a forum for re-affirming one's own identity. Meena talks about her father's mehfils, where 'our usual crowd plus a few dozen extra families would squeeze themselves in to our house to hear papa and selected uncles sing their favourite Urdu ghazals and Punjabi ok song' (Syal, 1996, p. 71). Meena's father like his friends are all marooned in England, they temper the traumatic memories of Indian partition and the racism they face now by visiting each other's houses, singing ghazals and exchanging jokes and gossip. It is significant that during these mehfils Meena learns a great deal of her parents' past as they discuss life during partition (Syal, 1996, p. 73) and life in Britain in the form of the racism they experienced. But Meena also feels rejection as her parents talk about a life and culture prior to her. Only Nanima's first visit brings tales and stories of life in India that Meena identifies with, saying, 'I desperately wanted to visit India and claim some of the magic as mine' (Syal, 1996, p. 211).

Whilst the text largely focuses on her parent's disapproval of their daughter's interaction with Anita, there are occasions when they favour this hybridisation of cultures. Daljit instructs Meena how to make use of the indigenous culture as she says, 'you take the best from their culture, not the worst' (Syal, 1996, p. 53) and rebukes her daughter on her use of English, 'just because the English can't speak English themselves, does not mean you have to talk like an urchin' (Syal, 1996, p. 53). Furthermore, Meena's parents generate a sense of cultural hybridity by celebrating not only Diwali, but also Christmas, as well as allowing Meena to attend church services. They believe the latter to be nothing extraordinary, justifying it by saying, 'every path leads to the same god' (Syal, 1996, p. 92) and besides, according to her father, 'they just read and play, nothing much religious really ... it keeps them out of the cold and out of mischief' (Syal, 1996, p. 92). However, a dissenting view is expressed through Aunty Shaila: 'you will confuse the girl' (Syal, 1996, p. 92), although Meena's parents choose to ignore her. For Meena the celebration of Diwali in the context of Britain is disappointing. Using the discourse of the majority to explain the minority fails to satisfy Meena who makes a comparison: 'No-one else in the world seemed to care that today was our Christmas, there was no holiday, no tinsel, or blinking Christmas trees ... no James Bond films or Disney spectaculars on the telly and nobody, not one person had wished me a happy Diwali ... everyone's indifference had stunned me' (Syal, 1996, pp. 91-2).

Syal also presents limits of cultural hybridity, when it becomes difficult and at times even impossible to challenge and negotiate differences across cultures. For instance, Meena's mother rejects gardening as just an 'English thing' (Syal, 1996, p. 33), and it is a constant source of embarrassment. She wants her family to fit in with the local villagers and have flowers in the garden. However Meena's attempts to persuade her mother fail as she rejects gardening on moral grounds and refuses to have anything whatsoever to do with it.

Whilst the text focuses on its protagonist Meena, the experiences of her parents are also revealed, especially with regard to their placement and displacement within Britain. Meena's mother, 'being a simple Punjabi girl ...' (Syal, 1996, p. 9) experienced dire conditions of post-immigration 'living in a shabby boarding house room with another newly arrived immigrant family' (Syal, 1996, p. 9) where Meena had to sleep in a drawer. Syal also reveals patriotism to the culture of origin. Even though India is the country the immigrants have left behind, the loyalty does not, however, die out; it is very much part of their lives in Britain. Meena recites the example of when Miss India won the Miss World competition, as she presents the excitement and admiration her parents' friends have at the news. The incident has more esteem and importance than the actual event as it counteracted popular belief and 'confirmed that Indian women were the brainiest and the most beautiful in the world' (Syal, 1996, p. 166). The whole text is imbued with a sense of patriotism and strong attachment to cultural identity.

From Novel to Film

The film adaptation of *Anita and Me,* directed by Metin Huseyin, was released at the end of 2002, six years after the novel was published. Together with *My Beautiful Laundrette*, *Bhaji on the Beach, East Is East* and *Bend it like Beckham, Anita and Me* forms the latest addition to a distinctively British South Asian genre. The earlier films have largely focused on the pains of growing up for young adults, whilst *Anita and Me* features an 11-12 year old girl. The passage from childhood innocence to young adulthood is a subject that has not often found expression in British films, aside from *Kes* and *Billy Elliot.* Yet when *Anita and Me* was screened in the cinemas it received a lukewarm reception in contrast to *Bend it like Beckham,* which emerged a few months before it.

As a film *Anita and Me* has been criticised as 'nothing but a messy and irritating jumble of a few reliable formulas' (Waldron-Mantgani, 2002). It has been criticised for containing the same recipe that was seen in those films which preceded it, and it is almost as if audiences had become bored with this formula. But as a film emerging from a novel the constraints might be related to the actual content of the original text as it is narrated by one young girl. However, as is apparent from the preceeding analysis the novel is a much richer text than the film, it contains such detail that the characters are more rounded and not one dimensional as they appear in the film. The novel conveys a sense of being grounded in social reality and real experiences, as it discusses issues of racism, community, generation, and migration that the film fails to address convincingly. The film remains a text about two girls and their friendship, and little else is developed to make the film more convincing. The novel seems more effective in that it has more detail regarding sub-plots that contextualise Meena's experiences and personal development, whereas the film jumps over these, treating them as mundane issues, which are often so important, to create more dramatisation for sensational purposes.

The movie seems to show Meena whining about how dissatisfied she is, how her parents do not understand her. In comparison, the book is far more perceptive. We are able to locate the character within the context about which she complains so vociferously, and consequently the reader is enticed to have more sympathy with her predicament. Because the film refuses to develop this empathy, it ultimately becomes tiresome after a while. It is difficult for the audience to understand why she gives her parents a difficult time, why she does not want to eat curry and prefers fish fingers instead, and questions her mother about not having a garden that equates to the gnome and flower-filled gardens of their neighbours. Such moods are those of a spoilt brat. In the film, Meena is in a constant state of resentment and dissatisfaction, and tries to make herself sound witty and deep. Although she learns to appreciate things more by the end, even then, she only changes to a certain extent, and it is difficult to feel any empathy for the character on anything but a theoretical level.

As a popular film shown to audiences in cinemas, it is hard to understand how the director expects the audience to identify with Meena. The concerns of the girl and her family are presented as being contained within the South Asian community, despite being the only Indian family in the village, so that the film deals with what have become predictable ingredients of British South Asian cinema, a young girl feeling stifled by her family and the ongoing racism, and the movement into new and much better horizons. For *Anita and Me* to achieve the successes of *Bend it like Beckham* would be difficult, as the better film was more appealing due to its very title – it had the name of a world famous footballer. *Anita and Me* is very different in that respect, having to rely on its 'stars' with a TV background, and the reputation of the novel for marketing.

The film appeals to some audiences through its use of nostalgia for the 1970s. The nostalgia of the film is apparent through its visual style. Huseyin uses slightly reddish, brownish filters that are supposed to remind us of 8mm home movies, so that it evokes a sense of nostalgia, and is reminiscent of the time in mining communities before the disintegration that followed in the wake of the 1984-5 miners' strike, which featured in *Billy Elliot*.

The casting of already known TV stars from British comedies works within the film, and is one of its main strengths for the audience. Syal from (*Goodness Gracious Me, The Kumars at No 42*) appears in the film as the terrifying Aunt Shaila, it also features Sanjeev Bhaskar (also from *Goodness Gracious Me* and *The Kumars at No 42*), Mark Williams (*The Fast Show*) and Kathy Burke (*Harry Enfield & Chums*, among others). However, none of these characters can quite break out of their stereotypes – Redgrave's shopkeeper, Williams' confused priest, Beesley's long-haired hippie. They all seem like stock characters who are well-used in the plot, but are not developed in a way comparable to the equivalent characters in the novel. The most convincing is Zohra Segal as Meena's grandmother. Using Meena Syal to play Meena's auntie fails to be convincing, as it is a caricature of an 'aunty ji'. These supporting performances are no more than adequate, perhaps because the screenplay fails to examine their characters in any great depth.

The characterisation of Meena's parents work well with Sanjeev Bhaskar and Ayesha Dharker playing convincing supporting roles; however, we are only told their story through Meena's perspective. The narration within the novel is effective with Meena, however, it is much less so within the film. The film never really presents the parents' perspective on events, only their dialogue and Meena's responses to them. For instance, when Meena asks her father if he fought in the war, his response is deep and meaningful 'We fought. We fought poverty, we fought the British, we fought those people who got through the short cuts. Nobody gave us medals.' Yet Meena's response is nothing except eye rolling showing her naivity.

Putting unknown faces in the main roles works well. Chandeep Uppal plays naive and immature Meena and Anita is played by Anna Brewster. Yet neither of them are exceptional to watch, they never really make the characters their own. Anita and Meena in the text of the original novel are far stronger than in the visual image. Anita in the film appears too adult. She is, according to Meena Syal, the embodiment of three of her friends rolled into one. However, Anita appears much more mature than Meena, such that one questions whether the relationship between them is believable. Anita is a blonde bombshell who struts around Tollington with her shiny plastic red coat, has sex and a more cynical outlook. In contrast, Meena appears as an average girl, who cycles around on her bike with a naive view of events around her. Anita is not fleshed out as a character, and also appears very distant, almost unknowable.

The film highlights how oblivious those living in Tollington are of issues around racism. Huseyin evokes a Tollington where political correctness has not yet been invented, as no one notices when Anita's mum (played by Kathy Burke) casually tells her youngest daughter the name of the black poodle she brings home one day is 'nigger'. Reading this in the novel is quite different to seeing the ignorance on screen.

The film mirrors *Bend it like Beckham* in that it shows Meena, like Jess, has hopes and desires that contrast with the conservative traditions at home. Both use mechanisms of first person narration to convey to the audience the protagonists' inner thoughts and emotions, as Jess talks to the image of Beckham, and Meena writes a diary. The voiceover in *Anita and Me* works to some extent, but in *Beckham* the narration is more effective when Jess verbalises her thoughts. The voiceover narration becomes too long and intrusive in *Anita and Me*.

The book *Anita and Me* functions as a serious novel as well as a comedy in the way it handles social issues; however, the film fails in this respect. The film flippantly presents these serious social and political issues. Whilst *Beckham* touched on the genuine problems of teenagers and their friendships and the questions of culture and ethnicity and betrayal, when the same issues are presented in *Anita and Me* they are handled differently. Meena's attraction to Anita is purely due to her rebellious nature. It is a more immature depiction of the issues that are presented more maturely in *Bend it like Beckham*.

The film is able to show sarcasm and humour; Meena's parents pride themselves in the area they live in. 'Look at the view', her father tells family friends who drop by to visit. Huseyin shows the view of two rows of terraced housing leading to a field which has rubble in the foreground, a factory beyond the field and a white family beating each other in the street outside the last house. Furthermore the Kumars speak English eloquently in contrast to the natives. When Deidre asks Meena's mother, 'Yow tin yower better den oos?' she responds back in proper English politely instead of the aggression she's just experienced. This contrast is used throughout the film and highlighted constantly to show the Indian family as more English than the English themselves. Meena's mother appears elegant and well refined, in contrast to Deidre who potters around in her heels and clothes that look two sizes too small for her.

What the film does is show a combination of comedy and seriousness. The scene when Meena performs 'Gimme Dat Thing' at one of her parents' mehfils follows a scene with an undercurrent of seriousness, with references to Enoch Powell and a subtle evocation of the casual racism of the period. For instance, the engineer attending the meal is later found beaten almost to death by the local racists. An event that is followed by Meena's mother's descent into depression. All this is seriously presented. Occasionally, Huseyin handles the switches between the two moods well (such as in the scenes with Meena's grandmother) but the film still feels uneven in places. Overall it lacks the dramatic bite to portray honestly the racial tensions of the period. In comparison, the novel works better in this respect.

Ultimately, Meena Syal's screenplay is flawed; the transition from book to screen has not been successful in a number of respects. The written text works much better than the visual text of the film. Whilst Meena heads off to new horizons there is no such luck for Anita. Brewster carries her flippant attitude through to the end of the film and leaves you with the impression that Anita is headed for self-destruction.

Because the film centres on the relationship between Anita and Meena, and the relationship fails to go anywhere, the narrative lacks a clear direction. In contrast, the novel is more complex and layered, and this substitutes for the lack of a clear resolution. The film retains the same narrator as the novel – Meena. However, incidents that precipitate a deeper understanding of characters or events seem no longer as effective in the film as in the text. The other characters as they appear in the film are one-dimensional.

Conclusion

The film adaptation of *Anita and Me* followed in the wake of those critical and commercial successes of British South Asian cinema *East is East* and *Bend it like Beckham*. Although it drew on the exceptional talents of a cast of widely known stars of British television comedies, the film was not as successful as its predecessors. What is significant here is that neither of the two earlier films was developed from novels, although *East is East* was developed from stage productions. Watching cinematic adaptations of novels has enraged audiences ever since they have been adapted into films. After having become acquainted with the characters, plot, and atmosphere of the story via the printed word, the audience has already developed preconceptions regarding these, and therefore measures the film adaptation against these expectations.

As the protagonist in *Anita and Me* is a child, she becomes part of the novel's social and political vision, which is controlled by its author as the novel is part auto-biography. Meena's experiences are not only crucial for her own personal development, but they are also an illustration of the novel's central theme of cultural confusion and insecurity. However, using a child as its protagonist has its drawbacks, as the child's view of life as documented in the novel is limited to her naive perceptions and awareness, which can often become frustrating for the reader. At times, the two groups focused upon are wearisomely predictable. The over-the-top clean-cut and cute Aunties are contrasted with the White working class women and the language that is used wavers between earthy words like 'lav-brush' and eleborate metaphors that are tiresomely long (O'Sullivan, 1996). The prose is sometimes stumbling and inelegant, perhaps deliberately to relay the honesty of what is being portrayed; nevertheless it is often vulgar at times when perhaps it need not be.

A progression towards maturity is explored through the theme of childhood within the text, in relation to both physical growth and perception. Syal endows Meena with a full complement of self-awareness, wit and intelligence. Her quality of perception improves so that she develops her ability to perceive the environment and those around her accurately. Innocence is brought through a rite of passage process into a realisation of identity, sexuality and responsibility. Syal also aims to bring out the confusion of British South Asian youth and the culture clashes involved, but she depicts confrontation and adjustment in simplistic terms. She polarises the culture clash between South Asian and White people, when in reality the clash occurs with the other races and cultures that make up Britain.

Chapter 8

Conclusion

This book has argued for the existence of a body of creative works in recent British literature and cinema that expresses the distinctive identities of British South Asian women. These creative products explore the issues of hyphenated identities, which are interwoven within the actual structure through motifs and the assimilation of untranslated words within texts.

It is significant that the emergence of this creative endeavour has reworked the language of representation. Women authors write themselves into their own history: they articulate differences in a narrative which is also expressed in their own terms of reference (Parmar, 1990). Among the themes they address are the different ways that aspects of the 'host' or 'majority' culture are perceived by women brought up and educated within that culture, compared to the perceptions and valued judgements of their elders. Culture, by definition, is acquired within a given social context or a given set of parallel contexts, within which the individual has to learn about such ideas as race and gender. The issues related to both gender and race have become the core issues within the writing of the British South Asian women's writings and films considered here. They are an underlying feature of their everyday lives. However, it is the way in which they deal with these issues of contention that is the essence of the writing, as it shows a battling of self-worth alongside preconceived notions of identity, which are interwoven within stereotypical notions of South Asian womanhood. Thus, the identity that is explored is not only specific and individual but embraces a collective identity of South Asian women in Britain.

The book has drawn upon recent theoretical debates around diaspora and cultural hybridity. These theoretical tools have been put to work in the interpretation of the texts and films created by British South Asian women. Furthermore, by drawing upon the contemporary sociology of ethnic minority communities in Britain and considering the developments within the Black feminist movement, these creative products have been re-located within the communities, political conflicts and social movements from which they originated. This has facilitated a very empirical approach to the politics of the authenticity (Gilroy, 1993) of these texts and films, particularly in terms of their thematic concerns and verisimilitude from the perspective of a South Asian woman.

Generational differences are central themes in the novels and films that have been considered. The context of these is the way in which the first generation have been shaped by the experiences of migration and racism. The second generation have been influenced by both the country which they have been born into, and the culture of their parents. Consequently, the second generation have become cultural navigators. Furthermore, this has been a highly gendered process, with women experiencing more constraints than their second generation male peers. The first generation still feel that they are temporary visitors, whilst for the second generation Britain really *is* home.

Social and political struggles, in the form of the Black feminist movement, have been central to the emergence of South Asian women's cultural voice in Britain. These struggles were not just about everyday grievances, but also raised fundamental issues about identity, the political meaning of 'Black', and 'South Asian'. The overall unity in the face of racism created a context within which women of diverse ethnic groups were able to explore their ethnicity and clarify the issues that were specific to their own communities. The movement was the midwife of their creativity. It provided the networks of support for authors and artists, sympathetic audiences, and even some early access to commercial, if small scale, publishing ventures. From today's perspective of commercial success for a few British South Asian women it would be easy to forget this history. Many of the themes and issues identified as grievances by the movement have been reflected within the literature produced by those associated with it.

The literature and films that have been the focus of the chapters above reveal the plurality of identities with in the category 'South Asian', and they challenge the dominant stereotypes of South Asian women in Britain. The discussion of the New Woman in South Asian and diasporic literature has drawn out the differences between the literature produced in the sub-continent and that produced in Britain. The literature from South Asia is mostly concerned with issues around femininity contained within a patriarchal society. In contrast, although femininity is a central theme of the literature produced by diasporic women, it is contained within the experience of migration, settlement, racism and ethnic identity in a hostile society. They share an attempt to represent the suffocation felt by many women due the prescription of their social roles. Hence the centrality of the New Woman in this literature who seeks to escape and to assert her own individuality against social constraints. South Asia functions as the cultural centre to the lives of first generation migrants in Britain. It is 'home'. However, for the second generation, South Asia functions not as 'home' but as a more abstract representation of ethnic identity. It defines their diasporic identity, their ethnicity within British society.

Films written and directed by British South Asian women have become increasingly popular. Together with other films by and about South Asians in Britain it is now possible to speak of a distinctive genre of British South Asian cinema that manages to be both authentic and popular. The experience of life in the diaspora is central to Gurinda Chadha's films considered here. The protagonists, their motivations, the themes, the use of music, and the very language of the dialogue mark this cinema as characteristically South Asian and British. Furthermore, her films take various icons and emblems of 'White Britain', for instance football, David Beckham and the seaside holiday, and redefine them as culturally plural, open to many cultural claims, so that David Beckham can be as inspirational to a South Asian girl as he can be to a White girl. In this way, Chadha's cinema has redefined what it means to be British, it has opened up the cultural space of Britishness to alternative identifications. It has desified British cinema.

Brick Lane explores a relatively new South Asian community in Britain. In locating itself within the Bangladeshi community themes of migration and changing gender roles are to the fore. The central character, Nazneen, undergoes a long transformation towards some kind of independence. However, there are several major flaws in the novel. It reads as if it is set entirely in the 1970s in the manner in which represents the everyday life of the Bangladeshi community, although much of it is set in the 1990s. Racism is represented symbolically through the graffiti and leaflets of right-wing groups, but the characters never come face to face with it unlike real South Asian people. *Brick Lane* sits astride the boundary between an authentic South Asian novel and the commercial demands of publishers to appeal to a wider largely White audience.

Meena Syal is one of the best known British South Asian celebrities due to her work in television. However, she is also an accomplished author, and her novel *Anita and Me* and the film adaptation of it have been the focus of the analysis here. Whilst the other novels and films concentrate on older teenagers or adults, the protagonist in *Anita and Me* is going through the confusions of later childhood and early adolescence. The novel and film are set in the 1970s at a peak of racist mobilisation and features Meena in a small mining village. Whilst she is outwardly accepted by the villagers, there is an undercurrent of racism that leads to confrontation. Meena has to create for herself a combination of her parents' culture and the one she is growing up in. The film adaptation was released some time after *Bend it like Beckham*, and it benefited from the earlier film's success.

These commercial successes have led to British South Asian women's creativity moving into different arenas. After the success of *Bend it like Beckham*, Gurinder Chadha's latest film *Bride and Prejudice* 'desifies' Jane Austen's *Pride and Prejudice.* No longer content in restricting her film productions to Britain, Chadha has set her new film in five different locations, London, Amritsar, Goa, Mumbai, and Los Angeles. Whilst this reflects the commercial appeal of her work, it also underlines the global reach of the South Asian diaspora. What Chadha is trying to do is to make it attractive to South Asian audiences, so that Austen's Bennets of the novel become the Bakshis in the film, and like the Bennets, the Bakshis are looking for suitable boys for their daughters. According to Chadha, the film, is a: 'global production as most of the people living in London are Punjabi British. I want to show a multicultural blend in the film' (Chadha, 2003).

Increasingly, South Asian and even British filmmakers in Britain are now venturing to make movies, Bollywood style, to create a 'British Bollywood'. The 'masala formula' consisting of melodrama, bursting into song, and action sequences are utilised by artists, for example Meena Syal's collaboration as the scriptwriter for Andrew Lloyd Webber's *Bombay Dreams*. It is an essentially western musical performed almost entirely in English, but drawing upon the spectacle of Bollywood. Its cast is largely South Asian yet the language is English with a couple of Hindi words.

In the 1970s, British South Asian women's literature was rather narrow in its concerns and audience. Principally concerned with the immediate impact of migration and closely associated with the Black feminist movement it was ignored by mainstream commercial publishing. However, during the 1990s and into the twenty-first century, the literature has attracted more attention from commercial publishers. The cultural activities of British South Asian women are now regarded to be of sufficient commercial significance as to attract the major investments that are required for film production.

Bibliography

Adams, C. (1987), *Across Seven Seas and Thirteen Rivers*, THAP Books, London.
Afsar, H. (1989), 'Gender Roles and the Moral Economy of Kin Among Pakistani Women in West Yorkshire', *New Community*, 15 (2), pp. 211-225.
Agard, S. (1987), 'The Blackbird', in Cobham, R. and Collins, M. (eds), *Watchers and Seekers*, Women's Press, London, p. 89.
Ahmad. F., Modood, T. and Lissenburgh, S. (2003), South Asian women and Employment in Britain: The Interaction of Gender and Ethnicity: Policy Studies Institute, London.
Ahmad, R. (1988), *Right of Way*, Women's Press, London.
Ahmad, R. (1991), 'What's Happening to the Women's Presses', *Spare Rib*, May, pp. 10-13.
Ahmad, R. (1994), *Flaming Spirit*, Virago, London.
Akram, A. (1974-75), 'Pakistani Migrants in Britain: A Note', *New Community*, 4 (1), pp. 116-118.
Alexander, C.E. (2000), *The Asian Gang: Ethnicity, Identity, Masculinity*, Berg, Oxford.
Ali, M. (2003), *Brick Lane*, Doubleday, London.
Alibhai-Brown, Y. (2000), *Who Do We Think We Are? Imagining New Britain*, London, Allen Lane/Penguin, pp. 216.
Amos, V. and Parmar, P. (1984), 'Challenging Imperial Feminism', *Feminist Review*, 17, pp. 3-20.
Anderson, M. and Buckley, M. (1988), *Women, Equality and Europe*, Macmillan, London.
Anthias, F. and Yuval-Davis, N. (eds) (1989), *Woman-Nation-State*, Macmillan, London.
Anthias, F. and Yuval-Davis, N. (1992), *Racialised Boundaries*, Routledge, London.
Anwar, M. (1998), *Between Cultures: Continuity and Change in the Lives of Young Asians*, Routledge, London.
Anwar, M. (1979), *Myth of Return: Pakistanis in Britain*, Heinemann Educational, London.
Aziz, R. (1997), 'Feminism and the Challenge of Racism: Deviance or Difference', in Mirza, H.S. (ed.), *Black British Feminism*, Routledge, London.
Bagguley, P. and Hussain, Y. (2003), 'Bend it like Beckham', *Feminist Media Studies*, pp. 359-61.
Bailey, C. (2003) *Bend a Blast: Bend it like Beckham Makes History*, www.nowtoronto.com/issues/2003-03-06/movie_reviews2.php.
Bailey, L.J. (1990), *Black Women's Writing and Its Significance for the Sociology of Gender, Race and Class*, MSc Dissertation, Bradford University.
Bains, J. and Johal, S. (1998), *Corner Flags and Corner Shops: The Asian Football Experience*, Gollancz, London.
Bald, S.R. (1995), 'Negotiating Identity on the Metropolis', in King, R., Connell, J. and White, P. (eds), *Writing Across Worlds, Literature and Migration*, Routledge, London.
Ballard, R. (ed.) (1994), *Desh Pardesh, The South Asian Presence in Britain*, Hurst, London.
Ballard, R. (1992), 'The South Asian Presence in Britain and its Transnational Connections', in Singh, H. and Vertovec, S. (eds), *Culture and Economy in the Indian Diaspora*, Routledge, London.
Ballard, R. (1994), 'Introduction: The Emergence of Desh Pardesh', in R. Ballard (ed.), *Desh Pardesh: The South Asian Presence in Britain*, Hurst and Company, London.
Barrett, M. (1980), *Women's Oppression Today*, Verso, London.

Barot, R., Bradley, H. and Fenton, S. (1999), 'Rethinking Ethnicity and Gender', in R. Barot, H. Bradley and S. Fenton (eds), *Ethnicity, Gender and Social Change*, Macmillan, London.
Bell, C. (1971), *Community Studies, An Introduction to the Sociology of the Local Community*, Allen and Unwin, London.
Bennet, T. (2000), *Popular Music and Youth Culture: Music, Identity and Place*, Macmillan, London.
Berthoud, R. (2000), *Family Formation in Multicultural Britain: Three Patterns of Diversity*, Institute for Social and Economic Research, Working Paper 2000-34, Essex, University of Essex.
Bhabha, H. (1994), *The Location Of Culture*, London, Routledge.
Bhachu, P. (1996), 'The Multiple Landscapes of Transnational Asian Women in Diaspora', in Amit-Talai, V. and Knowles, C. (eds), *Re-Situating Identities: The Politics of Race, Ethnicity, Culture*, Broadview, Canada.
Bhattacharyya, G. and Gabriel, J. (1994), 'Black British Film in The 1990s – Gurinder Chadha and the Apna Generation', *Third Text*, Summer.
Bhatti, G. (1999), *Asian Children at Home and at School: An Ethnographic Study*, Routledge, London.
Bhavnani, K.K. (1989), 'Complexity, Activism, Optimism, An interview With Angela Davis', *Feminist Review*, 31, pp. 66-81.
Bhavnani, K.K. and Coulson, M. (1986), 'Transforming Socialist Feminism, The Challenge of Racism in Socialist Feminist', *Feminist Review*, 23, pp. 81-92.
Bhavnani, K.K. and Phoenix, A. (1994), *Shifting Identities Shifting Racism*, Sage, London.
Bhopal, K. (1997), *Gender, 'Race' and Patriarchy. A Study of South Asian Women*, Ashgate, Aldershot.
Boxer, M.J. and Quataert, J.H. (1978), *Socialist Women: European Socialist Feminism in the Nineteenth and Early Twentieth Centuries*, Elsevier, Oxford.
Brah, A. (1988), 'Extended Review' *British Journal of Sociology of Education*, 9 (1), pp. 115-21.
Brah, A. (1992), *Working Choices: South Asian Young Muslim Women and the Labour Market*, Employment Department Research Paper Series, no. 91, London.
Brah, A. (1996), Cartographies of Diaspora, Routledge, London.
Brown, W. (2002), www.honestdog.com/may2002/films3.shtml.
Bryan, B., Dadzie, S. and Scafe, S. (1985), *The Heart of the Race, Black Women's Lives in Britain*, Virago, London.
Bryan, B., Dadzie, S. and Scafe, S. (1997), 'The Heart of the Race, Black Women's Lives in Britain', in Mirza, H.S. (ed.), *Black British Feminism*, Routledge, London.
Bunting, S. (1993), Rosemary Parse: Theory of Health as Human Becoming, Sage, London.
Carby, H. (1982), *Multi-Cultural Fictions*, Centre for Contemporary Cultural Studies, University of Birmingham, Birmingham.
Carby, H.V. (1997), 'White Woman Listen: Black Feminism and the Boundaries of Sisterhood', in Mirza, H.S. (ed.), *Black British Feminism*, Routledge, London.
Carmichael, S. and Hamilton, C.V. (1967), *Black Power: The Politics of Liberation in America*, Random House, New York.
Cashmore, E. (1982), *Black Sportsmen*, Routledge & Kegan Paul, London.
Cashmore, E. (1996), *Dictionary of Race and Ethnic Relations*, Routledge, London.
Cashmore, E. and Troyna, B. (eds) (1982), *Black Youth in Crisis*, Allen and Unwin, London.
Chadha, G. (1992), *Bhaji on the Beach*, Screenplay, Draft 6, Rochelle Stevens, London.
Chadha, G. (1994), *Bhaji On The Beach*, (Film), Channel Four Films, 1994.
Chadha, G. (2003), http://cgi.rediff.com/movies/2003/oct/02chadha.htm.

Chandra, S. (1995), 'The "New Woman" in Namita Gokhale's Gods, Graves and Grandmother', in Dhawan, R.K., (ed.) *Indian Women Novelists*, 6, Prestige, New Delhi.
Chatterjee, D. (1989), *I Was That Woman*, Hippopotamus Press, Frome.
Choong, D., Cole, W., Olievette, B. and Pearse, G. (1987), *Black Women Talk Poetry*, Black Women Talk Ltd, London, p. 7.
Choudhury, Y. (1993), *Roots and Tales of the Bangladeshi Settlers*, Birmingham, Sylhet Social History Group.
Clifford, J. (1997), 'Diaspora', in Guibernau, M. and Rex, J. *The Ethnicity Reader: Nationalism, Multiculturalism and Migration*, Policy Press, Cambridge.
Clifford, J. (1994), 'Diasporas', *Cultural Anthropology*, 9, 3, pp. 302-338.
Cobham, R. and Collins, M. (eds) (1987), *Watchers and Seekers, Creative Writing by Black Women in Britain*, Women's Press, London.
Coote, A. and Campbell, B. (1982), *Sweet Freedom: The Struggle for Women's Liberation*, Blackwell, Oxford.
Counter information Services (1981), *Women in the 80s*, Special Report.
Dabydeen, D. and Wilson-Tagoe, N. (1997), *A Readers Guide to West Indian and Black British Literature*, Hansib, London.
Dahya, B. (1973), 'Pakistanis in Britain: Transients or Settlers', *Race*, 14 (3), pp. 241-277.
Dahya, Z. (1965), 'Pakistani Wives in Britain', *Race*, 6 (4), pp. 311-321.
Dale, A., Shaheen N., Kalra, V. and Fieldhouse, E. (2002), 'Routes into education and employment for young Pakistani and Bangladeshi women in the UK', *Ethnic And Racial Studies*, 25 (6), pp. 942-68.
Davies, C.B. (1994), *Black Women, Writing and Identity*, Routledge, London.
Davies, C.D. and Ogundipe-Leslie, M. (1995), *International Dimensions of Black Women's Writing*, Pluto Press, London.
Davis, A. (1983), *Women, Race and Class*, Women's Press, London.
Desai, A. (1963), *Cry the Peacock*, Orient, New Delhi.
Desai, A. (1965), *Voices in the City*, Orient Paperbacks, New Delhi.
Desai, A. (1975), *Where Shall We Go This Summer*, Vikas, New Delhi.
Deshpande, S. (1980), *The Dark Holds No Terrors*, Penguin, New Delhi.
Deshpande, S. (1983), *Roots and Shadows*, Orient Longman, Bombay.
Dhawan, R.K. (1993), 'Introduction', in *Indian Women Novelists*, Set 1, vol. 1, Prestige, New Delhi.
Dhingra, L. (1987), 'Breaking Out of Labels', in Cobham, R. and Collins, M. (eds), *Watchers and Seekers*, Women's Press, London, pp. 30.
Dhingra, L. (1988), *Amritvela*, Women's Press, London.
Dhondy, F. (1976), *East End at your Feet*, Macmillan, Basingstoke, Hampshire.
Dhondy, F, (1978), *Come to Mecca*, Fontana Lions, London.
Drury, B. (1991), *Ethnic Identity and Ethnic Mobilisation in Britain*, Research Monograph No.5, Centre for Research in Ethnic Relations, University of Warwick, Coventry, p. 129.
Eade, J. (1989), 'Nationalism and the Quest for Authenticity: The Bangladeshis in Tower Hamlets', *New Community*, 16 (4), pp. 493-503.
Eade, J., Vamplew, T. and Peach, C. (1996), 'The Bangladeshis: the encapsulated Community', in C. Peach (ed.), *Ethnicity in the 1991 Census, vol 2, The Ethnic Minority Populations of Britain*, London: Office for National Statistics, pp. 150-60.
Eade, J. (1997), 'Keeping the Options Open: Bangladeshis in a Global City', in A. Kershen (ed.), London: *The Promised Land? The Migrant Experience in a Global City*, Aldershot: Avebury.
Emecheta, B. (1986), *Head Over Water*, Flamingo Fontana, London.
Emecheta, B. (1988), *Second Class* Citizen, Flamingo, London.

Ethnic Minority Communities Relations Council (1975), *Who Minds, Report On Working Mothers and Child Minding, Ethnic Minority*, Communities Relations Council.

Fryer, P. (1984), *Staying Power: The History of Black People in Britain*, Pluto Press, London.

Fuchs, C. (2004), *Those Kids were as Fast as Lightning – Conversation with Gurinder Chadha*, www.reelimagesmagazine.com/txt_features/conversations/reel_conversationbeyonce_knowles_copy%281%29.htm.

Gardner, K. and Shukur, A. (1994), 'Im a Bengali, I'm Asian, and I'm living here: The Changing Identity of British Identities', in R. Ballard (ed.), *Desh Pardesh: The South Asian Presence in Britain*, Hurst and Company, London.

Gardner, K. (1995), *Global Migrants, Local Lives*, Clarendon Press, Oxford.

Gardner, K. (2002), *Age, Narrative and Migration*, Berg, Oxford.

Gayle, N. (1987), 'Black Woman Out Dere', in Cobham, R. and Collins, M. (eds), *Watchers and Seekers*, Women's Press, London, p. 30.

Ghosh, A. (1989) 'The Diaspora in Indian Culture', *Public Culture*, 2, 1, pp. 73-8.

Gilroy, P. (1987), *There Ain't No Black in the Union Jack*, Hutchinson, London

Gilroy, P. (1993a), *Small Acts*, Serpents Tail, London.

Gilroy, P. (1993b), *The Black Atlantic*, Verso, London.

Grewal, S., Kay, J., Lewis, G., Lander, L. and Parmar, P. (1988), *Charting the Journey, Writings by Black and Third World Women*, Sheba, London.

Griffin, G. (1995), *Feminist Activism in the 1990s*, Taylor and Francis, London.

Gupta, R. (2003), *From Homebreakers to Jailbreakers: Southall Black Sisters*, Zed, London.

Hai, A. (2004), *Teaching Recent South Asian Women Writers: Issues of Gender in Literature and Theory*, http://womencrossing.org/hai.html.

Hall, S. (1990), 'Cultural Identity and Diaspora', in Rutherford, J. (ed.), *Identity*, Lawrence and Wishart, London.

Hall, S. (1992), 'Cultural Studies and its Theoretical Legacies', *Cultural Studies*, Lawrence Grossberg, Cary Nelson, and Paula A. Treichler (eds), New York: Routledge, pp. 277-294.

Hansari, H. (2002), *Muslims in Britain*, Minority Rights Group International, London.

Hiro, D. (1991), *Black Britain, White Britain: A History of Race Relations in Britain*, Grafton, London.

Hooks, B. (1982), *Ain't I a Woman: Black Women and Feminism*, Pluto Press, London.

Hooks, B. (1989), *Talking Back: Thinking Feminists, Thinking Black*, Sheba, London.

Humm, M. (1992), 'Asian, Black and Women of Colour Lesbianism/Feminism's', in *Feminism: A Reader*, Harvester Wheatsheaf, London.

Hussain, Y. (2004), 'Literature in a Cold Climate', in Ali, N. et al. (eds) *A post-Colonial People: South Asians in Britain*, Hurst, London.

Hussain, Y. and Bagguley, P. (2005), 'Citizenship, religion and cultural identity among British Pakistani Muslims since September 11th and the "riots" of 2001', in Abbas, T. (ed.), *Muslims in Britain: Communities in Crisis*, Zed Books, London.

Hutnik, N. (1991), *Ethnic Minority Identity*, Clarendon Press, Oxford.

Islam, S.M. (1997), *The Mapmakers of Spitalfieds*, Peepal Tree Press, London.

Jayawardena, K. (1982), *Feminism and Nationalism in the Third World: In Nineteenth and Early Twentieth Centuries*, Institute of Social Studies, The Hague, Belgium.

Jivani, A. (1994), 'Argy Bhaji', *Time Magazine*, 26 January, pp. 18-19.

Jones, T. (1992), *Britain's Ethnic Minorities*, Policy Studies Institute, London.

Joseph, G. (1981), 'The Incompatible Menage a Trois, Marxism, Feminism and Racism', in Sargent, L. (ed.), *The Unhappy Marriage of Marxism and Feminism*, Pluto Press, London.

Joseph G.I. and Lewis, J. (1981), *Common Differences*, Anchor Books, London.

Kabeer, N. (2000), *The Power to Choose; Bangladeshi Women and Labour Market Decisions in London and Dhaka*, Verso, London.
Kalra, S.S. (1980), *Daughters of Tradition: Adolescent Sikh Girls and their Accommodation to Life in British Society*, Diana Balbir Publications, Birmingham.
Kay, J. (1985), 'Am I A Mule', in Burford, B. et al. (eds), *A Dangerous Knowing: Four Black Women Poets*, Sheba, London, pp. 53-54.
Kenyon, O. (1991), *Writing Women: Contemporary Women Novelists*, Pluto, London.
Kershen, A. (ed.) (2000), *Language, Labour and Migration*, Ashgate: Aldershot.
Khan, V. (1976), 'Purdah in The British Situation', in Barker, L.D. and Allen, S. (eds), *Dependence and Exploitation in Work and Marriage*, Longman, London.
Khan, V.S. (1976), Pakistani Women in Britain, *New Community*, 5 (1-2), pp. 99-108.
Khan, V. (1977), in Watson, J. (ed.), *Between Two Cultures: Migrants and Minorities in Britain*, Blackwell, Oxford.
Khanum, S.M. (1994), *We just buy illness in exchange for hunger: experiences of health care, health and illness among Bangladeshi women in Britain*, Unpublished Phd thesis, Keele, Keele University.
King, R., Connell, J. and White, P. (1995), *Writing Across Worlds, Literature and Migration*, Routledge, London.
Landow, G. (1989), 'Women and the Hindu Tradition', in *Women in India: Manohar*, New Delhi, pp. 122-123.
Ledger, S. (1997), *The New Woman: Fiction and Feminism at the Fin Desiecle*, Manchester University Press, Manchester.
Lewis, J. (ed.) (1983), *Women's Welfare, Women's Right*, Croom Helm.
Liddington, J. and Norris, J. (1978), *One Hand Tied Behind Us: The Rise of the Women's Suffrage Movement*, Virago, London.
Lomas, G. (1973), *Census 1971, The Coloured Population of Great Britain – Preliminary Report*, Runnymede Trust, London.
Macauley, D.J. (1996), *Reconstructing Womanhood; Reconstructing Feminism, Writings On Black Women*, Routledge, London.
McNeil, D. (2003), 'Stand up and Sound Off', The Multiracial Activist, www.multiracial.com/readers/mcneil5.html.
Mehta, R. (1977), *Inside the Haveli*, Arnold Heinemann, New Delhi.
Milloy, J. and O'Rourke, R. (1991), *The Woman Reader*, Routledge, London
Mirza, H.S. (ed.) (1997), *Black British Feminism*, Routledge, London.
Mitchell, J. (1971), *Women's Estate*, Penguin, London.
Modleski, T, (1986), *Feminism Without Women's Culture and Criticism in a 'Post Feminist Age*, Routledge, London.
Modood, T. et al. (1994) *Changing Ethnic Identities*, PSI, London.
Nayman, N. (2003), 'She Shoots, She Scores', *Eye*, 6 March.
Ngcobo, L. (ed.) (1988), *Let It Be Told – Essays By Black Women in Britain*, Virago, London.
Nivien, A. (2003), *South Asian Diaspora Literature in Britain*, www.salidaa.org.uk/salidaa/Sections/collectionsLiterature.
O'Sullivan, C. (1996), 'Anita and Me', *Observer*, 21 April, p. 15.
Owaad, *Fowaad*, no. 1979.
Papastergiadis, N. (1997), 'Tracing Hybridity in Theory', in Werbner, P. and Modood, T. (eds), *Debating Cultural Hybridity; Multi-Cultural Identities and the Politics of Anti-Racism*, Zed Books, London.
Parmar, P. (1982), 'Gender, Race and Class: Asian Women in Resistance', in Centre for Contemporary Cultural Studies, *The Empire Strikes Back: Race and Racism in 70s Britain*, Routledge, London.

Parmar, P. (1990), 'Black Feminism: The Politics of Articulation', in Rutherford, J. (ed.), *Identity*, Lawrence and Wishart, London.
Phillipson, C., Nilufar, A. and Latimer, J. (2003), *Women in Transition: A Study of the Experiences of Bangladeshi Women living in Tower Hamlets'*, Policy Press, London.
Phizaclea, A. (1983), *One Way Ticket, Migration and Female Labour*, Routledge and Kegan Paul, London.
Prescod-Roberts, M. and Seele, N. (1980), *Black Women Bring it all Back Home*, Falling Wall Press, London.
Procter, J. (2000), *Writing Black Britain, 1948-1998: An Interdisciplinary Anthology*, Manchester University Press, Manchester.
Ramdin, R. (1999), *Reimaging Britain: Five Hundred Years of Black and Asian History*, Pluto Press, London.
Randhawa, R. (1987), *A Wicked Old Woman*, Women's Press, London.
Report of the Pakistan Commission on the Status of Women (1989), quoted in Samad, Y. and Eade, J. (2002), *Community Perceptions of Forced Marriage*, Community Liaison Unit, Foreign and Commonwealth Office.
Richmond, A.H. (1988), *Immigration and Ethnic Conflict*, Macmillan, London.
Riley, J. (1985), *The Belonging*, Women's Press, London.
Riley, J. (1988), *The Romance*, Women's Press, London.
Rodgers-Rose, (1980), *The Black Woman*, Sage Publications, London.
Safran, W. (1991), 'Diasporas in Modern Societies: Myths of Homeland and Return', *Diaspora*, 1, 1, pp. 83-99.
Sahgal, G. and Yuval-Davies, N. (eds) (1992), *Refusing Holy Orders: Women and Fundamentalism in Britain*, Virago, London.
Samad, Y. and Eade, J. (2002), *Community Perceptions of Forced Marriage*, Community Liaison Unit, Foreign and Commonwealth Office.
Sandhu, S. (2003), Book Review of Monica Ali's *Brick Lane*, www.lrb.co.uk/v25/n19/sand01_.html.
Sathupati, P.S. (1995), 'Conflict and Identity in Shashi Desphande's Novels', in *Indian Women Novelists*, Prestige, New Delhi.
Segal, L. (1987), 'Lynne Segal interviews Diane Abbott', *Feminist Review*, 27, pp. 55-60.
Sehgal, N. (2003), *Aspirations Vs. Culture – 'Bend It Like Beckham'*, www.the-south-asian.com/May-2002/Bend_it_like_Beckham.htm.
Seneviratne, S. (1987), 'Jealous', in Grewal et al. (eds), *Charting the Journey: Writings by Black and Third World Women*, Sheba, London, p. 18.
Shan, S.J. (1990), *In My Own Name*, Cambridge University Press, London.
Sharma, S. (2004), 'Asian Sounds', in Ali, N. et al. (eds), *A Post-Colonial People: South Asians in Britain*, Hurst, London.
Shaw, A. (1994), *Kinship and Continuity: Pakistani Families in Britain*, Harwood, Singapore.
Sheikh, F. (1991), *The Red Box*, Women's Press, London.
Shoshana M. and Landow, G. (1991), Changing Images of Women in South Asian Fiction *Anthropology*, 302, Princeton University.
Siddiqui, H. (1995), 'An interview with Hannana Siddiqui', in Griffin, G. (ed.), *Feminist Activism in The 1990s*, Taylor and Francis, London, pp. 79-89.
Spelman, E. (1988), *Inner Essential Woman: Problems of Exclusion in Feminist Thoughts*, Women's Press, London.
Spivak, G.C. (1988), 'Reading The World: Literary Studies in The Eighties', in *Other Worlds: Essays in Cultural Politics*, New York, Routledge.
Sulter, M. (1985), *As a Black Woman*, Akira Press, London.

Sulter, M. (1990), *Passion: Discourses on Black Women's Creativity*, Urban Fox Press, London.
Syal, M. (1996), *Anita and Me*, Flamingo, London.
Taylor, M.J. and Hegarty, S. (1985), *The Best of Both Worlds?: A Review of Research into the Education of Pupils of South Asian Origin*, National Foundation for Educational Research in England and Wales, Windsor.
Tololyan, K. (1991), The Nation-State and its Others: In Lieu of a Preface, *Diaspora*, 1, pp. 3-7.
Tololyan, K. (1996), 'Rethinking Diaspora(s): Stateless Power in the Transnational Moment', *Diaspora*, 5, 1, pp. 3-36.
Trivedi, P. (1984), 'Black Women Organising Autonomously', *Feminist Review*, 7, pp. 37-50.
Uberoi, N. (1965), 'Sikh Women in Southall', *Race*, 6, (1), pp. 34-40.
Verma, G.K. and Ashworth, B. (1986), *Ethnicity and Educational Achievement in British Schools*, Macmillan, London.
Vertovec, S. (1996), 'Diaspora', in *Dictionary of Race And Ethnic Relations* (4th Ed.), Routledge, London.
Vertovec, S. (2000), 'Religion and Diaspora', Paper presented at the conference on New Landscapes on Religion in the West, Oxford University.
Wade, B. and Souter, P. (1992), *Continuing To Think: The British Asian Girl*, Multilingual Matters, London.
Waldron-Mantgani, I. (2002), Review of *Anita and Me*, The UK Critic, www.rottentomatoes.com/click/movie-10002188/reviews.php?critic=all&sortby=default&page=1&rid=816915.
Wall, C. (1989), *Changing Our Own Words: Essays on Criticism, Theory and Writing by Black Women*, Routledge, London.
Washington, M.H. (1975), 'Introduction', in Washington, M.H. (ed.), *Black-Eyed Susan's, Classic Stories by and About Black Women*, Anchor Books, New York.
Watson, J. (1977), *Between Two Cultures: Migrants and Minorities in Britain*, Blackwell, Oxford.
Werbner (1990), *The Migration Process: Capital, Gifts and Offerings among British Pakistanis*, Berg Publishers, Oxford.
Werbner, P. and Modood, T. (1997), *Debating Cultural Hybridity*, Zed Books, London.
Werbner, P. (2002), *Imagined Diasporas among Manchester Muslims: The Public Performance of Pakistani Transnational Identity Politics*, Oxford University Press, Oxford.
Westwood, S. and Phizacklea, A. (2000), *Transnationalism and the Politics of Belonging*, Routledge, London.
Whipple, M. (2003), Book Review of Monica Ali's *Brick Lane*, www.reviewsofbooks.com/brick_lane/.
Williams, V. (1987), 'One Angry Woman', in Cobham, R. and Collins M. (eds), *Watchers and Seekers*, Women's Press, London.
Wilson, A. (1978), *Finding a Voice: Asian Women in Britain*, Virago, London.

Index

Abbott, Diane 46
Adams, C. 91, 99
African Americans 5, 43, 44, 51
African Caribbeans
    Black feminism 16, 33, 34, 35, 37–8, 51
    Chadha films 76
    immigration of 21
    New Women 60
    women writers 47, 48, 49
Agrad, Sandra 46
Ahmad, Rukhsana 50
Ahmed, Lalita 78
Akira Press 42
Ali, Altab 101
Ali, Monica 17, 91–109, 133
Alibhai-Brown, Y. 28
alienation 56, 58, 59, 67
Amos, Valerie 43, 44, 46
Amritvela (Dhingra) 11, 48, 65–8, 94
Angelou, Maya 43
Anita and Me (film) 112, 125–8, 133
Anita and Me (Syal) 9, 17, 46, 89, 94, 111–29, 133
Anthias, F. 43
Anwar, Mohammed 21, 102
Armenians 5
As a Black Woman (Sulter) 42
Asian Women Writers Collective 50
assimilation 12, 13, 20
authenticity 65, 68, 92, 109, 131

Bailey, L.J. 42
Ballard, R. 82, 102
Bambara, Toni Cade 51
Bangladeshis
    Brick Lane 17, 91–109, 133
    family reunification 22
    population in Britain 19
    second-generation 27
    South Asian identity 2
Beckham, David 82, 83, 88, 132

belonging 26, 48, 74
    Amritvela 65, 68
    Brick Lane 97, 98, 99
Bend it like Beckham (Chadha) 16, 72–3, 79–90, 125, 126, 127, 133
Bhabha, H. 12–13
Bhaji on the Beach (Chadha) 16, 72, 73–9, 89–90, 125
bhangra music 6, 11, 12, 14, 77, 83–4, 90
Bhaskar, Sanjeev 126
Birmingham Black Sisters 41
birth control 39–40
Black concept 16, 32, 33, 34, 35–6
Black culture 13
Black diasporas 6, 7
Black feminism 16, 33–52, 94, 131, 132
Black Women Bring It All Back Home (Prescod-Roberts and Seele) 24
Black Women out Dere (Gayle) 47
Black Women Talk 42
Black women's groups 25, 41
The Blackbird (Agrad) 46
Bloom, Valerie 47
Bollywood 78, 79, 133
Bombay Dreams (Lloyd Webber) 133
borders 8
Brah, A. 7, 9
Breaking Out of the Labels (Dhingra) 46, 47
Brewster, Anna 127
Brick Lane (Ali) 17, 91–109, 133
'bridari system' 102
Bride and Prejudice (Chadha) 133
Brixton Women's Group 41
Brown, William 81
Bryan, B. 45, 94
Burke, Kathy 126

Campbell, B. 40
Carby, H. 43, 44
Cashmore, E. 89
caste 15

Chadha, Gurinder 16, 71–90, 132, 133
Charting the Journey: Writings by Black and Third World Women (Grewal et al.) 33–4, 46, 94
Chatterjee, Debjani 47, 48
childhood 113–17, 125
Choudhury, Y. 91, 99
Christians 2
citizenship 27
class
  Anita and Me 122
  bipolar discourses 10
  Black feminism 33, 37, 40, 41
  Black women's literature 43, 44, 45
  Brick Lane 91, 103
  migrants 94
  personal identity 14
  power issues 8
Cobham, R. 34, 49, 94
Collins, Merle 34, 43, 47, 49, 94
colonialism 21, 38, 54, 94, 117–18
Come to Mecca (Dhondy) 92
communalism 59, 60, 61
Continuing to Think: The British Asian Girl (Wade and Souter) 46
Coote, A. 40
Cry The Peacock (Desai) 59–60
cultural codes 107, 108
cultural hybridity 6, 11–14, 61, 71, 82–4, 123–5
culture 3–4, 131
  diaspora concept 5
  minority/indigenous culture conflict 121, 122
  New Women 69
  patriarchal 29
  sociology of 3
curry houses 6, 12

The Dark Holds No Terrors (Deshpande) 56, 57
Davis, Angela 46
Depo-Provera campaign 39–40
deportation 24
Desai, Anita 55–6, 58–60
Deshpande, Shashi 56–7, 58, 59
desification of cinema 16, 71, 89, 132, 133
Dharker, Ayesha 126
Dhingra, Leena 46, 47, 48, 50, 65–8, 94

Dhondy, Farrukh 92
diaspora 5–11, 12, 31, 90, 97
difference 12, 15
discrimination 27, 35, 38
  Black women's literature 44, 46
  far right groups 103
  first-generation immigrants 19, 20
  New Women 62
  see also racism
Diwali 123, 124
domestic violence 24–5, 41, 96–7, 107
dress 28, 30, 77, 78, 105, 106
  see also hijab

East End at Your Feet (Dhondy) 92
East is East 81, 89, 125, 128
East-West encounter 66, 93, 94
education 14, 102–3
  New Woman 54, 57, 59
  second-generation South Asians 26, 27–8
Eliot, George 53
Emecheta, Buchi 42, 46
employment 20, 22–3, 24, 30, 38, 40–1
empowerment 31, 54
Englishness 32, 73–5, 76, 77, 78, 80
ethnicity 3, 5, 13, 15, 30
  Bend it like Beckham 79, 80, 86, 87, 88
  bipolar discourses 10
  Black women's literature 45, 47
  Brick Lane 91, 106–7
  diasporic identity 132
  see also race
ethnocentrism 1, 4, 22, 37, 39
exclusion 8, 9, 12, 37, 65, 114

family 2, 24, 30
  Anita and Me 113, 119, 121–2
  Bend it like Beckham 80–2
  Black feminism 37–8, 39
  New Woman 56
femininity 53, 84, 85–6, 87, 96, 108, 132
  see also gender; women
feminism
  Black 16, 33–52, 94, 131, 132
  critique of White feminism 33, 36–41, 44
  New Woman 53, 54, 68
  publishers 42–3, 51
Feminist Review 46

Index

festivals 109
film 3, 10, 132
   Anita and Me 112, 125–8, 133
   Bend it like Beckham 16, 72–3,
     79–90, 125, 126, 127, 133
   Bhaji on the Beach 16, 72,
     73–9, 89–90, 125
   Bollywood 78, 79, 133
   desification of cinema 16, 71, 89, 132, 133
Finding a Voice: Asian Women in Britain (Wilson) 24, 45, 94
Flaming Spirit: Stories from the South Asian Women Writers Collective 50
football 79–80, 84–6, 87–9

Gardner, K. 99
Gayle, Nefertiti 47
gender 3, 4, 8, 131
   Bend it like Beckham 79, 81, 83, 84–7
   bipolar discourses 10
   Black feminism 33, 41
   Black women's literature 43, 45, 51
   Brick Lane 95, 99–100, 104–5, 108
   migrants 94, 99
   New Woman 54, 56, 61
   see also femininity; feminism; women
Ghir, Kulwinder 83
Gilroy, P. 13, 92
globalisation 5, 9
Goodness Gracious Me 83, 126
Grewal, S. 34, 94
Gujaratis 2
Gupta, Rahila 50

Hall, S. 13
Hazeley, Iyamide 42
Head Over Water (Emecheta) 42
The Heart of the Race: Black Women's Lives in Britain (Bryan et al.) 45, 94
hegemony 7
hijab 28, 101, 102, 106
Hindus 2, 23, 27, 55
homeland 5, 7, 9, 47–8, 97–8
homosexuality 81
   see also lesbianism
Hooks, B. 43, 44
Hurston, Zora Neale 51
Huseyin, Metin 125, 126, 127, 128
hybridity 6, 11–14, 61, 71
   Anita and Me 123–5

Bend it like Beckham 82–4
Bhaji on the Beach 74, 77

identity 1, 2, 6, 19–32, 131
   Anita and Me 112, 117, 119, 121–5

   Bend it like Beckham 82, 84
   Bhaji on the Beach 74, 75, 77, 78
   Black feminism 16, 34, 43, 47, 51
   Brick Lane 91, 95–6, 97–8, 99, 100, 103–4, 106–7
   British 6, 15
   Chadha films 72–3, 74, 75, 77, 78, 82, 84, 89
   collective 4, 5, 10, 13, 34–5, 121
   diaspora concept 7
   first-generation 15–16, 19–21, 25, 31, 123
   hybrid 11–13, 14–15, 16, 26, 30, 121–5
   hyphenated 5, 9, 11, 12, 14, 26, 131
   localised 14
   Muslim 28
   New Woman 16, 54, 55, 57–9, 60–2, 64–5, 68–9
   racial 31–2, 46
   re-negotiation of 1, 51
   religious 31, 51
   second-generation 15–16, 26–7, 28–31, 82, 84, 99, 132
   South Asian women writers 3, 4, 10–11, 14, 15, 49–50
I'm English But... (Chadha) 71–2
imagined community 2, 7, 13, 121
immigration 1, 38, 121
   first-generation immigrants 19–20, 21, 24
   women's literature 47, 55
   see also migration
imperialism 20, 21, 24, 76
In My Own Name (Shan) 50, 94
independence 1, 22–3, 30, 57, 60, 65, 69
   see also self-determination
Indians
   Anita and Me 111–29
   first-generation immigrants 19, 21, 22
   New Woman in women's literature 55–60, 65–8
   population in Britain 19
   South Asian identity 2
   women in employment 22–3

individualism 22, 26, 60, 61
individuality 3, 4, 23, 30
   Brick Lane 106
   New Woman 56, 68, 69, 132
   Western values 1, 22, 69
Inside the Haveli (Mehta) 58, 59
inter-generational conflict 9, 15–16, 26–7
Islam *see* Muslims
Islam, Syed Manzurul 92
Islamophobia 101
'izzat' 29, 50

Jewish diaspora 5
Johnson, Amryl 47
journey theme 4, 7–8, 55, 60
Just Jealous (Seneviratane) 46

Kabeer, N. 91, 99
Kalra, S.S. 23
Kay, Jackie 47
Kher, Anupam 83
The Kumars at No 42 126

language 2, 11, 23, 27, 77, 90
lesbianism 10, 51, 85
literature 3, 10, 131, 133–4
   Anita and Me 9, 17, 46, 89, 94, 111–29, 133
   Black feminism 33–4, 36, 42–9, 51, 132
   Brick Lane 17, 91–109, 133
   emergence of British South Asian writing 49–50
   India women novelists 55–60
   New Woman 16, 53–69, 132
Lloyd Webber, Andrew 133

Mama, Amina 46
The Mapmakers of Spitalfields (Islam) 92
Markanday, Kamala 55–6
marriage 2, 11, 14, 27
   arranged 22, 29, 37, 39, 75
   New Woman 56, 57, 59, 62
Marshall, Paule 51
masculinity 84, 85
mass media 15
mehfils 115, 121, 123–4
Mehta, Rama 58, 59
migration 2, 5–6, 131

Brick Lane 91, 93, 94–6, 97, 99, 100
   literary representations of 51, 93–4
   New Woman 16, 60, 132
   see also immigration
modernity 56, 69
Morrison, Toni 51
Mukherjee, Bharati 60
multiculturalism 22, 72, 95
music 6, 11, 77, 83–4, 90
musicals 133
Muslims 2, 9, 11, 23
   festivals 109
   Islamophobia 101
   second-generation 27, 28
   women in the labour market 30
My Beautiful Laundrette 125

nationalism 32, 73
Naylor, Gloria 51
networks 20–1, 98, 102
New Woman 16, 53–69, 132
Ngcobo, Lauretta 43
Nice Arrangement (Chadha) 72
Nichols, Grace 47

Only Women Press 42
Organisation Of Women Of Asian And African Descent (OWAAD) 41

Pakistanis
   first-generation immigrants 19, 21, 22
   kinship loyalty 102
   population in Britain 19
   second-generation 27
   South Asian identity 2
   women in employment 23
Papastergiadis, N. 11–12
Parmar, Pratibha 43, 44, 46
patriarchy 29, 48–9, 54, 69
   Bangladesh 98
   Black feminism 37, 38, 41, 44
   see also sexism
patriotism 124, 125
Phizacklea, A. 43
post-colonial theory 13, 61
poverty 91–2, 100–1
Powell, Enoch 120, 121, 128
power relations 4, 8, 23
prejudice 20, 103
Prescod-Roberts, M. 24
publishing industry 42–3, 51

Punjabis 2

The Question (Chatterjee) 48

race 4, 5, 131
  Anita and Me 111–12, 121
  Bend it like Beckham 79, 83, 87
  Black feminism 33, 36, 37, 41
  Black women's literature 43, 44, 45, 51
  Brick Lane 91, 95, 99–100
  hybridity 12
  migrants 94, 99
  see also ethnicity
racism
  Anita and Me 111–12, 116, 117–21, 122, 123–4, 127, 128, 133
  Bend it like Beckham 81, 83, 88
  Bhaji on the Beach 75, 76–7
  Black feminism 33, 34–5, 37, 38, 39, 40, 132
  Black women's literature 43, 46, 48–9
  Brick Lane 95, 98, 101, 103–4, 133
  first-generation South Asians 20, 21, 131
  institutional 20, 22, 24, 35, 38
  migration in literature 94
  nationalism link 32
  New Woman 16
  power issues 8
  publishing industry 42
  'scientific' 11
  second-generation South Asians 27
  South Asian form of 15, 122
  women's employment 24
Randhawa, Ravinder 49, 50, 61–4, 94
rape 39
The Red Box (Sheikh) 12, 64–5
religion 9, 27, 28
  Bend it like Beckham 82
  fundamentalism 30–1, 51
resistance 38, 43
Rich Deceiver (Chadha) 72
Right of Way 50
Riley, Joan 43, 46, 47, 48–9
riots 6, 27, 104
rituals 109
The Romance (Riley) 48–9
Roots and Shadows (Deshpande) 56, 57

Sahgal, Nayanatara 55–6

Sandhu, S. 108
Second Class Citizen (Emecheta) 46
Seele, N. 24
Segal, Zohra 126
self-concept 1, 26
self-determination 10, 65, 69
  see also independence
self-discovery 60–1, 73
self-evaluation 58, 59, 60, 61, 65
self-identity 2, 4, 8
  body as expression of 79
  New Woman 55, 58, 59, 61
  see also identity
Seneviratane, Seni 46
sexism 15, 76, 77, 81
  see also patriarchy
sexuality 8, 10, 14, 51
  Bend it like Beckham 80, 81
  Black feminism 39–40
  migrants 94
  see also homosexuality; lesbianism
Shan, Sharan Jeet 50, 94
Shaw, A. 102
Sheba Feminist Press 42
Sheikh, Farhana 64–5
Sikhs 2, 23, 27, 79, 82
'Sita Savitri' stereotype 55
situatedness 7, 8
slavery 38, 39
So You Think I'm a Mule? (Kay) 47
social Darwinism 76
social learning 108
Souter, P. 46
Southall Black Sisters 25, 41
Spare Rib 46
Spelman, E. 43
Spivak, Gayatri 45
stereotypes 14, 27, 39
  Brick Lane 109
  'Sita Savitri' 55
  South Asian fathers 28
  South Asian womanhood 1, 4, 10, 22, 23, 131
suicide 29, 58
Sulter, Maud 42
Syal, Meera 15, 17, 46, 94, 111–29, 133

third space 12–14
Trivedi, Parita 23–4, 46

The Unbelonging (Riley) 46, 48

Uppal, Chandeep 127

values
  Chadha films 72, 77, 80
  colonialist 118
  second-generation South Asians 26
  Western 1, 22, 29, 69
Vertovec, S. 6
violence
  domestic 24–5, 41, 96–7, 107
  racial 20
Virago 42–3
Voices in the City (Desai) 58, 59

Wade, B. 46
Wadia, Nina 83
WAF *see* Women Against Fundamentalism
Waldron-Mantgani, I. 125
Walker, Alice 43, 51
Washington, Mary Helen 44
Watchers and Seekers, Creative Writing by Black Women in Britain (Cobham and Collins) 34, 49, 94
What's Cooking (Chadha) 72, 79
Where Shall We Go This Summer (Desai) 58
A Wicked Old Woman (Randhawa) 49, 61–4, 94
Williams, Mark 126
Wilson, Amrit 24, 45, 94
women
  Black feminism 16, 33–52, 93, 131, 132
  creative works 1–2, 3–4, 10–11, 14, 131
  cultural reproduction 123
  diaspora concept 9
  first-generation 15–16, 21–5, 131
  hybrid identities 14–15
  Muslim 28
  New Woman 16, 53–69, 132
  second-generation 15–16, 28–31, 132
  stereotype of South Asian womanhood 1, 4, 10, 22, 23, 131
  see also feminism; gender
Women Against Fundamentalism (WAF) 31
The Women's Press 42–3, 50

youth culture 6, 30, 101
Yuval-Davis, N. 43